JOURNAL FOR THE STUDY OF THE OLD TESTAMENT
SUPPLEMENT SERIES
316

Sheffield Academic Press

Determinism in the Book of Ecclesiastes

Dominic Rudman

Journal for the Study of the Old Testament
Supplement Series 316

Published by
Sheffield Academic Press Ltd
Mansion House
19 Kingfield Road
Sheffield S11 9AS
England

www.SheffieldAcademicPress.com

Typeset by Sheffield Academic Press
and
Printed on acid-free paper in Great Britain
by Antony Rowe Ltd
Chippenham, Wiltshire

British Library Cataloguing-in-Publication Data

A catalogue record for this book is available
from the British Library

ISBN 1-84127-153-5

CONTENTS

PREFACE

This book is based on a thesis entitled 'Determinism in the Book of Ecclesiastes', which was submitted to the University of St Andrews for the degree of PhD in 1997. I wish to acknowledge with gratitude the support of staff and students during my time as a research student there, and in particular my supervisor, Dr Robert Salters, whose patience and critical acumen turned my thesis into something considerably better than it might otherwise have been. I also express my gratitude to the British Academy for funding my PhD studentship, and the Leverhulme Trust for a subsequent research fellowship, during the tenure of which my thesis was revised for publication. Some sections of this work have appeared in print already in different forms: parts of Chapters 2, 6 and 7 first saw the light of day in *JNSL*, *JBL* and *CBQ* as 'The Translation and Interpretation of Ecclesiastes 8.17a', 'Woman as Divine Agent in Ecclesiastes', and 'A Note on the Dating of Ecclesiastes' respectively. I am grateful to the editors of those journals for permission for this material to appear here. Finally, and most importantly, my thanks are due to Cate for her support over the past five years. This book is dedicated to her with my love.

Dominic C. Rudman
University of Exeter
December, 1999

ABBREVIATIONS

AB	Anchor Bible
ABD	David Noel Freedman (ed.), *The Anchor Bible Dictionary* (New York: Doubleday, 1992)
AEL	M. Lichtheim, *Ancient Egyptian Literature* (3 vols.; Berkeley: University of California Press, 1971–80)
AHw	Wolfram von Soden, *Akkadisches Handwörterbuch* (Wiesbaden: Harrassowitz, 1959–81)
ANET	James B. Pritchard (ed.), *Ancient Near Eastern Texts Relating to the Old Testament* (Princeton: Princeton University Press, 1950)
ATD	Das Alte Testament Deutsch
ATSAT	Arbeiten zu Text und Sprache im Alten Testament
AV	Authorised Version
BA	*Biblical Archaeologist*
BASOR	*Bulletin of the American Schools of Oriental Research*
BDB	F. Brown, S.R. Driver, and C.A. Briggs, *A Hebrew and English Lexicon of the Old Testament* (Oxford: Clarendon Press, 1907)
BETL	Bibliotheca Ephemeridum Theologicarum Lovaniense
BHS	*Biblica hebraica stuttgartensia*
Bib	*Biblica*
BKAT	Biblische Kommentar: Altes Testament
BZAW	Beiheft zur *ZAW*
CAD	Ignace I. Gelb *et al.* (eds.), *The Assyrian Dictionary of the Oriental Institute of the University of Chicago* (Chicago: Oriental Institute, 1964–)
CBQ	*Catholic Biblical Quarterly*
D.	H. Diels (ed.), *Die Fragmente der Vorsokratiker* (Berlin: Weidmann, 1951–52)
DL	Diogenes Laertius
EncJud	*Encyclopedia Judaica*
ErIsr	Eretz Israel
EstBib	*Estudios Bíblicos*
HAR	*Hebrew Annual Review*
HAT	Handbuch zum Alten Testament
HB	Hebrew Bible

Hdt	Herodotus
HKAT	Handkommentar zum Alten Testament
HR	*History of Religions*
HS	*Hebrew Studies*
HTR	*Harvard Theological Review*
HUCA	*Hebrew Union College Annual*
ICC	International Critical Commentary
JAOS	*Journal of the American Oriental Society*
JB	*Jerusalem Bible*
JBL	*Journal of Biblical Literature*
JHI	*Journal of the History of Ideas*
JNES	*Journal of Near Eastern Studies*
JNSL	*Journal of Northwest Semitic Languages*
JQR	*Jewish Quarterly Review*
JSOT	*Journal for the Study of the Old Testament*
JSOTSup	*Journal for the Study of the Old Testament*, Supplement Series
JSS	*Journal of Semitic Studies*
JTS	*Journal of Theological Studies*
KAT	Kommentar zum Alten Testament
KHAT	Kurzer Hand-Commentar zum Alten Testament
KJV	King James Version
LSJ	H.G. Liddell, Robin Scott and H. Stuart Jones, *Greek–English Lexicon* (Oxford: Clarendon Press, 9th edn, 1968)
MUSKTF	Münchener Universitätsschriften Katholisch-Theologische Fakultät
NCBC	New Century Bible Commentary
NEB	*New English Bible*
NIV	New International Version
NRSV	New Revised Standard Version
NZSth	Neue Zeitschrift für systematische Theologie und Religionsphilosophie
OTG	Old Testament Guides
OTL	Old Testament Library
OTP	J. Charlesworth (ed.), *Old Testament Pseudepigrapha* (Garden City: Doubleday, 1983–87)
PColZen	W.L. Westermann and E.S. Hesenoehrl (eds.), *The Zenon Papyri, Business Papers of the Third Century dealing with Palestine and Egypt* (New York: Columbia University, 1934)
PCZ	O. Guérand and P. Jouguet (eds.), *The Zenon Papyri* (Cairo: Institut français, 1925–51)
P. Lips.	L. Mitteis (ed.), *Griechische Urkunden der Papyrussammlung zu Leipzig* (Leipzig: Teubner, 1906)
PSB NS	*Princeton Seminary Bulletin*, New Series
RA	*Revue d'assyriologie et d'archaeologie orientale*
RB	*Revue biblique*

REB	Revised English Bible
RSV	Revised Standard Version
RV	Revised Version
SCM	Student Christian Movement
SPCK	Society for Promoting Christian Knowledge
SVF	G. Von Arnim (ed.), *Stoicorum Veterum Fragmenta* (Leipzig: Teubner, 1903–24)
TDNT	Gerhard Kittel and Gerhard Friedrich (eds.), *Theological Dictionary of the New Testament* (trans. Geoffrey W. Bromiley; 10 vols.; Grand Rapids: Eerdmans, 1964–)
TDOT	G.J. Botterweck and H. Ringgren (eds.), *Theological Dictionary of the Old Testament* (trans. J.T. Willis; 10 vols.; Grand Rapids: Eerdmans, 1974–)
TECC	Textos y Estudios Cardenal Cisneros
UF	*Ugarit-Forschungen*
VF	*Verkündigung und Forschung*
VT	*Vetus Testamentum*
VTSup	*Vetus Testamentum*, Supplement Series
WBC	Word Biblical Commentary
ZAW	*Zeitschrift für die alttestamentliche Wissenschaft*
ZDMG	*Zeitschrift die deutschen morgenländischen Gesellschaft*
ZDPV	*Zeitschrift des deutschen Palästina-Vereins*
ZWT	*Zeitschrift für wissenschaftliche Theologie*

Chapter 1

ECCLESIASTES AND ITS HELLENISTIC CONTEXT

1. *Introduction*

Despite the identification made in early Jewish and Christian exegesis,[1] it is generally accepted today that Solomon was not the author of the book of Ecclesiastes. The reasons for this early identification of Qoheleth with Solomon hinged largely on the editorial superscription to the book in 1.1, in which Qoheleth is described as 'the son of David, king in Jerusalem' and on Qoheleth's own words in 1.12 in which he describes himself as 'king over Israel in Jerusalem'. Only two kings (David and Solomon) are noted to have ruled Israel from Jerusalem. Thereafter, the northern tribes broke away from the union, leaving Jerusalem the capital of Judah (1 Kgs 12.16-20) and ruled by the Davidic line.

The identification of Qoheleth as 'David's son' (i.e. Solomon) in the later superscription of 1.1 however, is not made in 1.12 nor anywhere else in Ecclesiastes. Nevertheless, it most likely arose from the description of the so-called 'Royal Experiment' in 1.12–2.12 where Qoheleth experiences all the trappings of wealth and pleasure appropriate to a king.[2] The depiction of the various luxuries enjoyed by Qoheleth is reminiscent of the Solomonic court (1 Kgs 10). This identification was made easier still for the editor by Qoheleth's claim to have 'increased in wisdom, more than all who were in Jerusalem before me'. Again, this was a statement that called to mind Solomon's legendary wisdom (1 Kgs 5.9-14 [ET 4.29-34]). Most modern commentators would agree however, that although the 'Royal Experiment' in 1.12–2.12 may be

---

1. Tg. Qoh. 1.1, 12; Midr. Qoh. to 1.1, 12; Clem. Alex. Strom. 6.11, 14, 15; Tertullian, *Adversus Valentinem* 2; *De Praescriptis Haereticis* 7.

2. R.N. Whybray, *Ecclesiastes* (NCBC; Grand Rapids: Eerdmans; London: Marshall, Morgan & Scott, 1989), p. 34.

intended to recall the glory of Solomon, Qoheleth seems not to have wished to cultivate the impression that the author of his work was Israel's most famous king.[3]

Although the seventeenth-century scholar Grotius is sometimes noted as being the first to suggest the unlikelihood of Solomonic authorship for Ecclesiastes, this distinction in fact belongs to Luther.[4] The conclusions of both in this regard were followed eagerly in the nineteenth century and indeed it has now become almost a cliché to cite the words of Franz Delitzsch in this regard: 'If the book of Koheleth were of old Solomonic origin, then there is no history of the Hebrew Language'.[5]

If Solomon is not the author of Ecclesiastes, when was the book actually written? Theories of the date of authorship vary wildly. E. Renan argued for a date as late as the first century BCE.[6] This has now been ruled out by the discovery of Ecclesiastes scroll fragments at Qumran, the earliest of which (4QQoh[a]) has been dated to the mid-second century BCE.[7] This provides a *terminus ante quem* for the work. In addition, many scholars have asserted some form of dependence for Ben Sira on Ecclesiastes.[8] Taking the date of Ben Sira as 180 BCE, this would suggest a date for the composition of Ecclesiastes prior to 200 BCE. A *terminus post quem* is suggested by the high proportion of Aramaisms and the appearance of two Persianisms in the book. Both point to a postexilic date.

---

3. R. Gordis, *Koheleth: The Man and his World* (3rd edn; New York: Bloch, 1968), p. 60.

4. H. Grotius (*Annotationes in Vetus Testamentum* [ed. G. Vogel; Halae: Curt, 1875–76], I, pp. 434-35) grounded his conclusions on the high proportion of Aramaisms in the book, pointing to a postexilic date. Luther (*Tischreden*, LIX, 6) ascribed authorship to Sirach and described it as a Talmud, probably composed from books in the library of Ptolemy IV Euergetes.

5. F. Delitzsch, *Commentary on the Song of Songs and Ecclesiastes* (Leipzig: Dörffling & Franke, 1875; Edinburgh: T. & T. Clark, 1877; repr., Grand Rapids: Eerdmans, 1982), p. 190.

6. E. Renan, *L'Ecclésiaste traduit de l'Hébreu avec une étude sur l'age et le caractere du livre* (Paris: Levy, 1882), pp. 51-54.

7. J. Muilenberg, 'A Qoheleth Scroll from Qumran', *BASOR* 135 (1954) pp. 20-28; F.M. Cross, 'The Oldest Manuscripts from Qumran', *JBL* 74 (1955), pp. 147-72 (153, 162).

8. A.H. McNeile, *An Introduction to the Book of Ecclesiastes* (Cambridge: Cambridge University Press, 1904), pp. 34-37; G.A. Barton, *Ecclesiastes* (ICC; Edinburgh: T. & T. Clark, 1908), pp. 53-56.

The current scholarly consensus would make Ecclesiastes a product of the early Hellenistic period, probably around 250 BCE.[9] This dating is based largely on socioeconomic evidence, but also to some extent on the grounds of the alleged presence of Greek thought in Qoheleth's work. Other scholars have argued that the reported parallels between the work of Qoheleth and Greek thought are so general as to provide no evidence whatsoever for a date in the Hellenistic period. Citing the lack of grecisms in Ecclesiastes as additional evidence for their view, dates in the Persian period have been proposed where the socioeconomic evidence is said to tally with the social background presupposed by the book.[10] This introductory chapter will therefore examine the linguistic and socioeconomic evidence before Qoheleth's worldview is discussed in more depth.

2. *The Language of Ecclesiastes*

In the past decade there has been renewed interest in the language of Ecclesiastes. Most recently, Seow has argued that linguistic considerations entirely preclude the possibility of dating the book later than the fourth century. For him, it is a product of the Persian period, specifically between the second half of the fifth century and the first half of the fourth. This conclusion is also defended by Seow on socioeconomic grounds.[11]

Even supposing a Hellenistic dating for the composition of Ecclesiastes, the lack of grecisms in Qoheleth's work should come as no surprise. In the book of Daniel, most certainly a product of the Hellenistic period, the use of Greek loanwords is limited to the musical instruments played at the dedication of Nebuchadnezzar's image in ch. 3 (קִיתָרֹס/קַיתְרוֹס = κίθαρις 'zither', פְּסַנְתֵּרִין/פְּסַנְטֵרִין = ψαλτήριον 'dulcimer', סוּמְפֹּנְיָה = συμφωνία 'orchestra, bagpipes' [Dan 3.5, 7, 10, 15]).[12] The intent behind the use of these Greek words is specifically to

9. D. Michel, *Qohelet* (Darmstadt:Wissenschaftliche Buchgesellschaft, 1988), p. 114; Whybray, *Ecclesiastes*, pp. 11-12; J.L. Crenshaw, *Ecclesiastes* (Philadelphia: Westminster Press, 1987), p. 50.

10. H.W. Hertzberg, *Der Prediger* (KAT, 16.4; Leipzig: Scholl, 1932), pp. 45-49.

11. C.L. Seow, 'The Socioeconomic Context of "The Preacher's" Hermeneutic', *PSB* NS 17 (1996), pp. 168-95 (171).

12. F. Rosenthal, *A Grammar of Biblical Aramaic* (Wiesbaden: Otto Harrassowitz, 1983), p. 59.

introduce an 'exotic' foreign element into the story of Daniel in a foreign court.[13] There are no grecisms in Daniel that might be construed as belonging to everyday speech. Nor do we find grecisms in Ben Sira or Hebrew texts from Qumran.

In contrast to the author(s) of Daniel, Qoheleth does not seek to create an 'exotic' foreign atmosphere in his work. That is not to deny the possibility of foreign influence on his thought, but the fact remains that Qoheleth expressed himself in a language that would be accessible to the contemporary (Hebrew) reader. It uses a form of Hebrew which is probably colloquial: certainly the epilogue says that Qoheleth 'taught *the people* wisdom'.[14]

Another important fact that should be noted is that Qoheleth's use of Persianisms does not preclude a Hellenistic dating. The term פתגם, although of Persian origin, occurs in Dan. 3.16; 4.14. The use of the Persian loanword פרדס in the context of the Royal Experiment is evidence just as valid for a Hellenistic background to Ecclesiastes as a Persian. Indeed, if one considers this particular passage, the context appears to fit the Hellenistic era rather better: Crenshaw asserts that the series of first person verbs in this passage, 'I built...', 'I planted...', 'I made...', is indicative of Qoheleth's 'personal involvement in a life of luxury at any expense',[15] but it is clear that Qoheleth is actually work- ing very hard in this passage. In the space of five verses (2.4-9), there are 11 first person verbs, covering every aspect of managing an estate. Qoheleth describes the material benefits which he enjoys as the just reward of hard work (וזה היה חלקי מכל עמלי—2.10).

Traditional interpretations of the 'Royal Experiment' focus solely on the sensuality of the objects described in that passage: the fruit trees in specially watered orchards (2.5-6), the material wealth, livestock and

---

13. J.A. Montgomery (*Daniel* [ICC; Edinburgh: T. & T. Clark, 1927], p. 201) remarks on the 'cosmopolitan' nature of the musical instruments in Daniel com- pared with the Temple music as found in 1 Chron. 25.1; 2 Chron. 5.12-13. N. Porteous (*Daniel* [OTL; London: SCM Press, 1979], pp. 57-58) also calls attention to the 'rhetorical effect' achieved by the repetition of the list of officials in 3.2, 3 (many of which are Persian loanwords: cf. Rosenthal, *A Grammar of Biblical Aramaic*, p. 58) and by the list of (largely Greek) musical instruments.

14. The point that Qoheleth uses a form of colloquial Hebrew is made by Seow himself ('Linguistic Evidence and the Dating of Qohelet', *JBL* 115 (1996), pp. 643-66) but was also previously suggested by Crenshaw (*Ecclesiastes*, p. 31).

15. Crenshaw, *Ecclesiastes*, p. 78.

servants that Qoheleth accumulates (2.7-8).[16] This is no pleasure dome however, but a thriving business. The Persian *paridaiḏa* (*par-te-taš*) from which the Hebrew פרדס and the Greek παράδεισος is derived seems mainly to refer to parks and pleasure gardens (Cant. 4.13; cf. *AHw*, p. 833; LSJ, p. 1308), but may also have a utilitarian function (Neh. 2.8). The usage of the Greek derivation παράδεισος in the Ptolemaic period as referring to an (economically productive) orchard, however, is also appropriate to the context of the 'Royal Experiment'. In the same context, an interesting parallel to Qoheleth's usage in an apparently economic context of the terms כרמים 'vineyards' (2.4), גנות 'gardens' (2.5) and פרדסים 'orchards' (2.5) occurs in P. Pet. 3.26: 'If an ox, or beast of burden, or sheep or any other animal trespass on another man's arable land, or orchard (παράδεισον), or garden (κῆπον), or vineyard (ἀμπελῶνα)...'[17]

Seow's article on Qoheleth's use of language will prove valuable in reopening the debate on the setting of Ecclesiastes, for he does much to show that Qoheleth might have written considerably earlier than the current consensus would suggest. By his own admission, however, almost all of the features of Qoheleth's vocabulary and syntax are common to both the Persian and Hellenistic eras. The exception to this is Qoheleth's use of √שלט in a legal/economic sense, which he argues is characteristic only of the fifth to fourth centuries and it is on this basis that he dates Qoheleth's work conclusively to the Persian period.[18]

As I have suggested elsewhere however, this conclusion is flawed.[19] Evidence exists for a sustained usage of √שלט in its technical legal/ economic sense well into the Christian era. Since an investigation into Qoheleth's use of this root forms the body of Chapter 7 of the present

16. e.g. A. Verheij, 'Paradise Retried: On Qohelet 2:4-6', *JSOT* 50 (1991), pp. 113-15; S. de Jong, 'Qohelet and the Ambitious Spirit of the Ptolemaic Period', *JSOT* 61 (1994), pp. 85-96. For a dating of the text to this period on very different (and almost certainly erroneous) grounds, cf. A.D. Corré, 'A Reference to Epispasm in Koheleth', *VT* 4 (1954), pp. 416-18.

17. H.L. Ginsberg (*Studies in Koheleth* [New York: Jewish Theological Seminary of America, 1950], p. 42) argues that παράεισος is not used in the sense which Qoheleth attributes to it until the third century BCE and that the same sense is not attributable to its usages in Cant. 4.13 and Neh. 2.8.

18. Seow, 'Linguistic Evidence for the Dating of Ecclesiastes', pp. 665-66.

19. D.C. Rudman, 'A Note on the Dating of Ecclesiastes', *CBQ* 61 (1999), pp. 47-52.

work, a full discussion on its use for dating the book of Ecclesiastes will be found therein.

3. *Sociohistorical Evidence*

1. *Numismatic Evidence*

In his article on the sociohistorical evidence for a dating of Ecclesiastes to the Persian period, Seow considers significant the fact that it was at this time that coins were introduced to Palestine. The 'daric' began to be minted from around 515 BCE onwards and coins of other denominations were minted in the provinces. In Seow's own words, 'Coins began appearing [in Palestine] during the Achaemenian period, although they did not become common until the second half of the fifth century. And numerous hoards have been found at various sites in Israel, all dating to the fifth century and later'.[20]

While it is true that the economy of the Persian Empire was to some extent based on the use of coinage, the economic documents that Seow adduces as evidence of this fact show that many financial transactions at this time were still made in terms of goods or services.[21] If Qoheleth's work can be said to reflect a thoroughly *monetarized* environment (5.9 [ET 10]; 7.12; 10.19), then that environment would better fit the Hellenistic era. Where barter did not prevail in the Persian period, transactions commonly took place involving weights of silver rather than coinage *per se*.[22] This must therefore cast doubt on whether money was utilized as widely as Seow would like to suggest. Hengel is certainly of the opinion that 'by and large one might say that minted money was finally

---

20. Seow, 'Socioeconomic Context', pp. 171-73. J.L. Kugel also dates Ecclesiastes to the Persian period, partially on economic grounds ('Qohelet and Money', *CBQ* 51 [1989], pp. 32-49 [46-49]).

21. Seow, 'Socioeconomic Context', p. 172.

22. E. Stern (*Material Culture of the Land of the Bible in the Persian Period 538–332 B.C.* [Warminster: Aris & Phillips, 1982], p. 215) citing Arad Ostraca No. 41; F.M. Cross, 'The Discovery of the Samaria Papyri', *BA* 26 (1963), pp. 110-20 (112). The earliest mention of coinage from Elephantine is in A. Cowley, *Aramaic Papyri of the 5th Century B.C.* (Oxford: Clarendon Press, 1923), pp. 130-31 (Papyrus 35, ll. 3-4 [400 BCE]). Another text from Egypt dated 402 BCE specifically mentions payment in 'money of Greece' (E.G. Kraeling, *The Brooklyn Museum Aramaic Papyri: New Documents of the Fifth Century B.C. from the Jewish Colony at Elephantine* [New Haven: Yale University Press, 1953], p. 271).

established in Palestine only through Ptolemy II, and largely superseded barter'.[23]

A remarkable aspect of Palestine's archaeology is that so far, no Persian darics have been found. Such coins as occur (and these are relatively scarce compared with finds from the Hellenistic era) are very often Greek drachms.[24] After 404 BCE, Persian governors minted their own copies of these coins.[25] Indeed, this state of affairs, in which Greek money was used either in preference to, or because of the scarcity of, the Persian daric in Palestine may be reflected in the appearance of a possible Greek loanword דרכמונים (= Gk. Gen. Pl. δραχμῶν) occurring in late (i.e. Persian period) texts such as Ezra 2.69; Neh. 7.69-71.[26] By way of contrast, the Ptolemies were careful to maintain a strict coinage monopoly, with foreign coins being called in and reminted.[27] In Palestine, finds of coins minted by Ptolemy II Philadelphus (283/2–246) exceed those minted by Ptolemy I Soter (323–283/2) by four to fivefold and of all other coins previously minted (Pre-Ptolemaic, Attic, Phoenician, Philisto-Arabian and those of Alexander) by eightfold.[28] This evidence become still more impressive when one compares Philadelphus's reign of 36 years against almost two centuries of the 'highly monetarized' Persian economy which Seow cites as evidence for a fifth to fourth century date for the composition of Ecclesiastes.

Thus, while a case can be made for a Persian background to Qoheleth's interest in money and for the economically advanced society that is represented in Qoheleth's work, a closer parallel may be found in the far more widespread use of coinage in Ptolemaic times, specifically under Ptolemy II Philadephus. Although Persian period documentation from Egypt and Mesopotamia indicates the growing importance of coinage in economic transactions, the physical evidence from archaeological finds does not support the thesis that its use was as widespread

23. M. Hengel, *Judaism and Hellenism* (2 vols.; London: SCM Press, 1974), I, p. 44, II, pp. 34-35, II, pp. 208-209.

24. K. Galling, *Studien zur Geschichte Israels im persischen Zeitalter* (Tübingen: J.C.B. Mohr, 1964), p. 101; Stern, *Material Culture*, p. 227.

25. Hengel, *Judaism and Hellenism*, I, p. 33.

26. Stern (*Material Culture*, p. 228) does not deny the existence of such a loanword, but argues that in these two contexts, the author meant to write אדרכונים 'daric'.

27. Hengel, *Judaism and Hellenism*, I, p. 36.

28. Hengel, *Judaism and Hellenism*, I, pp. 43-44.

in Palestine at this time as Seow suggests. In contrast, finds from the Hellenistic era are extremely rich and are suggestive of an economic background much the same as that which is presupposed in Ecclesiastes.

2. Trade and Industry

The question of whether the book of Ecclesiastes can be said to reflect any particular time in terms of the business atmosphere evoked by Qoheleth's writing is a notoriously difficult one and a good case can be made by commentators arguing for a Persian or a Hellenistic background: both eras experienced times in which there were substantial increases in trade, resulting in prosperity for at least some of the inhabitants of Palestine. M. Dahood has even used Qoheleth's interest in the world of business as evidence for a Phoenician origin to the work,[29] although his arguments for the same based on the language and orthography of the book have found little favour in more recent years.[30]

As examples of the growth of trade in Persian times, Seow cites the population expansion that appears to have taken place in coastal areas, particularly Sharon and archaeological evidence from Tell Dor, Tell Abu Hawam (Haifa) and Tell Shiqmona showing that these were centres of manufacture for textiles, purple-dye or for the storage of grain and wine. Inland, one finds evidence of foreign coins (unsurprising in view of the apparent scarcity of the daric in Palestine—see above), ceramics, precious metals and jewellery, glass and alabaster. This culture is, Seow argues, in line with the cosmopolitan Jerusalem described in Neh. 13.15-16.[31]

---

29. M. Dahood, 'Canaanite-Phoenician Influence in Qoheleth', *Bib* 33 (1952), pp. 30-52, 191-221 (esp. 220-21 for commercial background); 'Qoheleth and Recent Discoveries', *Bib* 39 (1958), pp. 302-18; 'Qoheleth and Northwest Semitic Philology', *Bib* 43 (1962), pp. 349-65; 'Canaanite Words in Qoheleth 10,20', *Bib* 46 (1965), pp. 210-12; 'The Phoenician Background of Qoheleth', *Bib* 47 (1966), pp. 264-82.

30. R. Gordis, 'Was Koheleth a Phoenician? Some Observations on Methods in Research', *JBL* 71 (1955), pp. 105-109; A. Schoors, 'The Use of Vowel Letters in Qoheleth', *UF* 20 (1988), pp. 277-86; J.R. Davila, 'Qoheleth and Northern Hebrew', *Maarav* 5-6 (1990), pp. 68-87 (70-72).

31. Seow, 'Socioeconomic Context', pp. 174-75. The problem with Seow's picture of population expansion is precisely that such expansion took place on the coast (and not, apparently, in the hill country). The building remains from the Persian period in Palestine are in fact remarkably scanty (E. Stern, 'The Archaeology

Unfortunately, little information exists about agricultural innovations in Palestine during the Persian period, although it is known that the Persians made unsuccessful attempts to establish their native fruit trees (apricot, peach and cherry) in Asia Minor.[32] In the Jordan valley, the Persians apparently also established balsam plantations. These were relatively small at the time of Alexander (Pliny, *Hist. Nat.* 12.111-23) but were significantly extended as the Hellenistic period went on.[33]

Rapid and sustained development of trade and agriculture in Ptolemaic controlled areas occurred in the early Hellenistic era. For example, the trade in commodities such as precious metals, textiles, ceramics and glass was an important feature of business life at this time and underwent considerable expansion.[34] The necessity of competing with the Seleucid power in the north meant that Ptolemaic Egypt became in the words of W.W. Tarn, 'a money making machine'.[35] The state in effect was the property of the king, who, as a result of the various royal monopolies in trade and agriculture, became immensely rich (a situation which may well be reflected in the Royal Experiment in 1.12–2.12).[36]

During the foundation years of the Ptolemaic period, particularly during the reign of Ptolemy II Philadelphus, Egypt and her provinces experienced an economic boom. Evidence for this assertion comes in part from the Zeno papyri, a series of letters from the representative of Philadelphus's διοίκητης (Finance Minister) to his master reporting on the state of the king's possessions in Palestine. For example, Gaza is

of Persian Palestine', in W.D. Davies and L. Finkelstein (eds.), *The Cambridge History of Judaism*. I. *The Persian Period* (Cambridge: Cambridge University Press, 1984), pp. 90-91.

32. H. Koester, *History, Culture and Religion of the Hellenistic Age* (Philadelphia: Fortress Press, 1984), p. 79.

33. Hengel, *Judaism and Hellenism*, I, p. 45.

34. Koester, *Hellenistic Age*, pp. 76-79.

35. W.W. Tarn and G.T. Griffith, *Hellenistic Civilization* (3rd rev. edn; London: Methuen, 1959), p. 179.

36. Hengel, *Judaism and Hellenism*, pp. 35-36; C. Préaux, *Le monde héllenistique: La Grece et l'Orient de la mort d'Alexandre a la conquête romaine de la Grece (232-146 av. J.-C.)* (Paris: Nouvelle Clio, 1978), pp. 208-12. In this context, see my article 'Qohelet's Use of לפני', *JNSL* 23 (1997), pp. 143-50, which argues that Qoheleth's statement that he attained more wisdom or wealth 'than all who were before me in Jerusalem' (1.16; 2.7, 9) refers to the king's ability to amass more wealth than his contemporaries: the expression היה לפני used in the context of kingship is actually an idiom meaning 'to be subject to' (cf. 1 Sam. 29.7, 8).

mentioned as an important centre for the trade of incense, myrrh, aromatic goods, spices and other luxury items.[37] Papyrus was planted in Palestine in this period.[38] Grain and olive oil were important Palestinian exports and the slave trade also played a lively part in the local economy.[39] Other goods, such as smoked fish, cheese, meat, dried figs, fruit, honey and dates, were also exported according to the Zeno archive (PCZ 59012-14). The cities of Jamnia and Ascalon were also founded or refounded at this time as a result of the Ptolemies' active sponsorship of urban building projects in Palestine (notably, such projects were not sponsored in Egypt itself).[40]

Just as archaeological evidence demonstrates a burgeoning Palestinian economy in Persian times, so the same can be said of the province under Ptolemaic rule. New agricultural settlements sprang up around Jaffa in the middle of the third century BCE and a Hellenistic warehouse incorporating among other things an oil press, dyeing equipment and a workshop has been found in the same area. A dye-works was built at Tell Mor around this time and the importance of this industry to the local economy is confirmed by evidence of a wholesale wool dyeing business found in the Hellenistic strata of Gezer. This also implies the presence of sheep farming and weaving industries.[41]

The Ptolemaic practice of planning the national economy is reflected by a range of technological innovations, such as improved oil and wine presses, the treadmill, the plough, and the introduction of new crops and improved breeds of livestock.[42] One such technological advance is the introduction of the wheel for raising water: a technique previously unknown in Egypt and Syria-Palestine. Artificial irrigation appears to have been unknown in Palestine before the Hellenistic period: it is notable that the first explicit mentions of such a practice occur in Ecclesiastes and Ben Sira (Eccl. 2.6; Sir. 24.30-31). While no archaeological evidence of such practices exist for Palestine in the Persian period, one finds at Adullam in Judaea in the Hellenistic period artificial

---

37. V. Tcherikover, *Hellenistic Civilization and the Jews* (Philadelphia: Jewish Publication Society of America; Jerusalem: Magnes Press, 1959), p. 70.
38. Hengel, *Judaism and Hellenism*, I, p. 46.
39. Hengel, *Judaism and Hellenism*, I, pp. 41-42.
40. Koester, *Hellenistic Age*, p. 209.
41. Hengel, *Judaism and Hellenism*, I, p. 46.
42. Hengel, *Judaism and Hellenism*, I, p. 47.

pools, terraces and canals much like those described by Qohelet in his 'Royal Experiment' (Eccl. 2.6).[43]

3. *Society*

The book of Ecclesiastes tells us much about the nature of society when Qoheleth was writing. It was apparently a time of frenetic commercial activity (2.4-9; 4.4, 8; 11.1-2). But it was also a time when there was a great divide between rich and poor (5.11 [ET 12]). While the wealthy could afford to indulge themselves in the luxuries that Qoheleth recommends, the poor suffered under heavy burdens and corruption was rife (3.16; 4.1). Nor was there much hope for the individual, apparently, in going to law. Justice could be, and seemingly was, denied to those who were lower down on the social scale (5.7 [ET 8]).

Kugel and Seow have both pointed out that this situation is or may be to some extent applicable to Palestinian society during the period of Persian domination.[44] To be sure, most of Seow's examples of parallels to the situation as described in the text of Ecclesiastes come from Egypt and Mesopotamia. However, parallels exist with the situation in Judah as described in the book of Nehemiah in which people were forced to take out loans against their property to buy food during a famine or to pay taxes (Neh. 5.3-4) or even giving their children as pledges for debt (5.5).[45] This was not an unusual situation, for Nehemiah goes on to remark on the heavy taxes exacted by former governors from the general populace (5.15).

On the other hand, the situation that we find in the Hellenistic period is also one in which these conditions occurred. Whereas very little is known for sure about the socioeconomic situation in Palestine during the *later* Persian period to which Ecclesiastes has been dated by Kugel and Seow, the situation during the Hellenistic period, as well as being inferred from Egyptian documents of the time, is described in Palestine by the Zeno archive. In a letter to Zeno, one of his Palestinian employees complains that his wages are unpaid by his Greek masters on a regular basis because 'I am a barbarian...and am not able to speak

43. Hengel, *Judaism and Hellenism*, I, p. 46.
44. Kugel, 'Qohelet and Money', pp. 35-37, 46-48; Seow, 'Socioeconomic Context', pp. 182-85.
45. Seow, 'Socioeconomic Context', p. 185; Hengel, *Judaism and Hellenism*, I, p. 49.

Greek (ὅτι οὐκ ἐπίσταμαι ἑλληνιοζειν)'.[46] In general, those natives who were prepared to 'hellenize' by learning to speak Greek fared much better than the non-Greek speaking 'barbarians' who were ruthlessly exploited by the Greek upper classes.[47]

Just as in the period of Persian domination, defaulting debtors in the Hellenistic era could be sold into slavery.[48] The Ptolemaic system which steered the economy also had a more insidious influence on society however. As we have seen, it could bring spectacular benefits for some (notably Greeks or Hellenized natives) but denied ordinary people a share in the benefits of the economic growth which took place in the third century. In the words of Koester:

> The primary cause [of social injustice and unrest] can...be found in the system of state monopoly, which continuously confronted the native working class with oppressive rules and regulations, but never granted a share in the proceeds of their labor and in the general wealth of the country.[49]

Such a scenario for society in Hellenistic times gives added irony to Qoheleth's words 'What profit is there for a man in all his labour which he undertakes under the sun?' (Eccl. 1.3, cf. 3.9). The *double entendre* behind Qoheleth's recurrent use of ענה√ ('to occupy', 'to afflict') in such statements as 'I have seen the business/affliction which God has given men to be occupied/afflicted with (ראיתי את העניין אשר נתן אלהים לבני האדם לענות בו—3.10, cf. 1.13; 2.23, 26; 4.8; 5.2 [ET 3]; 8.16) may also reflect this social setting and draw an implicit parallel between the actions of the oppressive Greek employers of the day and a deity who demands no less work of his subjects.

4. *Thought*

No author's work can be said to be entirely original. Everyone is to some extent dependent for their worldview on their cultural background and history. Indeed, Qoheleth himself might be said to concur with such a view in his statement 'that which has been is that which will be, that

---

46. PColZen 2,16, no. 66, 18, 21 cited by Hengel, *Judaism and Hellenism*, I, p. 39, II, p. 31.
47. Hengel, *Judaism and Hellenism*, I, p. 38.
48. Hengel, *Judaism and Hellenism*, I, pp. 49, 57.
49. Koester, *Hellenistic Age*, p. 55; Tcherikover, *Hellenistic Civilization*, p. 72.

which has been done is that which will be done: there is nothing new under the sun' (1.9).

Most commentators agree, however, that Qoheleth's thought is at times very different from anything that we find elsewhere in the Hebrew Bible.[50] Indeed, this fact was recognized at a very early stage. In Midrash Rabbah, we read: 'The sages sought to suppress the book of Qoheleth because they found in it words of heresy' (*Midr. Qoh.* to 1.3; 11.9).[51] This naturally gives rise to the question of what precisely is the cultural backgound that gave rise to Qoheleth's work.

1. *Ancient Near East (Mesopotamia)*

Similarities between Mesopotamian thought and that of Qoheleth have in the past been noted. This is particularly true in the case of the *Epic of Gilgamesh*, and almost all commentaries make an overt comparison between Eccl. 9.7-10 and the speech of Siduri the barmaid to Gilgamesh in the Old Babylonian version of this saga (Tablet 10.3 [*ANET*, p. 90]).[52] Affinities have also been noted with other Mesopotamian texts such as the *ludlul bel nēmeqi* ('I Will Praise the Lord of Wisdom' 2.10-38 [*ANET*, pp. 434-35]) which states that divine decrees are hidden from human sight (cf. Eccl. 3.11; 8.17) and that righteous and wicked may receive the same treatment from the gods (cf. 8.12-14). This view is also to be seen in 'A Dialogue about Human Misery' (27.276-80 [*ANET*, pp. 438-40]). Nevertheless, humanity's evils are against the will of the gods ([VIII] ll. 79-86, *ANET*, p. 439) and firmly rooted in human perversity. The essential problem is that the gods are remote and

---

50. D. Michel, *Untersuchungen zur Eigenart des Buches Qohelet* (BZAW, 183; Berlin: W. de Gruyter, 1989), p. 289; H.-P. Müller, 'Neige der althebräische "Weisheit": Zum Denken Qohäläts', *ZAW* 90 (1978), pp. 238-64; Crenshaw, *Ecclesiastes*, p. 52.

51. R.B. Salters, 'The Book of Ecclesiastes: Studies in the Versions and the History of Exegesis' (PhD dissertation; St Andrews, 1973), p. 3.

52. For a detailed treatment, see J. de Savignac ('La sagesse du Qôhéléth et l'épopée de Gilgamesh', *VT* 28 [1978], pp. 318-23). Cf., e.g., Hertzberg, *Der Prediger*, pp. 158-59; A. Lauha, *Kohelet* (BKAT, 19; Neukirchen–Vluyn: Neukirchener Verlag, 1978), pp. 169-70; Crenshaw, *Ecclesiastes*, p. 162; Whybray, *Ecclesiastes*, p. 143. Ranston's caution in asserting Qoheleth's dependence on this work is, as Whybray remarks, justified (M. Ranston, *Ecclesiastes and the Early Greek Wisdom Literature* [London: Epworth, 1925], p. 146).

interfere in human life only in the most general ways ([VII-VIII] 70-77; [XXIII] ll. 243-44; [XXIV] ll. 255-64, *ANET*, pp. 439-40). If some aspects of this text may be termed fatalistic, it is certainly not as thoroughgoing as in the work of Qoheleth. Another oft cited parallel occurs in the 'Pessimistic Dialogue between Master and Servant' (VIII ll. 55-60, *ANET*, pp. 438) which adopts an ambivalent attitude towards women, similar in some respects to that of Qoheleth.[53] Qoheleth's apparently contradictory attitude toward women (7.26; 9.9) will form the subject of one of the chapters of this book.

Among more recent commentators, O. Loretz has argued forcefully for a Semitic background to the thought of Qoheleth. For him, the parallels with Mesopotamian literature, although not enough to prove direct dependence, point to a shared worldview (Loretz is particularly impressed by the parallels between Eccl. 9.7-9 and the *Epic of Gilgamesh*).[54] It would be surprising if this were not the case, however. The question is, can a Semitic background account convincingly for all of Qoheleth's thought?

2. *Egypt*

Parallels also exist between the book of Ecclesiastes and Egyptian thought. This need not in itself be surprising, since Israelite wisdom was to some extent influenced by Egyptian ideas. For example, the dependence of Prov. 22.17–24.22 on the Egyptian 'Instruction of Amenemope' remains generally accepted, although some scholars have recently cast doubt on this hypothesis.[55]

With regard to the book of Ecclesiastes itself, the situation is altogether less clear. Comparisons have been made to such texts as the 'Instruction of 'Onchsheshonqy' (*AEL* 3:184-217), 'The Harper's Song' (*ANET*, p. 467) and the 'Dialogue between a Man and his Soul' (ll. 65-68, *ANET*, p. 405) with their injunction to enjoy life's material

---

53. Crenshaw, *Ecclesiastes*, pp. 51-52; R.E. Murphy, *Ecclesiastes* (WBC, 23a; Dallas, TX: Word Books, 1992), pp. xlii-xliii.

54. O. Loretz, *Qohelet und der Alte Orient: Untersuchungen zu Stil und theologischer Thematik des Buches Qohelet* (Freiburg: Herder, 1964), pp. 45-134.

55. R.N. Whybray, *The Composition of the Book of Proverbs* (JSOTSup, 168; Sheffield: JSOT Press, 1994), p. 132. Discussions on the influence of Egyptian thought on the wisdom of Israel may be found in W. McKane, *Proverbs* (OTL; London: SCM Press, 1970), pp. 51-208; R.J. Williams, 'The Sages of Ancient Egypt in the Light of Recent Scholarship', *JAOS* 101 (1981), pp. 1-19.

benefits in the face of uncertainty or death (cf. Eccl. 9.7-10; 11.7–12.7).[56] Others have argued that Ecclesiastes is a 'Royal Testament' in the vein of the teaching of Merikare (*ANET*, pp. 414-18),[57] although Qoheleth apparently drops his royal persona after 2.12. The idea of dependence *per se* between Egyptian wisdom and the work of Qoheleth has in fact never gained general acceptance, and though the works discussed in this section are frequently cited in commentaries, this is largely to demonstrate that thinkers in different cultures considering similar questions ('how much control do we have over our own fate?', 'how should we approach death?') tend to reach similar conclusions.[58]

3. *Greece*

The question of whether Qoheleth shows traces of Greek thought refuses to go away. H. Ranston argued that Qoheleth is dependent on early Greek philosophy, particularly the work of Theognis.[59] Comparisons have also been made with Heraclitus (fl. 500 BCE), whose philosophy exerted considerable influence on Stoic thought.[60] Others have sought parallels with the main philosophies of the Hellenistic era (notably Stoicism and Epicureanism).[61]

The most thorough treatment of the question of possible Greek

56. B. Gemser, 'The Instructions of Onchsheshonqy and Biblical Wisdom Literature', in *Congress Volume, Oxford, 1959* (VTSup, 7; Leiden: E.J. Brill, 1960), pp. 102-28. For a comparison with 'The Harper's Songs', see M.V. Fox, *The Song of Songs and Ancient Egyptian Love Songs* (Madison: University of Wisconsin Press, 1985).

57. K. Galling, *Der Prediger* (Tübingen: J.C.B. Mohr, 1969), p. 88; G. von Rad, *Wisdom in Israel* (London: SCM Press, 1972), pp. 226-37.

58. Crenshaw, *Ecclesiastes*, pp. 51-52.

59. Ranston, *Ecclesiastes and the Early Greek Wisdom Literature*, pp. 13-62. M. Strange argues strongly against this position, however ('The Question of Moderation in Eccl. 7:15-18' [STD dissertation; Catholic University of America, 1969], pp. 115-20).

60. E. Pfleiderer, *Die Philosophie des Heraklit von Ephesus, nebst Koheleth und besonders im Buch der Weisheit* (Berlin: Reimer, 1886).

61. T. Tyler, *Ecclesiastes* (London: Williams & Norgate, 1874), pp. 10-29; E.H. Plumptre, *Ecclesiastes* (Cambridge: Cambridge University Press, 1881), pp. 30-32; E. Bickerman, *Four Strange Books of the Bible* (New York: Schocken Books, 1967), pp. 141-49; J.G. Gammie, 'Stoicism and Anti-Stoicism in Qoheleth', *HAR* 9 (1985), pp. 169-87; J. Blenkinsopp, 'Ecclesiastes 3.1-15: Another Interpretation', *JSOT* 66 (1995), pp. 58-59, 62.

influence on Qohelet's work has been provided by R. Braun.[62] According to Braun, Qoheleth was indeed influenced directly by his Hellenistic environment in his choice of terms and phrases such as הבל (= τῦφος), יתרון (= ὄφελος), עמל (= πόνος), טוב לפני האלהים (= θεόφλος) and even indirectly (through a posited Phoenician borrowing from Greek) in the case of the phrase תחת השמש (= ὑφ' ἡλίῳ or ὑπὸ τὸν ἥλιον).[63] Braun also considers more general questions such as the style in which Greek philosophical thought was presented (e.g. the diatribe, an idea later put to use by Lohfink in his commentary) and philosophical concerns common to the general stock of Greek thought and that of the author of Ecclesiastes.[64] Braun's work has not won full acceptance, but it nevertheless still enjoys some measure of support from more recent commentators.[65]

Since the appearance of Braun's work, Lohfink has also appeared as a champion of the theory of widespread borrowing from Greek thought in the work of Qoheleth. Lohfink's dating of Ecclesiastes to the period 190–180 BCE is almost a necessary concomitant to his belief in heavy and diverse Greek influence on the work. In Lohfink's view, Ecclesiastes was written as a response to a religious crisis provoked by the Pro-Hellenist element in the upper classes and was designed to combine the best elements of Greek philosophy and Judaic religious belief.[66]

Parallels for this intention certainly exist: Aristobulus, writing in the mid-second century, attempted to write a commentary on the Pentateuch in the light of Stoic philosophy, and Philo of Alexandria also attempted to combine Greek (primarily Platonic but to a lesser extent Stoic) and Jewish thought in a series of works.[67] However, there are problems with Lohfink's position. First of all, he dates the book (deliberately) to a time of social tension. Syria-Palestine had recently been

62. R. Braun, *Kohelet und die frühhellenistische Popularphilosophie* (BZAW, 130; Berlin: W. de Gruyter, 1973).

63. Braun, *Kohelet*, pp. 44-55.

64. See n. 71 below.

65. O. Kaiser, 'Judentum und Hellenismus', *VF* 27 (1982), pp. 69-73; Fox states: 'Although many of the parallels Braun adduces are not persuasive, he has undoubtedly made the case that Qohelet was not isolated from his contemporary intellectual context' (M.V. Fox, *Qohelet and his Contradictions* [JSOTSup, 71; Sheffield: Almond Press, 1989], p. 16).

66. N. Lohfink, *Kohelet* (Würtzburg: Echter Verlag, 1980), pp. 7-15.

67. Koester, *Hellenistic Age*, p. 144; T.H. Tobin, 'Logos', *ABD*, IV, pp. 348-56 (350).

racked by wars between the Ptolemies and the Seleucids, having been temporarily overrun in 219 BCE by Antiochus III and finally coming under Seleucid control in 195 BCE, only five years before the proposed date of Qoheleth's work. Yet Ecclesiastes says nothing of the economic upheavals that must have accompanied these invasions. The socio-economic setting presupposed by Ecclesiastes is one of peace in which individuals may acquire considerable fortunes through business (2.4-11; 4.7-8; 5.9-10 [ET 11-12]). Fortunes are lost as well as made (5.12-14 [ET 13-15]; 11.1-2), but this is the result of unlucky speculation rather than the devastation of war.

Second, Lohfink perhaps goes too far in imagining an elaborate background for Qoheleth and his work. For example, he suggests that Qoheleth belonged to an important priestly family and that the Jerusa-lem Temple was used as an educational establishment in an attempt to counter the growing influence of Greek schools. One of the 'set texts' for study was what we now know as the book of Ecclesiastes.[68] In some respects, Lohfink's reconstruction resembles the detailed biography of Qoheleth built up by Plumptre.[69] The book of Ecclesiastes contains very little hard evidence about the author. The fact that respectable com-mentators can differ so profoundly about its setting illustrates that only the most general conclusions can safely be reached on the question of Qoheleth the man.

The difficulties with Lohfink's dating of Ecclesiastes lead us back to the third century BCE. This was, as we have seen, a time of peace and of economic expansion commensurate with the background presupposed by Qoheleth's work. It is at this point that an examination of the pos-sibility of influence from the main Greek or Hellenistic philosophies of that period is appropriate.

a. *Epicurean philosophy*

Many other commentators have argued for the influence of Greek philo-sophy on Qoheleth's work. Tyler accounted for the contradictions apparent in the book of Ecclesiastes by suggesting that Qoheleth com-bined elements of Stoicism and Epicureanism in his work. In doing so, Qoheleth sought to argue against them and so reassert the traditional Judaic faith.[70] Again, this is a position not unlike that of Lohfink who

68. Lohfink, *Kohelet*, p. 8.
69. Plumptre, *Ecclesiastes*, pp. 35-55.
70. Tyler, *Ecclesiastes*, pp. 10-29, 33.

posits that the contradictions in Ecclesiastes can be resolved by under-standing the book as a diatribe.[71] However, Podechard is correct in pointing out the problems with Tyler's theory of Epicurean influence on the work of Qoheleth.[72] Tyler argues that Qoheleth's recommendation to joy is in line with Epicurean belief and specifically links Eccl. 5.17-19 (ET 18-20) with the concept of ἀταραξία or tranquillity, which should be the goal of the Epicurean sage.[73] A closer inspection of Epi-curean thought, however, shows that where Qoheleth thought that the best that could be expected of joy would be that it would enable the individual to largely forget the supreme injustice of death (5.19 [ET 20]), the Epicureans faced death squarely and without qualms: 'death is nothing to us' (Epicurus, *Letter to Menoeceus* 124; Lucretius, *De rerum natura* 3.830). The state of ἀταραξία is not based on self-delusion. Nor is it the experience of what Epicurus would call 'kinetic' pleasure (cf. Qoheleth's recommendation to 'eat and drink' in 2.24; 3.13; 5.17; 8.15). Rather, it denotes the complete absence of fear or pain (Epicurus, *Letter to Menoeceus* 127-32).[74] The serene attitude to life and its vicissitudes which the Epicureans counselled is in fact utterly alien to Qoheleth.

b. *Cyrenaic philosophy*
Although a thorough investigation falls outside the boundary of this study, a much closer parallel to Qoheleth's exhortations to joy exists in the philosophy of the Cyrenaics. This school was active in the reign of Ptolemy II Philadelphus (283/2–246), and took its name from the province of Egypt where it originated. Their main tenets were that life was unknowable and unjust and that the correct human response was consequently to seek what happiness was attainable through material pleasure.[75] In this, they differed significantly from the followers of

71. Lohfink, *Kohelet*, p. 10, following Braun, *Kohelet*, pp. 36, 165, 179, and S. de Ausejo, 'El género literario del Ecclesiastés', *EstBib* 7 (1948), pp. 394-406.

72. E. Podechard, *L'Ecclésiaste* (Paris: Lecoffre, 1912), pp. 95-102.

73. Tyler, *Ecclesiastes*, p. 20.

74. A.A. Long and D.N. Sedley, *The Hellenistic Philosophers* (2 vols.; Cam-bridge: Cambridge University Press, 1987), I, pp. 121-25.

75. H.D. Rankin, *Sophists, Socratics and Cynics* (Beckenham: Croom Helm, 1983), pp. 200-201; W.K.C. Guthrie, *History of Greek Philosophy* (6 vols.; Cam-bridge: Cambridge University Press, 1969), III, pp. 493-94. For texts, see E. Man-nebach, *Aristippi et Cyrenaicorum Fragmenta* (Leiden: E.J. Brill, 1961), pp. 36, 40-41, 43-44 (fr. 145, 156-57, 161, 181-83).

Epicurus (Diogenes Laertius 10.136). They also advocated suicide as a legitimate response to the inequities of existence, in line with the statement of Theognis, 'Of all things to men on earth, it is best not to be born...or, once born, to pass as quickly as possible through the gates of Hades' (Theognis 425-27, cf. Eccl. 4.3). Cyrenaic philosophy quickly became one of the main philosophies of Ptolemaic Egypt in the time of Philadelphus and eventually had to be suppressed because of a sharp increase in the suicide rate.[76]

Unfortunately, we have little information about the Cyrenaics other than that derived from fragmentary quotations and reports. We cannot know whether Qoheleth was directly influenced by this philosophy. However, the Cyrenaics no doubt contributed to and were a reflection of the Hellenistic *Zeitgeist* of the third century BCE. If the generally accepted dating of Ecclesiastes to the mid third century or not long after is correct, we should not be surprised at the affinities between the thought of Qoheleth and the philosophy that had created such a stir elsewhere in the kingdom of Philadelphus.

c. *Stoic philosophy*

The area of possible Greek influence on the work of Qoheleth that has elicited most discussion is its relationship to the thought of the Stoics. The conclusions of Tyler as far as Stoic influence on Ecclesiastes was concerned were quickly accepted by Plumptre, Siegfried and Condamin.[77] However, doubts as to this theory surfaced early and Delitzsch and McNeile contended that everything in Ecclesiastes could be accounted a natural development of Semitic thought.[78] Barton also concurred with this view, claiming that such parallels as exist between Ecclesiastes and Greek philosophy prove '...at most that Qohelet was a Jew who had in him the makings of a Greek philosopher'.[79]

---

76. Mannebach, *Aristippi et Cyrenaicorum Fragmenta*, p. 57 (fr. 247a-b).

77. Plumptre, *Ecclesiastes*, pp. 30-32; C.G. Siegfried, 'Review of T. Tyler, Ecclesiastes', *ZWT* (1875), pp. 284-91; 'Der jüdische Hellenismus', *ZWT* (1875), pp. 469-89; *Prediger und Hoheslied* (HAT II, 3/2; Göttingen: Vandenhoeck & Ruprecht, 1898), pp. 8-10; A. Condamin, 'Etudes sur l'Ecclésiaste', *RB* 9 (1900), pp. 30-44.

78. F. Delitzsch, *Ecclesiastes* (Grand Rapids: Eerdmans, 1982); Renan, *L'Ecclésiaste*, pp. 62-63; McNeile, *An Introduction to Ecclesiastes*, pp. 43-44.

79. G.A. Barton, partially quoting McNeile, *Ecclesiastes*, p. 34.

In more recent times, Gammie and Blenkinsopp have also advanced the hypothesis of some form of Stoic influence on the author of Ecclesiastes.[80] Gammie's methodology is superior to that of many of his predecessors in that he largely limits his discussion to known Stoic belief of the third century BCE.[81] He attempts to resolve the discrepancies between Qoheleth's thought and that of the early Stoic leaders by arguing that Qoheleth accepts some Stoic ideas and argues against others. Similarly, Blenkinsopp suggests that the catalogue of times in 3.2-8 was produced by a Stoicizing Jewish sage, being quoted by Qoheleth in order to argue against it.[82] Although the consensus remains that Qoheleth was active in the third quarter of the third century BCE, the idea of Stoic influence on the book of Ecclesiastes has gained no firm acceptance.

Perhaps the most striking feature of Stoic philosophy is that it advances the concept of a highly developed form of determinism. This is the belief that everything in the cosmos is controlled by a single force, which may be termed 'God' or 'Fate'.[83] The consequence of such a belief as far as humanity is concerned is that the individual is not responsible for his/her own thoughts and actions. This has important moral repercussions when it comes to the question of human evil: should individuals be punished for their own wickedness, or should blame be allotted to the deity who controls their actions? This was a problem that preoccupied the second and third leaders of the Stoic school, Cleanthes and Chrysippus and their solution was to limit the influence of determinism over human actions (although the approach of each was fundamentally different).[84]

This problem was also current in Judaism around 180 BCE when Ben Sira was writing. Apparently, the wicked could justify their actions at the time by making an appeal to a highly developed and logical form of determinism which had gained some ground in Jewish thought at that time:

80. Gammie, 'Stoicism and Anti-Stoicism in Qoheleth', pp. 169-87; Blenkinsopp, 'Ecclesiastes 3.1-15', pp. 55-64.

81. Gammie, 'Stoicism and Anti-Stoicism in Qoheleth', p. 173.

82. Blenkinsopp, 'Ecclesiastes 3.1-15', p. 61.

83. R. Taylor, 'Determinism', in P. Edwards (ed.), *Encyclopedia of Philosophy* (London and New York: Macmillan, 1967), II, p. 359.

84. W.C. Greene, *Moira: Fate, Good and Evil in Greek Thought* (Cambridge, MA: Harvard University Press, 1944), pp. 344-50.

Do not say, 'The Lord is to blame for my failure'; it is for you to avoid doing what he hates.

Do not say, 'It was he who led me astray'; he has no use for sinful men.

The Lord hates every kind of vice; you cannot love it and still fear him.

When he made man in the beginning, he left him free to take his own decisions;

if you choose, you can keep the commandments; whether or not you keep faith is yours to decide.

He has set before you fire and water; reach out and take which you choose;

before men lie life and death, and whichever he prefers is his.

For in his great and mighty power the Lord sees everything.

He keeps watch over those who fear him; no human act escapes his notice.

But he has commanded no man to be wicked, nor has he given licence to commit sin.

(Sir. 15.11-20, NEB)

The precise relationship between Ben Sira and Ecclesiastes remains unclear, but the passage above may suggest that some parts of Stoic deterministic theory exerted an influence over Judaic thought before the Greek domination over Palestine came to an end. On the other hand, evidence also exists for a deterministic worldview in biblical texts that date from before the Hellenistic period. Under these circumstances, the explanation offered by the sinner for his actions in this passage from Ben Sira may be seen as being in line with purely Judaic thought.

Many commentators have argued that Qoheleth himself was a determinist.[85] No full agreement exists on the nature of this determinism, nor whether this can be shown to come ultimately from a source in Stoic philosophy, as opposed to a Hebraic source. The object of this study is therefore twofold: first, it aims to show that Qoheleth was indeed a determinist. It will also consider questions such as the problem of human evil and how Qoheleth explains this in the light of his deterministic belief. A natural corollary of this will be an investigation into the extent to which Qoheleth regards the human will as being free to make choices and how this is combined with determinism. Finally,

---

85. Delitzsch, *Ecclesiastes*, pp. 254-55; Ginsberg, *Studies in Koheleth*, pp. 37-38; R.B.Y. Scott, *Proverbs Ecclesiastes* (AB, 18; Garden City, NY: Doubleday, 1965), p. 221; Fox, *Contradictions*, p. 192; Murphy, *Ecclesiastes*, p. 33.

having built up a picture of Qoheleth's worldview, this will be compared with determinism as it is expressed elsewhere in the Hebrew Bible and with Stoic beliefs of the third century BCE in order to discover the probable source of Qoheleth's thought.

Chapter 2

QOHELETH AND FATE

1. *Introduction*

Was Qoheleth a determinist? Many commentators have suggested as much. Delitzsch, for example, despite dating Ecclesiastes to the Persian period, nevertheless saw key texts expressing Qoheleth's worldview such as Eccl. 3.1-15; 9.11-12 as deterministic, stating that '(Man) is on the whole not master of his own life'.[1] More recently, Fox has argued in much the same vein.[2] Other commentators more wary of committing themselves on this question have nevertheless hinted that at least some aspects of Qoheleth's work may be explicable from a deterministic angle. Thus, Crenshaw states: 'If we cannot determine our future, however much we try, God's disposition towards us becomes a matter of life and death... The inevitable consequence of such thinking would seem to be some form of determinism'.[3]

Some commentators such as Podechard have argued that determinism is not evident at all in Ecclesiastes. Many passages presuppose a certain amount of free will on the part of humanity.[4] Indeed, Qoheleth regularly uses the imperative form of the verb which implies that the reader has a choice of whether or not to follow Qoheleth's advice (4.17 [ET 5.1]; 5.1 [ET 2], 3 [ET 4], 5-7 [ET 6-8]; 7.9-10, 13-14, 16-17, 21, 27; 8.2-3; 9.7-10; 10.4, 20; 11.1-2, 6, 9–12.1). These are powerful arguments against understanding Qoheleth as a determinist, so the fact that so many commentators continue to see evidence of determinism in his work may appear surprising.

1. Delitzsch, *Ecclesiastes*, pp. 254-55, 365-67.
2. Fox, *Contradictions*, p. 192.
3. Crenshaw, *Old Testament Wisdom: An Introduction* (Atlanta: John Knox Press, 1981), p. 136. Whybray's position on the concept of 'gift' in Ecclesiastes is similar: 'God may give joy and pleasure; man can never achieve it for himself, however hard he may try' ('Qoheleth, Preacher of Joy', *JSOT* 23 [1982], pp. 87-98 [89]).
4. Podechard, *L'Ecclésiaste*, p. 192.

At a fundamental level, determinism and free will are incompatible concepts. Nevertheless, philosophers who we call determinist have tried to combine them. For example, Chrysippus, the third leader of the Stoic school, argued powerfully for the influence of determinism on all earthly events (Cf. e.g. *SVF* 2.997). Nevertheless, when confronted by the dilemma of whether this meant that human beings were not morally responsible for their own actions, he also found a place for a limited degree of human free will in his worldview (e.g. *SVF* 2.1000). The same might also be said of his predecessor Cleanthes (e.g. *SVF* 1.537; 2.993). Stoicism of the third century BCE therefore advanced a form of 'soft determinism' (the belief that humanity's actions are guided by a combination of predestination and free will), as opposed to 'hard determinism' (the belief that all human action is preordained and that free will is therefore an illusion).

In the Hebrew Bible itself, there also exists a tradition of determinism, as von Rad has pointed out.[5] However, what is noticeable about biblical determinism when compared to later beliefs, is that it is more concerned with expressing the idea of divine sovereignty over history than of pursuing the logic of its own thought to explain the relationship between the individual and the world. Instead, it is content to reaffirm traditional Hebraic thought in this regard. Thus, von Rad states: '...even when the use of the term "determinism" is justified, it is never a question of a complex of ideas that have been thought through philosophically and logically. Thus, for example, the individual's freedom of decision in religious and ethical matters is, strangely enough, scarcely affected.'[6]

Is Qoheleth advancing a form of soft determinism in line either with biblical or Stoic thought? Such an idea cannot be ruled out on the basis of Qoheleth's apparent belief in human free will elsewhere. This chapter will therefore explore Qoheleth's use of key terms in contexts where determinism might be implied.

2. *Key Terms in Ecclesiastes*

1. קָרָה / מִקְרֶה ('*occurrence, happening*'/'*to happen, befall*')

The noun מִקְרֶה occurs seven times in Ecclesiastes (2.14, 15; 3.19 [3×]; 9.2, 3), and its associated verb קָרָה three times (2.14, 15; 9.11).

5.	Von Rad, *Wisdom in Israel*, pp. 263-83.
6.	Von Rad, *Wisdom in Israel*, p. 263.

Elsewhere in the Hebrew Bible, these terms appear to have a neutral sense: in Ruth 2.3, the noun מִקְרֶה describes the happy accident of Ruth gleaning in the field of Boaz. In 1 Sam. 6.9 it is used to distinguish between divine retribution and ordinary misfortune. In 1 Sam. 20.26 it refers simply to a chance occurrence. All 19 usages of the verb קָרָה in the Hebrew Bible appear to carry this sense of 'chance' happening (cf. BDB, pp. 899-900). In Ecclesiastes however, √קרה occurs almost exclusively in the context of death (the only exception being 9.11 in which it seemingly denotes the occurrence of ill-fortune). This section will therefore investigate Qoheleth's understanding of this term against the backdrop of its usage elsewhere in the Hebrew Bible.

a. *The versions*
The Versions offer little assistance in our efforts to discover Qoheleth's intent. In all locations, the LXX renders the MT's, מִקְרֶה and קָרָה with συνάντημα ('meeting') and συνάντάω ('to meet') respectively. The Targum's אֵרְעוּן/אִירְעוּן and עֵרַע/עָרַע, and the Peshitta's ܓܕܫܐ and ܓܕܫ have the same meanings of 'event' and 'to happen, befall'. Only the Vulgate attempts a more context-driven rendering, translating the term מִקְרֶה with the noun 'interitus', 'death' (2.14; 3.19 [×2]), once with 'occasus', 'downfall, death' (2.15), and once with the more neutral 'conditio' 'circumstances' (3.19), although the occurrence of 'interitus' immediately preceding gives it a negative meaning. In 9.2, 3, for the remaining occurrences of the term מִקְרֶה, the Vulgate uses a circumlocution involving the verb 'evenio', 'to happen, befall'. Thus, the Vulgate's renderings have a generally negative slant which well illustrates the observation of Crenshaw that the term מִקְרֶה is primarily bound up with the concept of death.[7]

b. *Modern commentators*
Crenshaw's observation concerning קָרָה/מִקְרֶה that 'both the noun... and the verb...have an ominous nuance everywhere in Ecclesiastes with the possible exception of 9.11 which emphasises the unpredictability of events' is a useful one.[8] Nevertheless, the tendency in recent times is not to see the term מִקְרֶה as indicative of a belief in determinism on Qoheleth's part. Fox describes מִקְרֶה as '"fate" in the sense of what happens to someone, as opposed to what he does to himself (not in the

7. Crenshaw, *Ecclesiastes*, p. 85.
8. Crenshaw, *Ecclesiastes*, p. 85.

sense of what is predetermined)'.[9] While he is certainly correct in his assertion that מקרה is 'what happens to someone' (i.e. that it refers to events outside human control), this does not preclude the possibility of this term's reference to a predetermined event.

In the final analysis, √קרה as it is used in Ecclesiastes cannot refer to a chance occurrence. The fact of death, to which it refers in the great majority of cases, is not a matter of chance: it is the one event that is guaranteed to come to all. Nor is the timing of one's death down to chance, for Qoheleth uses the term עת ('appointed time') of death (3.2; 7.17). While Qoheleth is disturbed by this event, he also recognizes that it is an evil to which all must submit (8.8; 9.2-3, 10). Qoheleth's main concern with death seems to be the unpredictability of its timing (7.15; 8.14). The lack of any apparent causal connection between one's religion or morality and the length of one's allotted span only heightens the feeling that, somewhere along the line, the deity is dealing human beings a raw hand.

No more a product of chance is the element of unpredictability noted by Crenshaw behind the use of the verbal form יקרה 'happen' in 9.11. This is illustrated in the use of the term עת once more in 9.12: 'Human beings do not know their appointed time [עת]. Like fishes caught in an evil net [מצודה]; like birds taken in a snare [פח], so human beings are caught at the appointed time [עת] when it falls suddenly on them'. Quite apart from the reference to such events happening at an 'appointed time' (the very opposite of chance), the metaphor suggests a controlling force: a fisher or birdcatcher. While the term פח ('snare') is a neutral one, מצודה tells the identity of this fisherman: it is God. Elsewhere in the Hebrew Bible, the term occurs four times (Ps. 66.11; Ezek. 12.13; 13.21; 17.20). In three of these instances (Ps. 66.11; Ezek. 12.13; 17.20), it means 'net' (as in Eccl. 9.12) and in all three examples the use is a figurative one, illustrative of Yahweh's judgment. On the one occasion where it means 'prey' (Ezek. 13.21), it refers to the people of Judah as the prey of a foreign power through the acquiescence of Yahweh: again, a reflection of divine judgment.

While √קרה in Ecclesiastes is not itself a deterministic term, it does demonstrate Qoheleth's belief in the *unpredictability* of life's events (the semantic shift involved in understanding Qoheleth's use of the term מקרה to refer to an 'unpredictable' occurrence rather than a

---

9. Fox, *Contradictions*, p. 184.

'chance' occurrence is not great). The vocabulary with which it is used and the contexts in which it appears strongly support the idea that it is not human beings, but the deity who is in control of human life, and the time at which it ends. At any rate, its usage in Ecclesiastes indicates that Qoheleth did not believe in 'chance'.

2. פֶּגַע *('Meeting')*

The noun פֶּגַע occurs only once in Ecclesiastes (9.11), and once else-where in the Hebrew Bible (1 Kgs 5.18 [ET 4]). In 1 Kgs 5.18, it refers to a misfortune (the occurrence or not of which is evidently determined by God), although there it is modified by the adjective רַע ('evil').[10] In the same way, the verbal form can mean 'encounter (with evil intent)' or 'harm' (Josh. 2.16; Judg. 8.21), but it may also have the more neutral basic meaning of 'meet' (1 Sam. 10.5; Gen. 32.2). In MH, Jastrow emphasizes the connotations of misfortune that פֶּגַע often carries.[11] In Eccl. 9.11, the term פֶּגַע is typically translated 'chance' in English Bible translations.

The Hebrew text under consideration here reads:

שבתי וראה תחת השמש כי לא לקלים המרוץ ולא לגבורים המלחמה וגם
לא לחכמים לחם וגם לא לנבנם עשר וגם לא לידעים הן כי עת ופגע
יקרה את כלם

> 'So I turned and I saw under the sun that the race is not to the swift, nor
> the battle to the strong, nor yet bread to the wise, nor yet riches to those
> with understanding, nor yet favour to the skilful, but time and 'meeting'
> happen to them all'.

In view of the discussion which has just centred on the meaning of מִקְרֶה in Ecclesiastes (i.e. that it means '[unpredictable] happening' rather than 'chance happening'), it is significant that Qoheleth uses the verbal form יִקְרֶה in this verse to describe how 'time and meeting' manifest themselves in human life. This suggests in turn that the noun פֶּגַע does not refer to the influence of chance over human endeavour.

10. Fox (*Contradictions*, p. 261) remarks that in this particular instance, it is impossible to determine whether רַע is a necessary modifier to this term, or merely juxtaposed with פֶּגַע for emphasis.

11. M. Jastrow, *A Dictionary of the Targumim, the Talmud Babli and Yeru-shalmi, and the Midrashic Literature* (New York: Judaica, 1992), p. 1135.

a. *The versions*

The LXX's, ἀπάντημα ('meeting') remains close to the literal meaning of the Hebrew. It does not, however, immediately clarify Qoheleth's understanding of the term. The relationship of form between the LXX's ἀπάντημα for פֶּגַע and the LXX's συνάντημα for מִקְרֶה is noteworthy, however, since it would appear to suggest that the LXX translator saw the two concepts as interrelated. The Vulgate's 'casum', is to some extent ambiguous, since the noun 'casus' can mean either 'accident', 'event', 'occurrence' or 'mishap' depending on context. As far as the Versions are concerned, this translation is the odd one out since it appears to suggest explicitly an element of randomness in events (cf. the use of the ablative form 'casu', 'by chance' in Latin), but has nevertheless influenced all English translations (e.g. Gen. B, AV, RV, RSV, NRSV, NEB, REB: 'time and chance'). The Targum's, עֶרְעִיתָא ('meeting') is similarly neutral: like the Hebrew verb פֶּגַע, the Aramaic verb עֶרַע has the sense of 'to happen', 'to meet'. The Peshitta's rendering makes use of the Syriac cognate term פֶּגַע to translate the MT's פֶּגַע. In Syriac, this term has very much the same semantic range as its Hebrew equivalent (i.e. 'meet', 'befall', 'happen'), and in fact is regularly used to translate √פֶּגַע by the Peshitta.[12] Thus, it sheds no further light on the meaning of the term פֶּגַע in Eccl. 9.10.

b. *Modern commentators*

The alternative interpretative tradition represented by the Vulgate, that פֶּגַע refers to a 'chance occurrence' continues in the thought of most modern commentators. Thus, Crenshaw states: 'Chance governs human lives, according to Qohelet... No one can prepare for the unexpected or compensate for randomness'.[13] Such a reading of 9.11 is also reflected in the various translations offered for the term פֶּגַע by others: 'Zufall' (Zimmerli, Lohfink), 'Glück' (Hertzberg), 'bad luck' (Scott).[14] Glasser refers to the 'accidents' (in the sense of chance happenings) which govern life, as does Seow.[15] Whitley is in a minority in his suggestion

---

12. K. Brockelman, *Lexicon Syriacum* (Hildesheim: Georg Olms, 1966), p. 556.
13. Crenshaw, *Ecclesiastes*, p. 164.
14. D. Zimmerli, *Der Prediger* (ATD, 16.1; Göttingen: Vandenhoeck & Ruprecht, 1962), p. 223; Lohfink, *Kohelet*, p. 71; Hertzberg, *Prediger*, p. 160; Scott, *Proverbs Ecclesiastes*, p. 245.
15. E. Glasser, *Le procès du bonheur par Qohelet* (Paris: Cerf, 1970), p. 157; C.L. Seow, *Ecclesiastes* (AB, 18c; Garden City, NY: Doubleday, 1997), p. 308.

that while פֶּגַע may refer to a 'mischance' elsewhere, here it has the neutral sense of 'event' or 'happening'.[16]

As Fox points out, even if פֶּגַע in Eccl. 9.11 were semantically neutral, the occurrences that Qoheleth describes therein are examples of misfortune.[17] A פֶּגַע denotes something that prevents the strong from victory in war and the swift from winning the race. In other words, it deprives those with a peculiar talent from experiencing the just reward of that talent. Taken in isolation, these two examples might suggest single, isolated incidences of bad luck, yet Qoheleth goes on to say that the wise may not be able to earn their living, nor the intelligent riches, nor the skilful gain favour because of עֵת וָפֶגַע ('time and meeting'). These latter examples are indicative of more than a single piece of misfortune affecting the outcome of an action. They illustrate ill-fortune dogging entire lives, perhaps even the whole of existence.[18]

Murphy follows Ginsberg in seeing here a reference to death.[19] Murphy argues that:

> No matter what one's talents, because of events beyond human control, one never has a sure grip on success. The 'time of calamity' is an unfortunate time, a fortuitous event that happens when one cannot cope with it. It refers to death, but also to any serious adversity.

Although Murphy's interpretation of the verse as referring to death creates contextual problems, it is interesting to note that he focusses on the fact of the outcome of one's efforts being ultimately 'subject to events beyond human control'.[20] If such events which determine the outcome of one's efforts are not coordinated, then they may be denoted by the term 'chance'. If they are coordinated in some way, then the outcome of one's actions are subject to Fate.

---

16. C.F. Whitley, *Koheleth: His Language and Thought* (BZAW, 148; Berlin: W. de Gruyter, 1979), p. 80.

17. Fox, *Contradictions*, pp. 260-61.

18. Glasser, *Qohelet*, p. 152.

19. H.L. Ginsberg (*Qoheleth* [Jerusalem and Tel Aviv: Newman, 1961], p. 116) argues that עֵת וָפֶגַע refers specifically to the time of death in Eccl. 9.11. This assertion is influenced by the appearance of עֵת רָעָה in v. 12, a passage which is frequently interpreted thus. In this he follows Barton (*Ecclesiastes*, p. 164) and ultimately the Metzudath David. While the thought that he sees in 9.11 is not alien to Qoheleth, it does not explain why those with a peculiar talent do not enjoy the reward thereof in life. Ginsberg's position is also adopted by A. Barucq (*Ecclésiaste* [Paris: Beauchesne, 1968], p. 163) and Murphy (*Ecclesiastes*, p. 94).

20. Murphy, *Ecclesiastes*, pp. 93-94.

In this context, it is particularly striking that in none of the examples
for the noun פֶּגַע or the verb פָּגַע given above is the event which it
denotes a random occurrence or meeting. In the case of Josh. 2.16 and
Judg. 8.21 there is intent behind both uses of the verb: Josh. 2.16 speaks
of pursuers 'meeting' their prey and Judg. 8.21 of Gideon 'meeting', or
falling on Zebah and Zalmunna following their challenge, with the
intent of killing them. In those examples of a more neutral meaning for
the verb, we see God's angels 'meeting' Jacob in the wilderness in Gen.
32.2 and the prophecy of Samuel in 1 Sam. 10.5 that the spirit of God
will come upon Saul when he meets a company of prophets. Neither of
these meetings can be said to be chance: on the contrary, they are
intended by at least one of the parties involved. Even the single usage
of the noun in 1 Kgs 5.18 (ET 4) is reflective of the same: the non-
appearance of a פֶּגַע to trouble Solomon's reign is attributed to God.
Similarly, the implication for Eccl. 9.11 is that the inexplicable adver-
sities in life which beset human endeavour are the product not of life's
randomness but of its orderliness: if the wise do not earn enough to survive and the swift fail to win their race, it is because it is intended thus.
Qoheleth would probably have agreed with Anatole France that chance
is 'the pseudonym of God when He did not want to sign'.

3. עֵת *('Time')*

The importance of the term עֵת to Qoheleth's worldview may be seen in
the fact that it occurs 40 times in Ecclesiastes (3.1, 2 [×4], 3 [×4], 4
[×4], 5 [×4], 6 [×4], 7 [×4], 8 [×4], 11, 17; 7.17; 8.5, 6, 9; 9.8, 11, 12
[×2]; 10.17). We have seen examples of how the term is used in conjunction with מִקְרֶה 'occurrence' and פֶּגַע 'meeting' in contexts where
some form of divine intervention in human affairs is being asserted by
Qoheleth. The object of this section will be to explore how Qoheleth
uses this term in isolation.

Since 30 of the 40 occurrences of the term עֵת occur in the passage
3.1-11, the investigation of this text will form a large part of this section. Thereafter, its usage will be considered in 7.17; 8.9; 9.8; 9.12;
10.17.

The passage 3.1-11 is crucial for our understanding of what Qoheleth
means when he speaks of עֵת ('time'). The views of modern commentators on the passage vary. Some see in 3.1-11 a deterministic
worldview expounded by Qoheleth: others an unrealized and unrealiz-
able ideal of acting at the appropriate moment which was so much a

part of Israelite Wisdom. Within this passage, vv. 2-8 provide a list of opposite or near-opposite actions which may occur in the course of a human lifetime. Although this section does have a degree of importance for this study, and will be commented upon in due course, it will not immediately yield the thought behind the term עת as used by Qoheleth. This investigation will therefore focus initially on 3.1 and 3.11.

a. *The versions*

Both זמן 'time' and חפץ 'business' are unusual terms, and may be indicative of the relatively late Hebrew of Ecclesiastes. זמן 'time', 'appointed time' (so BDB, pp. 273-74) occurs elsewhere in the Hebrew Bible only in Neh. 2.6; Est. 9.27, 31. All of these occurrences have the idea of an appointed time for some event. In Neh. 2.6, Nehemiah tells the king at what time he will return from his visit to Jerusalem. In Est. 9.27, 31, the appointed times for Jewish festivals are described. חפץ in the sense of 'business', 'matter', 'thing', may also be a late usage, occurring three times outside Ecclesiastes (Isa. 58.3, 13; Prov. 31.13) and three times in Ecclesiastes (Eccl. 3.1; 5.7; 8.6). In Isa. 58.3 the context is of furthering one's affairs by fasting, in Isa. 58.13 it is used of business that breaks the sabbath, and in Prov. 31.13 of the business that the diligent wife pursues.

The structure of 3.1 suggests that לכל זמן and לכל חפץ עץ are parallel in meaning. Thus עת for Qoheleth would also have the meaning of 'appointed time'. This is indeed suggested by the LXX which translates עת with καιρος in 3.2, 3, 4, 5, 6, 7, 8, 11, yet in 3.1 uses χρόνος for the MT's עת and καιρος for the MT's זמן. The Vulgate's 'tempus' is also used to translate the MT's זמן in 3.1, while in 3.2, 3, 4, 5, 6, 7, 8, 11 it translates the MT's עת. In 3.1, the Vulgate translates the MT's עת with the noun 'spatium' ('period of time'). The Targum meanwhile, uses the equivalent Aramaic terms for 'appointed time': זמנא for the MT's זמן and עידנא for the MT's עתו. It thus affords little help from a lexical perspective in interpreting this passage. The Peshitta's ܪ܏ܒܢ, which is equivalent to the Hebrew זמן is used twice to translate both the MT's זמן and עת in 3.1. The Versions therefore support the conclusion that עת and זמן mean the same thing, namely 'appointed time'.

By whom are these times appointed? All commentators, whether they argue that the catalogue of times is an expression of the wisdom ideal of attempting to act at the appropriate moment, or whether they understand it in a deterministic sense, understand the times of 3.1-8 as appointed by God.[21]

b. *Modern commentators*

The term עת has been viewed by commentators in a number of ways. In 3.1-8, it is seen by some commentators as exemplifying the ideal of doing the right thing at the right time, which pervaded wisdom literature,[22] and which also occurs in Greek thought.[23] Others understand it in a sense halfway towards determinism and have seen in this passage the Stoic concept of living according to reason, or the logos.[24] This is not dissimilar to Whybray, who argues concerning 3.1-8 that:

> the things which happen to a man (for example birth and death) and the opportunities which are given to him (for example, planting and uprooting, keeping and throwing away) occur at the time...which God has determined.[25]

The majority of commentators, however, argue that 3.1-11 should be understood in a deterministic sense. Thus Fox comments:

> The rightness or opportuneness of a particular time is not at issue here. The teaching of 3.1-9 is rather that the occurrence of all human events is

---

21. Siegfried, *Prediger*, pp. 39-41; M. Devine, *Ecclesiastes or the Confessions of an Adventurous Soul* (London: Macmillan, 1916), p. 56; Glasser, *Qohelet*, p. 61; D. Kidner, *A Time to Mourn and a Time to Dance* (Leicester: Inter-Varsity Press, 1976), pp. 38-39; Whybray, *Ecclesiastes*, p. 73; Seow, *Ecclesiastes*, p. 171.

22. Loretz, *Qohelet und der Alte Orient*, pp. 252-53. Cf. also Podechard, *L'Ecclésiaste*, p. 285.

23. Ranston (*Ecclesiastes*, p. 43) citing Theognis 402. Plumptre (*Ecclesiastes*, p. 127) also mentions the maxim of Pittacus in this connection: Καιρὸν γνῶθι 'Know the right season for everything', and the fact that Demetrius Phalerus, the librarian of Ptolemy Philadelphus wrote a treatise entitled περὶ καιροῦ 'Of opportuneness' (Diogenes Laertius 1. 4.6).

24. Gammie ('Stoicism and Anti-Stoicism in Qohelet', p. 175) treads a middle path, stating that 'Fate, is comparable to Qoheleth's understanding of divine causation (Qoh 3:11; 7:13)', but argues that the catalogue of seasons shows that there are some things over which human beings do have free will, an idea which is also expressed by Blenkinsopp ('Ecclesiastes 3.1-15', pp. 58-59). This view ultimately goes back as far as Tyler (*Ecclesiastes*, pp. 11-12) and Siegfried (*Prediger*, p. 39) however.

25. Whybray, 'Preacher of Joy', p. 89. A similar view is suggested by Devine (*Ecclesiastes*, p. 56), arguing specifically against a full deterministic rendering.

beyond human control, for God makes everything happen in its proper time (proper, that is, from his viewpoint).[26]

Jastrow reads similarly, stating that 'Koheleth's thought is, that everything is preordained and the time for its occurrence fixed. Why then toil and worry: Things will happen anyway at the appointed time'.[27] Yet while many commentators will agree with the first part of this reading, the force of the rhetorical question in 3.9 seems to be rather: 'what do human beings get out of all the toil (denoted by 3.1-8) which the deity forces them to do'?

The same position is taken by Delitzsch, who sees 3.1-8 as essentially deterministic in character:

> ...all happens when and how God wills, according to a world plan, comprehending all things which man can neither wholly understand, nor in any respect change... All that is done here below is ordered by God at a time appointed, and is done without any dependence on man's approbation.[28]

This line of thought is also followed by Ginsberg, Scott and Murphy.[29]

Podechard mentions such deterministic readings of 3.1-8 and other parts of Ecclesiastes. However, he is also quick to point out that many other parts of the Hebrew Bible 'contiennent des affirmations tout aussi inquiétantes pour la liberté humaine' (or 'contains statements just as disturbing for human freedom') and that human free will is presupposed in many parts of Ecclesiastes (3.16; 4.1; 7.15-17; 8.10-15; 9.2-3).[30] Podechard's argument in these passages about the problem of free will in Ecclesiastes centres on the freedom of humankind to commit actions that Qoheleth views as wicked or evil. Human beings appear from Qoheleth's experience to be given free rein to oppress their fellows and God appears to have no predictable system to mete out just reward and retribution.

Although God's system for reward and retribution may not be predictable, this is not the same as saying that such a system does not exist. God punishes the sinner and rewards the good (2.26), though Qoheleth

---

26. Fox, *Contradictions*, p. 192.

27. M. Jastrow, *A Gentle Cynic* (Philadelphia: Lippincott, 1919), p. 210 n. 41.

28. Delitzsch, *Ecclesiastes*, pp. 254-55.

29. Ginsberg, *Studies in Koheleth*, pp. 37-38; *idem, Koheleth*, pp. 73-74; Scott, *Proverbs Ecclesiastes*, p. 221; Murphy, *Ecclesiastes*, p. 33.

30. Podechard, *L'Ecclésiaste*, p. 192.

is unable to predict what makes the individual 'good before God'.[31] God would appear to be the missing comforter for the oppressed in 4.1.[32] Good times and bad follow hard upon each other in the life of the individual at the behest of God, without reference to the individual's morality or piety (7.14). Qoheleth's God is far from absent in the world, despite Qoheleth's statement that 'God is in Heaven and you upon Earth' (5.1 [ET 2]). Here Qoheleth emphasizes God's power, manifested precisely in his ability to punish those who displease him (5.5 [ET 6]). In fact, for many commentators, it is in the arbitrary nature of God's actions that Qoheleth comes closest to an assertion of determinism.[33] Fate is an unpredictable force. Although Qoheleth's Jewish culture tells him that there is a God who cares for the righteous and punishes the wicked (3.17; 8.12-13), his own observations tell him that frequently the innocent suffer and the wicked triumph (3.16; 4.1; 5.7 [ET 8]; 7.15; 8.9-11). The logical conclusion to be drawn from this discrepancy would therefore be that either God does not exist, or that God does not take part in the world's affairs. Qoheleth, however, draws no such conclusion: he concludes that there is a God, but that he distributes his gifts in a random, unpredictable way (2.26; 5.18 [ET 19]; 6.2).

The arguments in favour of the position that 3.1-11 is a deterministic text are given by Fox: in 3.11 the text states that God makes everything happen 'in its time', while 3.14 suggests that God is the cause of everything that happens. In 3.17, the action occurring at a certain 'time' is clearly that of God's judgment. Here again, the focus is not on the opportuneness or otherwise of human actions, but on a specific activity carried out by the deity.[34]

---

31. Scholars such as Siegfried (*Prediger*, p. 38), McNeile (*Ecclesiastes*, p. 24), Barton (*Ecclesiastes*, p. 84), Podechard (*L'Ecclésiaste*, p. 284), Lauha (*Kohelet*, p. 58) and Whybray (*Ecclesiastes*, p. 64) have, for various reasons (usually involving the attribution of the verse to a glossator), understood 2.26 to have a moral content. The majority of recent commentators, however, assign the verse to Qoheleth and understand the terms in the sense of 'pleasing to God' and 'displeasing' (so Hertzberg, *Prediger*, pp. 82-83; Zimmerli, *Prediger*, pp. 161-62; Fox, *Contradictions*, pp. 188-90; Crenshaw, *Ecclesiastes*, p. 90; Murphy, *Ecclesiastes*, p. 27).

32. Glasser, *Qohelet*, p. 74.

33. Crenshaw, *Old Testament Wisdom*, p. 136.

34. Fox, *Contradictions*, p. 192.

c. *The wider context (Ecclesiastes 7.7; 8.9; 9, 12; 10.17)*

If the wider context is considered with reference to Qoheleth's usage of the term עת, it is possible to come to some provisional conclusions about Qoheleth's usage of this term in the catalogue of seasons. A range of views exist on the interpretation of this passage, each of which hinges on he meaning of the term עת. If 3.1-11 is taken in isolation, a good case can indeed be made for it referring to an ideal time for each human activity in accordance with which human beings are unable to act. However, evidence from the wider context suggests that Qoheleth's use of the term עת refers to the divinity's imposition of his will on human affairs, making humanity act in a certain way at the time which he has determined.

In 7.17, Qoheleth advises against being 'overly wicked' with the rhetorical question 'why should you die before your time (בלא עתך)?' Qoheleth's thinking here is that human wickedness will lead to the ultimate punishment of death from the divinity.[35] In this situation, עת cannot refer to an impossible ideal. Rather, it is to the termination of the span of time which the deity has allotted to the individual for his life. The implication is that God chooses the 'time' at which one dies, but that this may be revised in the light of subsequent behaviour.[36] The idea that one's death has an '(appointed) time' is also evident in the phrase עת למות 'a time to die' in the catalogue of seasons (3.2). The timing of one's death is not usually considered as something over which human beings have any control, and indeed this idea is reflected in Qoheleth's statement in 8.8: 'No-one has power over the spirit to retain the spirit, nor can one exercise proprietorship in the day of death. There is no substitution in that war...'

As shall be demonstrated later, the thought of 8.9-10 is intimately bound up with the usage of שלט√. Recently, Seow has pointed out that Qoheleth typically uses this root in its technical legal/economic sense of delegated authority.[37] It is God who gives to the individual שלטון

---

35. Barton (*Ecclesiastes*, p. 144) and Jastrow (*A Gentle Cynic*, p. 225) imply acceptance of a certain amount of wickedness on Qohelet's part: it is excess which leads to punishment.

36. This indeed is the idea in Job 22.16, cited by Crenshaw (*Ecclesiastes*, p. 141), although he sees the death of the wicked individual as the result of action by 'angry fellows' or the 'authorities' rather than God as such.

37. Seow (*Ecclesiastes*, p. 284) sees the term in 8.9 in its technical sense but makes the connection with human authorities as givers of שלטון rather than God.

('proprietorship, authorization') over goods in 5.18 (ET 19); 6.2. Thus, Qoheleth's remark in 8.9 that 'there is a time (עת) in which one man exercises proprietorship (שׁלט) over another to his detriment' can be understood as an expression of the inscrutability of the deity's rule. The nature of Qoheleth's complaint is that God allows one individual to oppress another, so that the deity becomes implicated in human wrongdoing. Thus it is that Qoheleth can say in 8.10 that he saw 'wicked people approaching and even entering the holy place and they went about the city priding themselves on having done right'.[38]

The context of 9.8 is on the face of it not overtly deterministic, for it is one in which Qoheleth offers advice to the disciple: 'at all times (בכלעת) let your garments be white and let your head lack no oil'. (On the other hand, it is the deity who gives the opportunity for joy to human beings. In 3.13, for example, 'the gift of God' is the ability 'to eat and to drink and to experience the good of all one's toil').[39] However, the real idea of this verse is that one should utilize the means for having pleasure whatever happens in one's life.[40] The 'times' which together make up the life of the individual are beyond human control. The deity alone determines what happens to us, and, by and large, the actions which we perform. However, this text implies that at least some of humanity are given enough freedom to make a choice as to whether to find pleasure.

The thought of 9.12 has been considered to some extent in the context of Qoheleth's usage of the phrase עת ופגע in 9.11, but it is worth recapitulating briefly the ideas contained in this passage. The text of 9.12 may be translated

> No man knows his time (עתו), like fishes caught in an evil net and like birds caught in the snare, so are human beings trapped by the evil time (עת רעה) when it falls upon them suddenly.

The term עת in this context cannot possibly refer to an ideal time in accordance with which human beings cannot act. The point of this passage is that 'time' seeks out and finds human beings rather than vice

---

38. So NEB, based on a suggested emendation by G.R. Driver ('Problems and Solutions', *VT* 4 [1954], pp. 224-45 [230-31]). The question of the meaning of 8.9 and its relationship to 8.10 will be discussed in more detail in Chapter 4 of this book.

39. Whybray, 'Preacher of Joy', p. 90; R.K. Johnston, 'Confessions of a Workaholic: A Reappraisal of Qoheleth', *CBQ* 38 (1976), pp. 14-28 (25).

40. Whybray, *Ecclesiastes*, p. 144.

versa.[41] As such, the use of the term עת has a clearly deterministic flavour: it catches (√אחז) and ensnares (√יקש') human beings. The entrapment imagery of 9.12 captures perfectly how the divinely appointed 'time' restricts human freedom.

The deterministic flavour of this passage is brought out still further by the use of the term מצודה which is typically used of the divine net that is wielded by Yahweh and by means of which he executes judgment upon the human world (Ps. 66.11; Ezek. 12.13; 17.20, cf. מצוד in Job 19.6).[42] Gordis rightly points out that the adjective רעה applied to the 'net' and the 'time' has no moral content. Rather, both are 'evil' from the standpoint of the victim, which Qoheleth adopts.[43]

The use of the term עת in 10.17 does not appear to have deterministic overtones. The text, which may be translated, 'Happy the land when its king is nobly born, and its princes feast at the appointed time (בעת), for strength and not for drunkenness' nevertheless does not express the wisdom ideal of acting at an 'ideal time'. If one considers this concept in the wisdom tradition, the idea of performing an action at the right time is to maximize its effect. Here, the 'appointed time' for the action of his subjects is imposed by the king who rules wisely. In this respect, there is a clear parallel to the action of God who enforces 'appointed times' for all actions on his human subjects.

d. *Conclusion*

Although the thoughts of commentators as to the meaning of 3.1-11 differ significantly, it is possible to reach some initial conclusions about the passage based on Qoheleth's use of the term עת elsewhere. Qoheleth never uses this word elsewhere to denote the idea of an ideal time in accordance with which human beings *should* act. Rather, it occurs in the sense of an 'appointed time' which is imposed from without, in accordance with which the object *must* act. Many of the passages in which the term occurs imply the role of the deity in the imposition of

---

41. J.A. Montgomery ('Notes on Ecclesiastes', *JBL* 43 [1924], p. 243) in fact translates עת here as 'fate' and makes specific reference to 3.1 in this context. Cf. McNeile (*Ecclesiastes*, p. 79) who calls the passage 9.11-12 'a poetical expression of the thought of iii 1-9'.

42. Rudman, 'Woman as Divine Agent in Ecclesiastes', *JBL* 116 (1997), pp. 411-27.

43. R. Gordis, *Koheleth: The Man and his Word* (New York: Bloch, 1968), p. 298.

these times, although 10.17 forms an exception to this rule. Even here, however, the sense of a time that is enforced is paramount. This would therefore appear to suggest that the catalogue of seasons represented by 3.1-8 should be interpreted as expressing the idea of a wide ranging deterministic influence in human affairs.

One way in which this conclusion about 3.1-8 might be refuted is by the suggestion that the catalogue of times and seasons is a text that is quoted by Qoheleth and reinterpreted in 3.9-15. Thus one might argue that the sense in which עת occurs in 3.1-8 differs from Qoheleth's own usage elsewhere. This particular idea is a relatively old one. However, Blenkinsopp has recently used it to argue against the idea that Qoheleth's deterministic worldview is as all-inclusive as this passage would appear to suggest (although he does accept the idea that Qoheleth advances the concept of a limited form of determinism else-where).[44] This view, and the arguments against it, will be considered in Chapter 4.

4. משפט ('Judgment')

The noun משפט occurs six times in Ecclesiastes (3.16; 5.7 [ET 8]; 8.5, 6; 11.9; 12.14). Of these usages, two clearly refer to examples of human injustice (3.16; 5.7 [ET 8]), one forms part of the final editorial addition to the book, asserting a traditional view of divine judgment (12.14),[45] and another is probably a gloss influenced by this editorial addition (11.9).[46] Whereas broad agreement exists on the meaning of all these examples, Qoheleth's usage of the term משפט in 8.5-7 has failed to attract a similar consensus.[47] It is notable, however, that Qoheleth uses the term parallel to עת ('appointed time') in both verses. Having argued in this chapter that the latter term is indicative of a belief in determinism on the part of Qoheleth, an examination of 8.5-7 is therefore necessary to consider whether Qoheleth's use of the noun

---

44. Blenkinsopp, 'Ecclesiastes 3.1-15', pp. 55-64.

45. Crenshaw, *Ecclesiastes*, p. 192. Lauha (*Kohelet*, p. 223) suggests in fact that the reference in 12.14 is to a judgment after death.

46. Siegfried, *Prediger*, p. 73; Barton, *Ecclesiastes*, p. 185; McNeile, *Ecclesiastes*, p. 26; Podechard, *L'Ecclesiaste*, p. 452. More recently, some commentators have argued for the retention of 11.9b, including Gordis (*Koheleth*, p. 336) and Whybray (*Ecclesiastes*, p. 162).

47. Siegfried (*Prediger*, p. 63), McNeile (*Ecclesiastes*, p. 25) and Barton (*Ecclesiastes*, p. 150) also attribute 8.5-6a to the same חסיד glossator as 11.9b.

מִשְׁפָּט in these locations may also have deterministic overtones.

The Hebraic concept of judgment in which punishment or reward are meted out by the deity, is in some respects similar to fate. This resemblance becomes more pronounced in the work of Qoheleth, who considers that divine justice is ineffable and that God rewards whoever pleases him without respect to moral worth. This is a theme upon which Crenshaw remarks:[48]

> If we cannot determine our future, no matter how hard we try, God's disposition towards us becomes a matter of life and death... Men and women possessed no control over the goods which God dispensed in his own time and manner. Not even morality purchased the best gifts, and often good people waited in vain for signs of divine favour, while rich rewards speedily greeted evil acts. In short, the trouble with gifts was that God retained control over them. In a sense then, God forced men and women to rely on him for everything... The inevitable course of such thinking would seem to be some form of determinism.

Many commentators recognize, for example, that when Qoheleth speaks of the one who is 'good before God' (טוֹב לִפְנֵי הָאֱלֹהִים) and the sinner (חוֹטֵא) in Eccl. 2.26, he does not use these terms in a conventional moral sense. Rather, the situation which Qoheleth describes is illustrative of God's inscrutable judgment.[49] As Murphy remarks, 'the import of the verse is to claim sovereign freedom for God in imparting gifts'.[50] Those, such as Podechard, who would seek to retain a moral dimension to these terms, are forced to to recognize a gloss in 2.26a (by a pious copyist seeking to tone down the content of Qoheleth's assertions).[51]

Can the difficult passage 8.5-7 be understood in the light of such a deterministic concept of judgment, or should the phrase עֵת וּמִשְׁפָּט ('time and judgment') occurring in both be applied to the courtly wise man's savoir faire, his ability to act in the proper time and manner and hence to escape the wrath of the despotic king depicted in 8.2-4? In

---

48. Crenshaw, *Old Testament Wisdom*, p. 136.

49. H.L. Ginsberg ('The Structure and Contents of the Book of Koheleth' in M. Noth and D.W. Thomas [eds.], *Wisdom in Israel and the Ancient Near East* [VTSup, 3; Leiden: E.J. Brill, 1955], pp. 138-49), states that these terms 'mean respectively (as is today generally recognized) "pleasing to God" or "displeasing", or "lucky" and "unlucky"—not "righteous" and "wicked". This applies not only in ii 26, but also e.g. in vii 26'.

50. Murphy, *Ecclesiastes*, p. 27.

51. Podechard, *L'Ecclésiaste*, p. 284.

order to determine this, these two verses will now be considered and then related to the wider contexts of the preceding verses and Qoheleth's thought elsewhere in Ecclesiastes.

8.5-7

> The keeper of a commandment shall know no evil thing, for a wise man's mind[52] knows time and judgment. Because to every purpose there is time and judgment, human misery weighs heavily: they do not know what will happen, and when it will happen who can tell them?

a. *The versions*

No agreement as to the meaning of this passage exists between the Versions. The Peshitta offers a literal rendering of these verses, while that of the Targum is too free to be of any significant help. The LXX and Vulgate, however, bear witness to two conflicting interpretative traditions which are reflected in the work of modern commentators.

A significant difficulty of this passage is understanding precisely what Qoheleth means when he says that 'the wise man's mind knows time and judgment'. Should we suppose that the author of Ecclesiastes is alluding to the possibility of some form of divine judgment on wickedness either on earth, or after death? Or does this statement refer to the wise man's own 'judgment' by which he reacts appropriately to a changing situation?

The latter interpretation is suggested by the Vulgate, which reads, 'Tempus et responsionem cor sapientis intelligit' ('The heart of the wise man understands time and the reply'). Here, the term מִשְׁפָּט is understood in its rare sense of 'proper procedure' (Isa. 28.26; 40.14; 1 Kgs 5.8)—an interpretation that is favoured by Gordis, who refers the statement to the wise man's ability to respond appropriately to the whims of a despotic master (cf. Eccl. 8.2-4).[53]

The LXX follows a very different path when it translates: καὶ καιρὸν κρίσεως γινώσκει καρδία σοφοῦ ('...and the heart of the wise knows the time of judgment'). If this rendering does not understand the phrase עֵת וּמִשְׁפָּט as a hendiadys (and given the LXX's Aquilan character and the fact that the same Hebrew phrase in 8.6 is translated καιρὸς καὶ

---

52. Gordis (*Koheleth*, p. 289) translates: 'a wise heart'. Whether or not this reading is accepted makes no material difference to the exegesis here.

53. Gordis, *Koheleth*, pp. 289-90.

κρίσις ['time and judgment'], this would seem likely), it suggests that the LXX translator used a variant manuscript in which the conjunction on מִשְׁפָּט was deficient (15 Hebrew MSS contain this particular reading).

Although the omission of this conjunction may appear a minor difference, it is one which has considerable significance for the interpretation of this passage. Fox, for example, follows the line that עֵת וּמִשְׁפָּט is indeed a hendiadys equivalent to עֵת מִשְׁפָּט ('time of judgment'),[54] arguing that the phrase עֵת וּמִשְׁפָּט refers to divine judgments on human evil (again connected with the despotic king of 8.2-4).[55] The wise man knows that 'God will judge the righteous and the wicked' (3.17) and will obey the king's orders, biding his time in the sure knowledge that his master will be punished. This interpretation is doubly attractive because not only is it in line with Qoheleth's thought in 3.17, it also retains the idea of עֵת as a time appointed by God for a purpose. Alternatively, the LXX may, like the Vulgate, be understanding מִשְׁפָּט as 'proper procedure', in which case we might translate, 'the wise man's mind knows the time for appropriate action'.

The real test of any interpretation of 8.5 must lie in how well it relates to its immediate context as well as that of Qoheleth's thought as a whole, and it is here that both versions run into serious difficulties. Apart from a minor variant, the LXX of 8.6 gives a literal translation of the MT: "Ότι παντὶ πράγματί ἐστι καιρὸς καὶ κρίσις, ὅτι γνῶσις τοῦ ασνθρώπου πολλὴ ἐπ' αὐτόν ('For to everything there is time and judgment, for the knowledge[56] of a man is great to him'). The mention of 'knowledge' here suggests that the LXX translator is indeed understanding מִשְׁפָּט as 'proper procedure': presumably, what is meant in the LXX is that the wise man is able to determine the appropriate time for action and manner of procedure because human beings are intrinsically clever. However, not only does this interpretation rely on what is probably a simple copyist's error (דַעַת for רָעַת—the latter reading is supported by all the other Versions), Qoheleth denies any such thing in 8.7!

54. Fox, *Contradictions*, pp. 247-48. Against this, Crenshaw (*Ecclesiastes*, p. 151) points to the LXX translation of the same phrase in 8.6 (καιρὸς καὶ κρίσις) as evidence for the correctness of the MT.

55. So also Plumptre, *Ecclesiastes*, pp. 176-77; Lauha, *Kohelet*, p. 149; Seow, *Ecclesiastes*, p. 281.

56. The LXX evidently reads דַעַת for רָעַת here, although the MT is to be preferred.

The Vulgate reading, 'Omni negotio tempus est et opportunitas et multa hominis afflictio' ('For every business there is a time and appropriate moment, and great is the distress of man') is at first glance more successful. The MT's לכל חפץ would seem to be an echo of 3.1, suggesting a similar interpretation of the noun עת should be made in this passage, and in fact the Vulgate's translation of the term משפט by 'opportunitas' appears to be an attempt to link this verse with both its interpretation of 8.5 as indicative of the wise man's ability to respond appropriately to events, and with the catalogue of times and seasons in 3.1-8. However, it should also be noted that the translator of the Vulgate has been forced to translate the term משפט in two different ways in order to maintain a coherent exegesis. Whereas 'responsionem' in 8.5 refers to the wise man's reaction to events, his own subjective 'judgment' as it were, 'opportunitas' in 8.6 refers objectively to the fixed time itself. Thus, either the translator does not translate 'judgment' in 8.6 or he understands it as God's judgment which establishes the fixed time, in accordance with which the wise man should act. The contextual difficulties of these two verses have therefore been solved by an exegetical sleight of hand.

b. *Modern commentators*
Most commentators recognize some form of relationship between 8.5-7 and 3.1-8 and/or 3.17 regarding Qoheleth's use of the term עת, 'time', even if they disagree as to the precise meaning of the following term משפט.[57] However, the case for understanding the latter term to refer to a 'proper procedure' here is weakened by the fact that in the four other locations in the book where it occurs (3.16; 5.7 [ET 8]; 11.9; 12.14), it refers to 'judgment' or 'justice'.[58] One may object to this that at least 11.9, 12.14 have long been suspected of being editorial glosses, but the context provided by the use of √שפט in 3.16-17 is a strong indicator that it should be interpreted with its usual sense of (legal) judgment in 8.5-6.

---

57. A few commentators (e.g. Murphy, *Ecclesiastes*, p. 83; Whybray, *Ecclesiastes*, pp. 131-32) argue that 8.6-7 serves as an attack by Qoheleth on the conventional wisdom expressed in part or all of 8.5. Despite the lexical links between this verse and 8.2-4 (שומר and דבר רע occur in both passages), both distance 8.5 from its preceding context to achieve this reading.

58. Seow, *Ecclesiastes*, p. 281.

As Fox has observed, these verses consciously echo the language of 3.17.[59] Qoheleth states in 3.17:

אמרתי אני בלבי את הצדיק ואת הרשע. ישפט האלהים כי עת לכל חפץ
ועל כל המעשה שם

I said to myself (lit. 'in my heart'), 'the righteous and the wicked, God will judge', for there is a time for every purpose and concerning every work there

Thus we see the use in one verse of the four significant terms חפץ, 'purpose', עת, 'time', שפט√, 'judge' and לב, 'heart' which feature in the verse under consideration. In 3.17, Qoheleth demonstrates the truth of his statement in 8.5 that 'the wise man's heart knows time and judgment'. However, the essence of Qoheleth's concept of עת is that the point at which an appointed time for action will occur is unknowable. This is explicitly stated in 9.12, but is also reflected in 8.7, 'for he knows not that which shall be, for who can tell him when it shall be?'

However, Fox's understanding of the phrase עת ומשפט in 8.5 as a hendiadys meaning 'time of judgment' cannot be transferred to 8.6. The resultant translation, 'Because to every business there is a time of judgment, therefore human misery is great', makes little sense. The idea that God might judge all human action in the traditional way would be comforting to Qoheleth, who complains elsewhere on the tardiness of such action on God's part (8.11).

It is for this reason that Fox, following Ginsberg, is forced to emend the text of 8.6 by deleting ומשפט as an addition made under the influence of 8.5.[60] This is a rather desperate measure: the more so since Fox has already suggested a quasi-emendation to 8.5 in order to harmonize with his view of what Qoheleth ought to be saying. The resultant text of 8.6-7, 'Because to every business there is an appointed time, therefore humanity's misery is great: for he knows not what will happen, and when it will happen who will tell him?' makes perfect sense, and is entirely in keeping with Qoheleth's thought as it is expressed in the catalogue of times in 3.1-8. However, the term משפט in 8.6 provides an important link with the thought of 8.5. If it is deleted, then 8.6-7 is left in isolation and without context. Before taking such drastic action, it is as well to consider whether the term משפט can be retained

---

59. Fox, *Contradictions*, p. 247.
60. Fox, *Contradictions*, p. 248; Ginsberg, *Qohelet*, pp. 106-107.

in 8.6 and understood in a way consonant with Qoheleth's thought elsewhere.

Almost all commentators who understand the term מִשְׁפָּט to refer to divine judgment would agree that it refers to the intervention of God in the here and now (as opposed to a judgment after death). This judgment is of the familiar form in which a specific human action is met with a corresponding response of reward or retribution from God. However, if all (or nearly all) human actions are controlled by the deity, then the rationale for such a system falls away. One might reasonably argue that this is simply one more of Qoheleth's contradictions, yet Qoheleth juxtaposes the terms מִשְׁפָּט and עֵת, thereby emphasizing the connection between the concept of judgment and his deterministic thought.

Thus the best way of understanding these verses is to connect them with the catalogue of times and seasons in 3.1-8 and to understand them deterministically (as Fox does). One might paraphrase 8.6-7, 'Because all human business is predetermined by God, human beings are in a distressing position: for they do not know what will happen or when anything will happen'.

One may object that this interpretation does not interpret the term 'judgment' and that therefore מִשְׁפָּט should be deleted in 8.6. This is not so, however, for the imposition of 'appointed times' is in fact based on God's inscrutable judgment of the individual. In 2.26, Qoheleth speaks of God giving 'wisdom, and knowledge and joy' to 'the one who is good before God', while God 'gives to the sinner toil: to gather and to heap up to give to one who is good before God'. It is perhaps no accident that this passage, with its series of infinitives denoting the divinely determined עִנְיָן ('toil') given to the sinner, immediately precedes the עִנְיָן (3.9) represented by the catalogue of times (3.1-8). Likewise, in 7.26, whether the individual male is trapped by woman is determined by whether he is 'good before God' or a 'sinner'. Whether one loves or not (cf. 3.8 'a time to love') is a consequence of how one is viewed and judged by the deity in this passage. The activities that human beings are made to perform (and their outcome) are a direct consequence of whether they are viewed by him as טוֹב ('good') or חוֹטֵא ('worthless'). Thus, one can say that 'to every business there is time and judgment'.

What of the preceding passage, 8.2-4? Can this view clarify the advice offered by Qoheleth in a courtly context? Since I have argued that the statement 'to every business there is time and judgment' refers in a general way to God's activity in the world and is expressing the idea that one's position and the activity one carries out is a reflection of divine favour or disfavour, it is interesting to note that God is mentioned in connection with the king in the very first verse of this passage (8.2):

אני פי מלך שמור ועל דברת שבועת אלהים.

I counsel you to keep the king's commandment, in regard to the oath of God'

This passage will in fact be considered in more depth in Chapter 7, which explores Qoheleth's conception of free will. For now, it is worth noting that both Tyler and Hertzberg have advanced an interpretation of the verse in which Qoheleth advises obedience to the king because of God's oath concerning kingship.[61] That is, the king has a specially favoured status with respect to God, and one should therefore 'keep' (שמור) the king's law. In 8.5, Qoheleth says 'one who keeps [שמור] (the king's) commandment will not experience problems: the heart of a wise man knows "time and judgment" '. In the light of the king's special position with God and Qoheleth's consequent advice to be obedient in 8.2, one can interpret 8.5 as saying 'a wise man will obey the king because his situation, like everyone else's, is divinely ordained'. In effect then, 8.5 would be a restatement of the thought of 8.2, and 8.6-7 would be not so much a contradiction of the thought of 8.5 as a coda based on the term 'time and judgment', widening its application from a courtly situation to existence in general: just as the wise man is powerless before the human king, so humanity as a whole is powerless before the divine one.

5. חלק *('Portion')*

Another way in which Qoheleth's deterministic worldview can be seen is in the concept of חלק, or 'portion'. This term occurs eight times in Ecclesiastes (2.10, 21; 3.22; 5.17-18 [ET 18-19]; 9.6, 9; 11.2) but is also common throughout the Hebrew Bible. However Qoheleth again, as shall be demonstrated, uses this term with a nuance of meaning and in contexts different to those in which it is found elsewhere.

61. Hertzberg, *Prediger*, pp. 141-43. The essential details of Tyler's reading (*Ecclesiastes*, pp. 101-102, 139-40) are the same as mine: (1) that the King is a divine viceregent and symbol of law; (2) that this provides the rationale for Qoheleth's advice to obey the king, and (3) that the phrase עת ומשפט 'Season and Law' refers in a general way to God's determinative activity in existence.

Tsevat describes the primary meaning of the term חלק as:

> '...the portion coming to one by law and custom.' From this meaning
> develops the meaning 'the portion in life determined by God,'
> 'destiny'.[62]

In the great majority of usages, חלק has important social overtones,
having to do with the organization of the community or the family
(Prov. 17.2; Neh. 13.13; 2 Sam. 19.30 [ET 29]). Very often, the division
involved in the use of the term חלק is one of arable land, as opposed to
pasture (מגרש). Yahweh, however, is the original owner of Palestine
(e.g. Deut. 12.10), so that whoever receives a portion of this land (Num.
26.53; Josh. 18.5; 19.51) has a portion in Yahweh's own property, and
whoever renounces his portion of the land has no portion in Yahweh
(Josh. 22.25, 27).[63]

Thus, the way in which Qoheleth uses this term, is, as Tsevat points
out, 'peculiar to Ecclesiastes'.[64] Elsewhere in the Hebrew Bible, it is
unusual for God to be overtly made the subject of the action (though he
may be the object [e.g. Num. 18.20]). Exceptions to this rule occur in
Deut. 4.19; 29.25 [ET 26] in which Yahweh apportions other gods to the
nations. Nowhere in the Hebrew Bible other than in the book of
Ecclesiastes does God grant to the individual human being a 'portion'.
Can this usage, however, be construed as indicative of a deterministic
usage on Qoheleth's part?

a. *The versions*

Of the eight occurrences of the noun חלק in the book of Ecclesiastes,
the LXX translates seven times with the term μερίς (2.10, 21; 3.22; 5.17;
9.6, 9; 11.2) and once by μέρος (5.18). Both of these terms have the
basic meanings 'part', 'portion', 'share', and thus serve as theologically
neutral but nevertheless literal translations in keeping with the LXX's
Aquilan character. Generally speaking, the same may also be said of the
Vulgate which translates everywhere with the neutral term 'pars' ('portion', 'part'). However, in 2.21 it is striking that it renders חלק with the
term 'quaesita' ('acquisition', 'gain'). In this case, the translator may be

---

62. M. Tsevat, 'חלק', *TDOT*, IV, pp. 447-51 (448).

63. G. von Rad, 'The Promised Land and Yahweh's Land in the Hexateuch',
ZDPV 66 (1943), pp. 191-204 (191-92).

64. Tsevat, 'חלק', pp. 450-51.

guilty of exegesis: if the contexts in which the term 'pars' is used is considered, it would appear that it denotes either 'portion' in a neutral sense (11.2), or in the sense of the rightful reward for one's labour (2.10; 3.22; 5.17, 18; 9.6, 9). The term 'quaesita' appears in the sense of a 'portion' of which the individual is undeserving. This distinction may be intended to preserve the deity to some extent against accusations of injustice. The Targum translates the term חלק with its Aramaic cognate חולק in all locations, offering no further insight, while the Peshitta translates the MT's חלק with ܬܐܪ in all locations. This particular term is a loanword derived from the Latin: 'moneta'. As such, it is most often used in the financial sphere and has the basic meaning of 'money' or 'cash'. A development from this meaning is the sense of 'reward',[65] which is most appropriate to the context of the majority of its usages in Ecclesiastes. While the use of the term ܬܐܪ cannot be said to offer a literal translation of the Hebrew חלק, it does have a semantic range broad enough to cope with both 2.10, where חלק may indeed be construed as 'reward', and 2.21, in which חלק may simply refer to the material goods acquired during one's lifetime (cf. Vulgate). The term ܬܐܪ in the sense of 'reward' may also carry the implication that one's חלק may be allotted by God in exchange for labour.

b. *Modern commentators*

Crenshaw argues concerning Qoheleth's use of the term חלק that:

> its essential meaning for him is limitation, a part of something rather than the whole thing. One's portion in life is the share of desirable or undesirable experiences which come along, not as the direct result of good or bad conduct but purely by chance.[66]

Crenshaw's view appears reasonable, yet few commentators indeed would argue that 'portion' is a chance thing, for it is God-given as the lot of humanity (e.g. 5.17-18 [ET 18-19]). There is a difference, albeit a subtle one between arbitrariness and chance.

Galling also sees 'portion' as intimately linked with human life and ultimately defined by the deity. For him, it is 'gerade zu *terminus technicus* für den der menschlichen Existenz zugeweisenen Raum' (or

---

65. Brockelman, *Lexicon*, p. 395.
66. Crenshaw, *Ecclesiastes*, p. 82. Whybray (*Ecclesiastes*, p. 55) emphasizes the often positive nature of חלק however. Murphy (*Ecclesiastes*, p. lx) points out that any positive meaning of portion is limited strictly to this world.

roughly translated: equivalent to a technical term for the space allotted to human existence).[67] Not all locations in which חלק is used, however, permit Galling's general interpretation of it as 'the space allotted to human existence', as Fox points out.[68] Glasser in a footnote on 2.10, remarks on the resemblance of חלק to certain ideas of fate. For him, it is 'le bonheur limité que Dieu distribue à sa guise aux hommes. On serait tenté de parler d'un "lot", car le bonheur, constate Qohelet, est une loterie.' (In translation: 'one would be tempted to speak of a lottery because happiness, according to Qoheleth, is a lottery.')[69] This view approaches the definition offered by Crenshaw, while at the same time taking account of the deterministic nature of the term חלק as we find it in Ecclesiastes.

Glasser's understanding of the term חלק as referring to 'le bonheur limité' (or limited happiness) in 2.10 is well founded. The text in question states: 'And whatsoever my eyes desired, I kept not from them. I did not withhold my heart from any joy, for my heart rejoiced in all my labour, and this was my portion [חלק] of all my labour'. It is noteworthy that in this verse, no overt reference is made to the material possessions that Qoheleth has accumulated in the course of the 'Royal Experiment'.[70] Rather, the subject of this verse is the joy that Qoheleth has derived from his labour, emphasized by the repetition of √שמח ('rejoice') as the verbal form שׂמח ('rejoiced') and the noun שמחה ('joy'). Joy, rather than material possessions per se, is the due reward for Qoheleth's hard work.[71]

This conception of חלק is also reflected by Qoheleth's words in 3.22: 'So I saw that there is nothing better than that a person should rejoice in their own works, for that is his portion: for who shall bring him to see what shall be after him?' Here the 'portion' of humankind, that they should rejoice in their labour, is reaffirmed. This is perhaps the only positive conclusion of Qoheleth as a result of his search, yet it is also shown here to be a 'second best' option. It is the alternative to the

---

67. Galling, *Der Prediger*, p. 89. Cited also by Tsevat, 'חלק', p. 451. Most recently, Galling has been followed by Seow (*Ecclesiastes*, p. 151).

68. Fox, *Contradictions*, p. 58.

69. Glasser, *Qohelet*, p. 48.

70. It could be argued that here the term עמל refers to 'goods obtained by labour' rather than labour itself (so Fox, *Contradictions*, p. 181). If so, however, this would only emphasize the position of joy as 'my portion from all my עמל'.

71. Delitzsch, *Ecclesiastes*, pp. 242-43.

knowledge of existence that Qoheleth seeks: the ability 'to see what shall be after him'. This therefore illustrates the definition of חלק as the 'limited good'/'limited happiness' of which both Crenshaw and Glasser speak.[72]

Again, in 5.17 (ET 18) the same link between joy and 'portion' is made by Qoheleth:

> Behold what I have seen: it is good and comely to eat and to drink, and to enjoy the good of all his labour which one takes under the sun all the days of his life which God has given him, for it is his portion.

In this passage, the term חלק is specifically pinned down as 'the enjoyment of the good in one's labour'. It is also, perhaps, worthy of note that the term יפה ('beautiful') is used to describe the taking of one's portion, the only other occurrence outside 3.11 in which it is used to describe the irresistible nature of Fate.[73] The theme of 'portion' as joy is made more explicit still in 5.18 (Eng. 19), where 'to rejoice in one's labour' (לשמח בעמלו) is parallel to the phrase 'to take one's portion' (לשאת את חלקו).

The *Sitz im Leben* of the term חלק therefore appears to be in the realm of human emotions.[74] This is also reflected in 9.6, in which Qoheleth considers the situation of those who have died: 'Their love, their hatred and their envy are now perished; neither have they any more a portion forever in anything which is done under the sun'. Thus far, the term 'portion' has been considered merely as 'joy' in one's labour or the benefits derived therefrom. In this verse however, 'portion' appears also to designate any human emotion. 'Love' and 'hatred' certainly appear in the list of predetermined actions and emotions in 3.1-8. 'Envy' is intimately bound up with human toil in 4.4; so much so that it appears almost as if human progress is ultimately little more than a beneficial by-product of rivalry. Likewise in 9.9, the admonition to

---

72. Crenshaw, *Ecclesiastes*, p. 82; Glasser, *Qohelet*, p. 48. Delitzsch (*Ecclesiastes*, p. 272) describes portion in the sense of joy as 'the best which (man) has of life in this world'.

73. Murphy, who to some extent understands 3.1-11 as a deterministic text, notes a parallel between God making an action 'beautiful in its time' (יפה בעתו) in 3.11 and the characterization of portion as 'beautiful' in 5.18 (ET 19) (*Ecclesiastes*, pp. 32-35, 53). In actual fact however, it it the action of taking one's portion that is 'beautiful'.

74. That such may be the case is partly suggested by Fox (*Contradictions*, p. 59).

'experience life with the woman you love' is backed up by Qoheleth's assertion that such is one's 'portion'. Although √שׂמח does not appear in this verse, the verb אהב ('love') does. Once again, the location of the term 'portion' is to be found firmly in the realm of human emotions.

Apart from the neutral use of the term חלק in 11.2 (in which the giver of a portion is clearly intended to be the reader), the only significant departure from Qoheleth's usage of חלק in the context of human emotion occurs in 2.21: 'For there is one whose earnings were acquired by wisdom and by knowledge and by skill;[75] yet he must give them as his portion to one who has not toiled for them' (cf. 2.22).[76] Even here, the 'portion' to which Qoheleth refers might well be the pleasure arising from the use of the wealth accrued by the first man.[77]

Thus, Qoheleth uses the term חלק in a way fundamentally different to its usage elsewhere in the Hebrew Bible. It is something which is given by God, and one can say with Crenshaw that it is indeed a 'limited good' which is allotted to humankind in life. Being as it is a gift, it has little or nothing to do with the individual merit of the recipient. It may be granted freely or withheld, even transferred to another, at God's discretion (cf. 2.21-26).[78] The term חלק refers to human emotions, primarily to the enjoyment of life. However, Eccl 9.6 suggests that חלק may apply in fact to the whole range of human emotions. Some evidence for this view is also provided by 9.9, where one's portion is to love a woman. Although חלק cannot be defined as 'Fate', it is a concept that illustrates the deterministic nature of Qoheleth's worldview. If human feelings are subject to the will of God, then the whole concept of human free will is called into question.

6. מעשׂה שׁנעשׂה תחת השׁמשׁ/מעשׂה האלהים *('The Work which is Done Under the Sun'/'The Work of God')*

In Eccl. 1.14, Qoheleth makes the surprising claim, 'I have seen [ראה] all the works which are done under the sun, and behold, all is absurdity and shepherding the wind'. At first sight, this appears to contradict his

---

75. Translating the term כשׁרון as 'skill' with Whitley (*Koheleth*, p. 27).

76. Understanding חלקו as a predicate accusative with Hertzberg (*Prediger*, p. 80) and Podechard (*L'Ecclésiaste*, pp. 277-78).

77. So Crenshaw (*Ecclesiastes*, p. 88), who sums up the mood of the verse: 'I earned the wages and therefore am entitled to derive satisfaction from them'.

78. Cf. the comment of Whybray, 'God may give joy and pleasure; man can never achieve it for himself' ('Preacher of Joy', p. 89).

statement in 8.17 that 'Nobody can find out [מצא] the work which is done under the sun'.[79] That Qoheleth's original statement is not simply a vain boast that he revises in the light of his investigations is suggested by his comment in 8.9, in which he states, 'All have I seen [ראה], and applied my mind to every work which is done under the sun'.

Qoheleth thus appears to make a fundamental distinction between 'seeing' and 'finding' the events that go to make up existence: Qoheleth first observes events, and then applies his mind to interpret, or 'find out' their meaning, thereby hoping to gain an insight into the workings of the world. This distinction is underlined if 1.13, 'I applied my mind to seek and to search out by wisdom, concerning all which is done under heaven' is compared with the statement 'I have seen all the work which is done under the sun' in 1.14, which underlines his qualifications for the investigation which he proposes.

The language of seeking and finding is largely restricted to a few passages in which Qoheleth alludes to the intent of his search (cf. esp. 1.13; 3.11; 7.23-29; 8.17). The verb דרש ('investigate') occurs only in 1.13, but תור ('search') occurs in 1.13; 7.25. More common terms are בקש ('seek') (3.6, 15; 7.25, 28, 29; 8.17; 12.10) and מצא ('find out') (3.11; 7.14, 24, 26, 27 [×2], 28 [×3], 29; 8.17 [×3]; 9.10, 15; 11.1; 12.10). From the contexts in which these terms appear, it seems that very often they have to do with the acquisition of knowledge, particularly when the object of the verb is the term חשבון ('the sum of things'—7.25, 27, 29) or formulaic phrases involving the term מעשה ('work'), such as מעשה האלהים, 'the work of God' (3.11) or מעשה אשר נעשה תחת השמש, 'the work which is done under the sun' (8.17). This link between these verbs and the acquisition of knowledge is reflected in Whybray's understanding of the verb מצא as having the meaning 'find out', Crenshaw's translation 'fathom', or that of Gordis, 'discover'.[80]

This connection is also evident in the parallel usage of the verbs תור/בקש ('seek'/'search') and ידע ('know') in 7.25 and מצא/בקש ('seek'/'find out') and ידע in 8.17. Qoheleth plays on this theme in

79. Whybray (*Ecclesiastes*, p. 49) suggests that 'all the works which are done under the sun' in 1.14 may simply refer to the actions which Qoheleth performs in the course of his investigation. This is a minority view, however.

80. Whybray, *Ecclesiastes*, p. 74; Crenshaw, *Ecclesiastes*, pp. 91, 153; Gordis, *Koheleth*, pp. 156, 186.

9.10: 'Whatever your hand finds to do, do mightily; for there is no work, nor device, nor knowledge [דעת], nor wisdom in Sheol where you are going'. Likewise, Qoheleth's statement in 3.11, 'also [God] has put eternity in their minds so that no one finds out the work which God does from beginning to end' is followed by a positive statement of what knowledge is available to Qoheleth despite his failure to 'find out' the work of God: 'I know [ידע] that there is nothing better than to rejoice and to fare well during life' (3.12).

Thus, Qoheleth is able to 'see' all the events that go to make up existence (1.14; 8.9), but though he may apply his mind to their interpretation (1.13; 8.9), he confesses 'nobody can find out the work which is done under the sun...even if a wise man claims to know it, he is not able to find it' (8.17).

Gordis, Fox and Murphy all point out that for Qoheleth, 'the work of God' (מעשה אשר עשה האלהים/מעשה האלהים—3.11; 7.13; 8.17; 11.5) is identical with 'the work(s) which is/are done under the sun' (מעשה רע אשר נעשה/המעשה שנעשה/מעשים שנעשׂו תחת השמש—1.14; 2.17; 4.3; 8.17).[81] Qoheleth views 'all the work of God' (8.17) and can order the reader to do likewise (7.13), but this work cannot be 'found out' (מצא—3.11) or 'known' (ידע—11.5). Likewise, Qoheleth and others can 'see the work which is done under the sun' (1.14; 2.17; 4.3), but it cannot be 'found out', i.e. interpreted to give a meaningful pattern to existence (8.17).

Modern commentators apparently follow GKC §117h in understanding the particle כי in Eccl. 8.17a, וראיתי את כל מעשה האלהים כי לא יוכל האדם למצוא את המעשה אשר נעשה תחת השמש as initiating an object clause, and accordingly translate, 'then I saw all the work of God, *that* no-one can find out the work which is done under the sun'. However, if Gordis, Fox and Murphy are correct in identifying 'the work that is done under the sun' and 'the work of God' as one and the same, a serious contextual problem arises. Although God evidently restrains human beings from discovering the 'works which are done under the sun' in 8.17, the apparent statement that this preventive act is '*all* the work of God' must be called into question.

---

81. Gordis, *Koheleth*, pp. 298-99; Fox, *Contradictions*, p. 175; Murphy, *Ecclesiastes*, p. 13.

a. *The versions*

Although the translation of כִּי as 'that' in Eccl. 8.17a is supported by the LXX's ὅτι, the Peshitta's מֶטֻל ד, 'because' implies that the Syriac translator understood the particle כִּי causally (GKC §148b). This is true also of the Targum, which adds extra material to the Hebrew of 8.17 in order to clarify the meaning of the verse:

וחזית אנא ית כל אובד גבורתא דיי ארום דחילא הוא ולית ליה
רשו לאנש
לאשכחא ית עובד גבורתא דיי דאתעביד בעלמא הדין תחות שמשא

I saw every mighty work of the Lord for it is awesome, and a human being is not permitted to find out the mighty work of the Lord which is done in this world under the sun.

Part of the reason for the causal rendering of כִּי by אֲרוֹם ('for') is seemingly contextual, for the translation of the Targumist demonstrates that he, like modern commentators, equates 'the work of God' with 'the work which is done under the sun'.

The Vulgate's, 'et intellexi quod omnium operum Dei nullam possit homo invenire rationem eorum quae fiunt sub sole' ('And this I understood of all the works of God: that a human being can find no reckoning of those things which are done under the sun') is suggestive of a similar contextual problem which this translator had in equating 'all the work of God' with the prevention of human beings from attaining knowledge. Rather, the prohibition is portrayed as a single aspect of God's work. Although כִּי is not concretely represented, being rather implicit in the relative pronoun 'quod' (i.e. 'this I understood... [that]'), it seems clear that the translator of the Vulgate attempted to balance contextual considerations with his desire to follow the LXX in understanding כִּי as the beginning of an object clause.

Of the versions, only LXX both retains something approaching the original structure of the Hebrew and interprets כִּי as the beginning of an object clause: most likely, this has more to do with the Aquilan character of the LXX translation of Ecclesiastes than with hermeneutical accuracy. The translators of the Vulgate, Peshitta and Targum appear to be, to a greater or lesser extent, baffled by the structure and sense of the Hebrew of this passage. At the very least, a contextual problem is implied by the approaches of the Vulgate and Targum, and the causal renderings of כִּי by the Peshitta and Targum (the Semitic versions) may be suggestive of a grammatical problem with the modern understanding of כִּי as introducing an object clause.

b. *Modern commentators*

In Eccl. 8.17a, most commentators understand the particle כִּי as initiating an object clause (GKC §157b, 117h), and English-speaking scholars accordingly translate the Hebrew:

רָאִיתִי אֶת כָּל מַעֲשֵׂה הָאֱלֹהִים כִּי לֹא יוּכַל הָאָדָם לִמְצוֹא אֶת הַמַּעֲשֶׂה
אֲשֶׁר נַעֲשָׂה תַחַת הַשָּׁמֶשׁ

Then I saw all the work of God: that no-one can find out the work which is done under the sun.[82]

The same approach can be seen in the work of French commentators such as Podechard and Glasser. They translate כִּי with 'que', although Podechard's translation, 'alors, j'ai reconnu (au sujet de) toute l'oeuvre de Dieu, que l'homme ne peut découvrir l'oeuvre qui se fait sous le soleil' (or translated, 'so I recognized [concerning] all the work of God, that Man cannot discover the work which is done under the sun'), implies a recognition that the human inability to discover wisdom is just one aspect of 'the work of God'.[83] Barucq also sees a problem with this usage, and omits an equivalent for כִּי from his translation of the passage: 'alors j'ai considéré l'oeuvre de Dieu. L'homme ne peut saisir l'oeuvre qui s'accomplit sous le soleil' ('so I considered the work of God. Man cannot grasp the work which is accomplished under the sun'), rightly going on to remark about Qohelet's consideration of 'the work of God' in this passage, 'il ne dit pas ce qu'est cette action, en quoi elle consiste' ('he does not say what this activity consists of').[84]

German scholars take their cue from Luther's translation of 8.17a: 'Und ich sah alle Werke Gottes, daß ein Mensch das Werk nicht finden kann, das unter der Sonne geschieht' ('And I saw all the works of God, that a man cannot find out the work which is done under the sun'). The translation of כִּי by 'daß' ('that') is evident, for example, in the work of Strobel,[85] although Ellermeier adopts a special epexegetical rendering of the subordinate clause in 8.17a and translates כִּי with 'nämlich'

---

82. Fox (*Contradictions*, pp. 253-55), following F. Ellermeier (*Qohelet* [Herzberg: Erwin Jungfer, 1967], pp. 295-300), alone among English-speaking authors translates 'that is'.

83. Podechard, *L'Ecclésiaste*, p. 406; Glasser, *Qohelet*, p. 136 n. c.

84. Barucq, *Ecclésiaste*, pp. 153, 156.

85. A. Strobel, *Das Buch Prediger (Kohelet)* (Düsseldorf: Patmos, 1967), p. 134.

('namely').[86] Lohfink's translation, '...da sah ich ein, daß der Mensch... das Tun Gottes in seiner Ganzheit nicht wiederfinden kann, das Tun, das unter der Sonne getan wurde' ('when I saw that Man cannot find out the work of God in its entirety, the work that happens under the sun') also translates כי with 'daß' but removes 'das Tun Gottes' (מעשה האלהים, 'the work of God') from the main clause to the subordinate clause, equating it with 'das Tun, das unter der Sonne getan wurde' (המעשה אשר נעשה תחת השמש, 'the work that happens under the sun').[87]

With few exceptions therefore, modern translations suggest that Qoheleth's meaning in Eccl. 8.17a is that 'all the work of God' is entirely taken up with preventing human beings from discovering wisdom: those few commentators, such as Barucq and Lohfink, who sense a contextual problem are forced into a position in which they must rearrange the passage, or leave the crucial word כי untranslated.

c. *Grammatical evidence*

The notion that כי in 8.17a is used epexegetically, or that it introduces an objective clause, may also be questioned on grammatical grounds. While it is true that an objective clause governed by a transitive verb such as ראה may be introduced by the particle כי (GKC §157b), in such cases the subordinate clause is the sole object of the verb, for example, Gen. 6.5, וירא יהוה כי רבה רעת האדם, 'and Yahweh saw *that the wickedness of humankind was great*'. A second object may also be expressed by such a clause (GKC §117h): in such constructions the object of the main clause becomes the subject of the subordinate clause.

Examples of this phenomenon cited in GKC §117h are given below, with the object of the main clause underlined and the subject of the subordinate clause italicized. Thus:

Gen. 1.4

וירא אלהים את האור כי טוב

and God saw *the light*, that *it* was good

Exod. 32.22

אתה ידעת העם כי ברע היא

You know *the people*, that *they* are set on evil.

---

86. Ellermeier, *Qohelet*, p. 299.
87. Lohfink, *Kohelet*, p. 63.

Examples of the same phenomenon with the verb ידע ('know') are cited for 2 Sam. 3.25; 17.8; 1 Kgs 5.17. Examples involving the verb ראה ('see') are cited for Gen. 6.2; 12.14; 13.10; 49.15; Exod. 2.2; Ps. 25.19; Prov. 23.31; Job 22.12; Eccl. 2.24; 8.17.[88]

This pattern is followed without fail in all of the examples cited, except in Eccl. 8.17:

וראיתי את כל מעשה האלהים כי לא יוכל האדם למצוא

את המעשה

אשר נעשה תחת השמש

> Then I saw all the work of God, that humankind cannot find out the work which is done under the sun.

If כי were to mean 'that', initiating an objective clause, we should expect the subject of the clause to be המעשה אשר נעשה תחת ('the work which is alone under the sun'), השמש מעשה האלהים ('the work of God'), or more likely הוא ('it'), referring to את כל מעשה האלהים ('all the work of God') in the main clause. Instead, the subject is האדם ('humankind').

An alternative proposal has been made by Fox, building on the detailed treatment of the syntax of this verse by Ellermeier.[89] Fox suggests that the usage of כי in 8.17a is a special one, introducing Qoheleth's epexegesis of the expression מעשה האלהים. As support for this hypothesis, he cites as a parallel Jon. 3.10

וירא האלהים את מעשיהם כי שבו מדרכם הרעה

> God saw their works, that they repented of their evil way.

Yet constructions involving כי appear to be subject to rigid rules. In order to illustrate how כי is used in this passage, (part of) the object of the main clause is underlined and the subject of the main clause italicized: 'God saw the works *of them*, that *they* had repented of their evil way'. On the analogy of this example, we should expect Eccl. 8.17a to say something along the lines of 'Then I saw all the work *of God*, that *he*...'

Although the usage of כי in Jon. 3.10 is unique, it is not entirely dissimilar to occurrences introducing an objective clause:

---

88. Gordis (*Koheleth*, p. 298) specifically cites Gen. 1.4 as a usage of כי parallel to that in Eccl. 8.17a.

89. Fox, *Contradictions*, p. 255; Ellermeier, *Qohelet*, pp. 295-300.

Gen. 6.2.

ויראו בני האלהים את בנות האדם כי טבת הנה

And the sons of God saw the daughters-of-men, that they were fair.

Here it is the 'nomen regens' of a genitive construction which becomes the subject of the subordinate clause. In Jon. 3.10, it is what would be the 'nomen rectum' in an equivalent construction.

A possible reason for this strange use of כִּי in Jon. 3.10 is that it seems to serve as a substitute for the relative pronoun אֲשֶׁר ('who, which') since the thought of this verse would more normally be expressed in Hebrew:

וירא האלהים את מעשי עם נינוה אשר הם שבו מדרכם הרעה

And God saw the works of the people of Nineveh, who had repented of their evil way.

Since the putative מַעֲשֵׂי עַם נִינוֵה ('the works of the people of Nineveh') is condensed to מַעֲשֵׂיהֶם ('their works'), the relative pronoun אֲשֶׁר cannot be used since it would then refer to the actions which had been performed, rather than to their doers. The use of כִּי here resolves that problem with a simple circumlocution. אֲשֶׁר and כִּי frequently have the same sense in object clauses (GKC §157a). If we compare Eccl. 8.17a, וְרָאִיתִי אֶת כָּל מַעֲשֵׂה הָאֱלֹהִים כִּי לֹא יוּכַל הָאָדָם לִמְצוֹא, it is clear that הָאָדָם ('humanity', 'man') as the subject of what is thought to be the subordinate clause bears no relation to the object of the main clause, contrary to every other usage of כִּי in this sense in the Old Testament. One is forced to seek an alternative translation of כִּי.

The grammatical and contextual difficulties involved in understanding כִּי as initiating an object clause in 8.17a underly the loose translation of this verse by the Vulgate and the causative renderings ('because') of כִּי by the Peshitta and Targum. It is, however, difficult to see how a causative rendering can help to clarify the meaning of the verse as we have it in Hebrew. Nor can כִּי in Eccl. 8.17a be rendered adversatively by translating as 'but', since כִּי can be used in this sense only after a negative clause (GKC §163). The best solution is therefore to understand the particle affirmatively (GKC §159ee). Such an interpretation is in keeping with Qoheleth's own usage, since most commentators understand כִּי as used in this manner by Qoheleth in one or all of 4.16; 7.7, 20.[90] Thus, one may translate Eccl. 8.16-17:

---

90. Crenshaw, *Ecclesiastes*, pp. 112, 132, 140; Fox, *Contradictions*, p. 209; Gordis, *Koheleth*, p. 162; Murphy, *Ecclesiastes*, p. 41.

> When I applied my mind to know wisdom, and to see the business which
> is done upon the earth (my eyes seeing sleep neither by day nor by
> night), then I saw all the work of God. Surely no-one can find out the
> work which is done under the sun: for though a man labour to seek it out,
> yet he shall not find it. Moreover, though a sage claim to know it, yet he
> shall not be able to find it.

The affirmative כִּי in 8.17a underlines Qoheleth's findings about the
unattainability of wisdom previously made in 7.23-25, and is consonant
with the emphatic tone of 8.17 as a whole. Introducing the results of
Qoheleth's observation, it paves the way for his very definite conclusions about humanity's inability to discover true knowledge, further
emphasized by the appearance of such phrases as בְּשֶׁל אֲשֶׁר ('for
though'), גַּם אִם ('moreover'), the double use of the noun הָאָדָם
('humanity', 'man') and the phrase לֹא יוּכַל ('cannot'), and the threefold repetition of the verb מָצָא ('find out') which occurs in this verse.

d. *Implications for determinism*

The contextual evidence adduced in this section suggests that 'the work
of God' can be said to be coextensive with 'the work which is done
under the sun' in Ecclesiastes as Gordis, Fox and Murphy have suggested, despite the problems posed by the traditional translation of
8.17a, which appears to differentiate between the two concepts. This
tension has now been to some extent resolved by demonstrating the difficulties (not least grammatical) associated with the traditional understanding of 8.17 and offering an alternative solution.

The case for understanding 'the work of God' and 'the work which is
done under the sun' as essentially one has been strengthened, but some
questions remain unanswered: what implications does this identification
have for understanding Qoheleth's overall theory of determinism? Why
does Qoheleth use two different phrases to express the same idea? Perhaps the difference between the two concepts is simply one of emphasis: 'the work which is done under the sun' refers to human action and
thought (cf. 4.1, 3). The parallel phrase 'the work of God' refers to
divine activity. Because Qoheleth is a determinist, human action and
thought is controlled by the deity, and any real distinction between
human and divine actions therefore disappears. This, then, explains why
Qoheleth uses the same language when speaking of both, makes both
the goal of his search, and thereby identifies both as one and the same
thing.

Qoheleth's conclusion regarding the search for 'the work of God/the work which is done under the sun' is that a successful outcome is impossible. By contrast, Qoheleth advises humanity that they should 'find pleasure in *their own* works' (יִשְׂמַח הָאָדָם בְּמַעֲשָׂיו—3.22). Though God may act to prevent human beings from finding out 'the work of God', Qoheleth bases his advice to find pleasure on the fact that 'God has already approved *your* works' (כְּבָר רָצָה הָאֱלֹהִים אֶת מַעֲשֶׂיךָ—9.7). In other words, if you are able to do it, it has been permitted by God. This same emphasis on concerning oneself with one's own actions (as opposed to those of God or the rest of humanity) is also implicit in the tone of the Royal Experiment:

> *I made great my works* (הִגְדַּלְתִּי מַעֲשַׂי)...*I made myself* gardens and orchards (עָשִׂיתִי לִי)...*I made myself* pools of water (עָשִׂיתִי לִי)...*I got myself* male and female singers (עָשִׂיתִי לִי)...then I looked *on all the works which my hands had done* (בְּכָל מַעֲשַׂי שֶׁעָשׂוּ יָדַי) and *on the labour which I had laboured to do* (וּבֶעָמָל שֶׁעָמַלְתִּי לַעֲשׂוֹת), and behold all was vanity... (2.4-11)

The impossibility of human attempts to break free of divine control is only underlined by Qoheleth's remark that 'I know that whatever God does will be eternal: *nothing can be added to it nor anything taken from it...*' (עָלָיו אֵין לְהוֹסִיף וּמִמֶּנּוּ אֵין לִגְרֹעַ—3.14). The divine plan cannot be altered by human actions.[91] More importantly, because 'the work of God' is expressed in human actions, this verse suggests that human beings are unable to 'add to' the work of God by acting on their own initiative, nor can they 'take away from' God's work by failing to perform the actions which he has determined for them.

The equivalence of 'the work of God' with 'the work which is done under the sun' is of great importance in understanding the nature of Qoheleth's deterministic worldview. In this context, Qoheleth's use of √עשׂה referring to the actions of individuals is also significant, for Qoheleth's conclusion is that since one cannot understand 'the work of God' or break free from its power, one should allow oneself to find pleasure in 'one's own works' (3.22). This indeed is the essence of Qoheleth's message.

---

91. Murphy (*Ecclesiastes*, p. 35) notes the unusual nature of Qoheleth's reference to the divine *deed* rather than the divine word.

Chapter 3

'TO EVERYTHING THERE IS A SEASON': THE DETERMINATION
OF THE COSMOS AND HUMANITY IN ECCLESIASTES 1.3-8

1. *Introduction*

Thus far, this investigation into the extent to which determinism may be
present in Qoheleth's work has been concerned entirely with its
presence in human life and the implications this has for humanity's
interaction with the world. However, in Eccl. 1.3-8. which is often seen
as the prologue to the book of Ecclesiastes, the author initially focuses
on the natural world itself (cf. esp. vv. 4-7). This passage is typically
understood by commentators to embody the essence of Qoheleth's
thought in the rest of the book. Accordingly, the present study will
consider the implications of this passage for the hypothesis that the
author of the book of Ecclesiastes held a deterministic worldview.

The theme of determinism as applied to human beings in the Hebrew
Bible is extremely rare: only a handful of texts allude to the possibility
that human behaviour might be controlled by the deity. Indeed, one
might even say that it is the deity's actions that are determined by
humanity to the extent that the scheme of reward–retribution restricts
divine action to reacting to human deeds. This is a point that von Rad
noted with respect to prophetic texts (e.g. Jer. 18.7-10), but such is also
the case in certain portions of the wisdom tradition (e.g. Prov. 2.9-10;
3.33-35).

Even if the concept of determinism does not play an important part in
depictions of the relationship between human beings and the deity in
the Hebrew Bible, numerous texts speak of the cosmos as being subject
to divine decree. The Priestly writer, for example, saw the sun as performing the divinely instituted role of ruling the day (Gen. 1.14-19, cf.
Jer. 31.35; Pss. 74.16; 137.7-9) though it remains under the control of
God, who may order it not to rise (Job 9.7) or to stand still (Josh. 10.12)
or to move backward (2 Kgs 20.11//Isa. 38.8). The moon likewise is

said to have been created by the deity and to remain under his control (Gen. 1.14; Pss. 8.4; 104.19; 136.7, 9; Sir. 43.6-8) and, like the sun, is subject to change by the deity (Deut. 33.14; Josh. 10.12-13; Isa. 13.10; Jer. 31.35; Ezek. 32.7-8; Joel 2.10; 3.4; 4.15; Hab. 3.11; Job 25.5).

God's control of the day to day workings of creation finds continued emphasis. Rain may be given (1 Kgs 17.14; Job 37.6; Jer. 5.24; Ezek. 34.26) or withheld (Amos 4.7; Zech. 14.7). Crops may flourish (Lev. 26.4; Hos. 2.10 [ET 8]; Joel 2.19) or fail (Hos. 2.11 [ET 9]; Joel 1.10). The waters of the deep may be restrained (Ps. 33.7; Isa. 51.10), or allowed to flood the earth (Gen. 7.11; Ezek. 26.19). The winds are equally under the control of God (Exod. 10.13, 19; Jer. 49.36; 51.1; Hos. 13.15; Ps. 135.7) and on occasion are personified as his messengers (מלאכים—Ps. 104.4 cf. ἄγγελοι—Rev. 7.1). God's control over the cosmos is far-reaching indeed.

It is generally accepted by commentators that the depiction of the cycles of nature in Eccl. 1.4-7 serves as a metaphor for human activity. Just as the sun, wind, rivers, and to some extent the earth are in constant motion (vv. 4-7), so, the argument runs, humanity labours unceasingly with little or no gain accruing to themselves (v. 3). This in turn is said to illustrate Qoheleth's comment in v. 9 that 'there is nothing new under the sun'.

While I would suggest that such a reading may be essentially correct, it also seems that a significant aspect of the analogy between the natural world and humanity—indeed, what may have been the main point of the passage for Qoheleth—has been overlooked. Not only do the elements engage in continuous and wearisome activity, they follow preordained paths in doing so. The 'generations' of 1.4 pass away only to return; the sun of 1.5 travels east–west accross the sky and reappears in exactly the same place each morning; the wind of 1.6 follows a course north–south and back again in a great loop; the rivers of 1.7 flow through their accustomed channels to the sea, returning to bubble up once more through their original springs. All perform the activities and follow the paths set for them. This observation then, begs the question as to whether the passage is intended to suggest that the course either of humanity as a whole or of the individual is likewise subject to divine decree.

2. Text and Context

(3) What profit is there for human beings in all their labour at which they labour under the sun? (4) A generation goes, and a generation comes, but the earth lasts forever. (5) The sun rises and the sun sets, panting to its place. There it rises. (6) Heading north, then circling south, circling, circling, goes the wind, and on its circuits the wind returns. (7) All rivers flow to the sea, yet the sea is never full. To the place from which the rivers flow, thither they return to flow. (8) All things are weary: a man cannot speak. The eyes are not sated with seeing, nor the ears full from hearing (Eccl. 1.3-8).

1. Ecclesiastes 1.3

Although commentators on Ecclesiastes largely agree on the editorial nature of the superscription to the book in 1.1, opinion is divided as to whether the prologue to Qoheleth's work begins in vv. 2, 3 or 4. It has long been observed that 1.2 forms an inclusio with that of 12.8, and may therefore have an editorial function, although most commentators nevertheless ascribe the statement that 'all is הבל' ('vanity') to Qoheleth's own hand.[1] Even among those who separate vv. 2-3 from what follows, there is a strong tendency to read the section on the cycles of nature in the light of these verses.[2] The only exception to this is Whybray, who understands vv. 4-7 in a positive sense. For him, the natural cycles do not represent pointless labour, since their activity sustains the cosmos.[3]

The flaw in such an argument is that whether or not the movement of the elements has a positive or useful purpose as regards the overall scheme of creation, this does not necessarily mean that any benefits from such activity accrue to them. One may toil for 16 hours a day employed in an occupation useful to others but nevertheless be underpaid and find oneself asking, 'How do *I* benefit from what I am doing?'. Thus, the observations of the majority therefore still stand: the cyclical

---

1. Those who take the beginning of the passage to be 1.2 include F. Hitzig, *Der Prediger Solomo's* (KHAT; Leipzig: Weidmann, 1847), p. 129; Delitzsch, *Ecclesiastes*, p. 211; Barton, *Ecclesiastes*, p. 69; Hertzberg, *Prediger*, p. 57; Seow, *Ecclesiastes*, pp. 100, 111.

2. Podechard, *l'Ecclesiaste*, p. 235; Galling, *Prediger*, p. 85; Lohfink, *Kohelet*, p. 21; Crenshaw, *Ecclesiastes*, p. 61.

3. Whybray, *Ecclesiastes*, pp. 39-40.

motion of the elements may serve in a very real sense as an exemplar of the fruitlessness of their own activity, and, in a more general sense, of human toil. This is a subject to which I shall return shortly. Of those commentators who separate vv. 2-3 in whole or in part from the subsequent verses then, there persists the awareness that the cycles of the elements should be read in the light of Qoheleth's opening statements. My own reading of the passage understands its beginning to be v. 3, in common with Lauha and Fox, although it remains coloured as with the rest of the book by the opening thematic statement in v. 2.[4]

The rhetorical nature of Qoheleth's opening query: 'What profit accrues to human beings (מה יתרון לאדם) in all their toil that they undertake (בכל עמלו שיעמל) under the sun?' has been noted from a relatively early stage in the history of the book's exegesis. *Eccl. R.*, for example, understood 'their toil' to be that labour that human beings undertake on their own account as opposed to the study of Torah, with the corresponding implication that there was no advantage to such mundane activity.[5] The insight that Qoheleth's question is essentially a rhetorical one is also to be found in many commentaries of the nineteenth and twentieth centuries.[6] However, it was left to Crenshaw to undertake a study of the use of another of Qoheleth's favourite queries מי יודע ('who knows...?') in the rest of the Hebrew Bible to furnish concrete evidence for the use of the rhetorical question in Ecclesiastes.[7] Just as Qoheleth uses [מי יודע] to mean 'nobody knows', so here the question 'what profit...?' is a roundabout way of saying 'there is no profit...'. Qoheleth in fact makes this highly negative evaluation of human existence explicit in 2.11, judging his work (מעשׂה) and its products (עמל) with an emphatic אין יתרון ('there is no profit').

Of what kind of profit is Qoheleth thinking? The noun יתרון ('profit') occurs in Ecclesiastes 10 times (1.3; 2.11, 13 [×2]; 3.9; 5.8 [ET 9], 15 [ET 16]; 7.12; 10.10, 11), while the related term יותר occurs seven times (2.15; 6.8, 11; 7.11, 16; 12.9, 12) and מותר ('superiority', 'profit') once (3.19). יתרון has been described as 'that which remains— the surplus, if any, on the balance-sheet of life', a metaphor deriving

---

4. Lauha, *Kohelet*, p. 31; Fox, *Contradictions*, pp. 168-69.

5. The same is true of the Targum and Rashi.

6. Plumptre, *Ecclesiastes*, p. 104; Podechard, *L'Ecclésiaste*, p. 204; Glasser, *Qohelet*, p. 21.

7. J.L. Crenshaw, 'The Expression *mî yôdēaʻ* in the Hebrew Bible', *VT* 36 (1986), pp. 274-88.

from the world of commerce.[8] Notably, the context of Qoheleth's usage of the related terms derived from the √יתר is quite restricted. Qoheleth evidently *did* believe that wisdom was profitable (2.13; 7.11; 10.10-11), at least in contrast to folly. However, he is equally insistent that there is no profit in human activity (1.3; 2.11; 3.9; 5.15 [ET 16]). Under the circumstances, Fox's suggestion that the term יתרון refers in a concrete sense to an 'adequate gain' in life may provide the best way of understanding Qoheleth's thought.[9]

Human beings then, derive no adequate gain from the 'labour' that they undertake in the world. Again, however, we must define more clearly the term עמל. The context provided by its usage elsewhere in Ecclesiastes allows us to go some way in answering this question also. Gordis argued that עמל in Ecclesiastes referred to 'laborious toil, hard labor' on the basis of its usage in late Hebrew.[10] However, this word is applied by Qoheleth to any and all human activity. In 3.9, for example, the noun עמל refers to the range of life's activities as these are displayed in 3.2-8. Planting, uprooting, building, demolishing, weeping, laughing, loving, hating: all are in their own way examples of עמל. The parallel is underlined when 3.12 ('I know that there is nothing better for them than to rejoice *and to experience pleasure in their life* [ולעשות טוב בחייו]') is compared with 2.24 ('There is nothing better for humanity than to eat and drink and *to make themselves experience pleasure in their toil* [והראה את נפשו טוב בעמלו]', where עמלו 'their toil' has a meaning equivalent to חייו 'their life' in the former passage. As Fox observes, Qoheleth's use of √עמל, particularly in texts such as 2.22, 24; 3.9; 4.9; 8.15; 10.15 is 'a way of showing life's activities in a special perspective, speaking of them as if they were all part of a great wearying task'.[11]

Life, then, for Qoheleth, is seen in some respects as a burdensome, toilsome activity. In 1.13, he uses a different term, 'business/affliction'

---

8.   Plumptre, *Ecclesiastes*, p. 104. This position is followed by Lauha (*Kohelet*, p. 33); Crenshaw (*Ecclesiastes*, p. 59) and is borne out to some extent by the observation of Dahood that the term חסרון, which Qoheleth uses in 1.15, means (economic) loss ('Phoenician Background', p. 266; 'Canaanite-Phoenician Influence', p. 221). Qoheleth's use of the term חשבון in 7.24-29 and 9.10, which could be rendered 'sum total' may also be telling in this respect. Cf. also tadf III, 2.11.6, cited by Seow (*Ecclesiastes*, p. 103).

9.   Fox, *Contradictions*, pp. 54-55.

10.   Gordis, *Koheleth*, p. 205.

11.   Fox, *Contradictions*, pp. 54-55.

(עְנְיָן) to express the same idea: 'It is a bad business/affliction (עִנְיָן) that God has given humankind to be occupied with (עָנוֹת)'. If human labour is divinely imposed as Qoheleth seems to imply, well might one ask, 'What profit does humanity derive from all their toil...?' There is 'profit' for God, for human activity plays a role in the workings of the cosmos, but whether those who toil gain anything for themselves is altogether less clear for Qoheleth—particularly since death nullifies everthing.

The statement that human beings gain nothing *'from all* (בכל) their labour' works on two levels.[12] On one hand, it gives an impression of *quantity* (as if to say, 'all that hard work, and nothing to show for it'); on the other, it implies reference to the *variety* of activities that human beings may undertake. However, no immediate clarification is given by the text as to why Qoheleth thinks that human toil is profitless. This chapter will argue that Qoheleth's point is vividly illustrated in the extended natural metaphor of 1.4-7. Just as the human generations, sun, wind and rivers follow a path that is set for them, and from which they cannot deviate, so human action is tightly circumscribed by the deity. The sun races across the sky, circles beneath the earth to return 'panting' to the place where it originally arose. It gains no advantage from its wearisome labour—it performs the task set for it by God without question. The winds gust unceasingly, 'circling, circling' in an similar image of fruitless activity, while the rivers flow seawards, only to end by bubbling up from the same springs to continue their journey. All of these activities can justly be called עמל ('toil'), and all are part of the natural law that makes up existence. Just as God imposes this labour on the elements and controls it, so he also imposes activity on human beings. By this reading, humanity's actions, like the activity of the elements, are subject to deterministic decrees that are beyond their control. Hence they have no real stake in what they do. The 'profit' is not ours, but God's. Both Fox and Crenshaw go some way towards this view when they argue that human activity is profitless because human beings can produce nothing new.[13]

---

12. It is possible to read the ב in בכל עמלו as a beth pretii, that is, what do human beings get 'in exchange for all their labour?' Whitley (*Koheleth*, pp. 52-53) followed by Crenshaw (*Ecclesiastes*, p. 59) argue for the meaning 'from' however. No significant difference is made to the meaning whichever translation is adopted.

13. Crenshaw, *Ecclesiastes*; Fox, *Contradictions*, p. 169.

2. *Ecclesiastes 1.4*

Although scholars may have observed that the unceasing toil of nature is a metaphor for human existence, the consequences of comparing humanity to, for example, a heavenly body following its set course, have gone largely unnoticed. The implication of Qoheleth's use of the natural metaphor is that human life is simply part of a larger pre-determined whole.

The meaning of the statement that 'a generation goes, and a generation comes' is disputed. Traditionally, this has been related to generations of human beings passing away and being replaced by subsequent generations (cf. e.g. Jerome, Rashi). However, Whybray argues on the basis of the root meaning of דור ('circle') that the term דור refers to the generations of natural phenomena depicted in vv. 5-7. Hence, the thought of Qoheleth would be that even though these phenomena may appear to pass away for good, they will always providentially return and the earth will continue as it has always done.[14]

While one can see the force of this argument as it applies to the sun (which is hidden from view at night), it is difficult to see how one might think the rivers or the wind could pass away for good when their activity is continuous (notably, the verb בא ('come') is not used of their activity). Elsewhere in Ecclesiastes, the term בא and הלך ('go') denote the birth and death of human beings (5.14 [ET 15]; 6.4). The verb הלך on its own also has the sense of 'die' in 3.20; 6.6; 9.10; 12.5.[15] Contextually then, there is little to prevent a reading of the verse that understands the generations described as referring to humanity.

The main argument against such a position might hinge on the overall application of the natural cycles of 1.4-7 to human existence. Does it make sense for Qoheleth to undermine his 'natural' metaphor by making reference to human beings as early as v. 4? At first sight, one might well think not. However, humanity is not specifically mentioned. Indeed, the point of reference in 1.4 may be to all living things, since Qoheleth elsewhere equates human beings with animals in the light of their common fate (3.18-22). Moreover, the depiction of the generations in 1.4 acts on the macro-level—if not on that of living things generally, at least on that of the species. The inference to be drawn from 1.4-7

14. R.N. Whybray, 'Ecclesiastes 1.5-7 and the Wonders of Nature', *JSOT* 41 (1988), pp. 105-12 (106-107).

15. Murphy, *Ecclesiastes*, p. 7; Seow, *Ecclesiastes*, p. 106.

(that all is determined) appears to operate on the micro-level—that of the individual, the course of whose life is similarly mapped out by the deity.

The significance of this vignette of living generations disappearing into the earth and rising out of it thereafter is that it serves as a concrete example of the earth, like the other three elements, in motion in a constant and regular fashion.[16] This observation is supported by the fact that Qoheleth shares the biblical view that human beings are creatures of dust, and turn to dust when they die (12.7, cf. Gen. 3.19). It is not difficult to see how the image of 1.4 may have suggested itself to the author of Ecclesiastes.

3. Ecclesiastes 1.5

In Ps. 19.6 (ET 5), the sun's triumphant progress across the heavens is described. Here the emphasis falls on a different aspect of its activity. As in the previous verse, the constant movement of the elements is conveyed through a string of participles: זורח...זורח...בא...שואף ('rises...sets...panting...rises'), which takes us on the full circuit of the sun's course.[17] Its arrival at the place from which it must rise once more is denoted by an emphatic שׁם ('there') as the last word of the verse. Qoheleth would, one imagines, have known that the sun does not follow exactly the same course across the sky throughout the year. However, there are clearly defined limits to this variation and the whole process is repeated on an annual basis. Even if the sun does not follow exactly the same course every day, the fact remains that the course which it pursues is predictable both on a general (east–west), and a specific level. In the same way, the catalogue of seasons in 3.1-8 demonstrates that though human activity may allow of variety, all activities are subject to the vicissitudes of time (עת).

The verb שׁאף ('pant') used of the sun as it completes its circuit of

16. Qoheleth's work predates by many centuries the discovery of the earth's rotation or its circuit round the sun (cf. 1.5!). Indeed this text, in which the earth 'stands', was used as evidence in the Inquisition's case against Galileo. I cannot think of any other metaphor involving the earth in constant and repetitive motion that would have been available to Qoheleth and that would have struck a chord with his audience.

17. The first word זרח, presents a problem in that it is pointed as a qal perfect third person male singular. Most likely, this intended to be a participle זורח, the waw having been displaced by metathesis.

the cosmos occurs elsewhere in the Hebrew Bible in the sense of panting with desire (Ps. 119.131; Job 5.5; 7.2) or with over-exertion (Jer. 14.6). Although Whybray understands the sun as panting eagerly in anticipation of its next rising,[18] most commentators take the verb in its negative sense.[19] In view of the constant activity the sun is described as performing and the apparently negative context provided by 1.2-3, the latter option seems preferable in this instance. The sun's wearisome, continuous, and above all preordained activity serves as a metaphor for that of creation as a whole, including humanity.

4. *Ecclesiastes 1.6*

Qoheleth's device of using participles to give the impression of unceasing movement is further accentuated here by the repetition of the forms סובב ('circling') (three times) and הולך ('heading', 'goes') (twice). In this context, Crenshaw's comment that the appearance of the three successive participles סובב סובב הולך immediately before the introduction of the subject הרוח ('the wind') gives the impression of being 'caught in a rut' is a particularly apt observation.[20] Yet the point is not that the wind is 'ineffectual', as Crenshaw puts it: the wind performs exactly as it is supposed to. The issue for Qoheleth is that the wind remains 'in its circuits'—that is, that it does not go outside the boundaries established for it.[21]

In addition to the idea of determinacy generated by the description of the wind eternally circling, an impression of totality is created by mention of the north–south movement of the wind. In combination with the east–west travel of the sun, Qoheleth has now covered the four main points of the compass. This reinforces the use in the passage of a whole of the four elements—the building blocks of the cosmos according to the ancient philosophers—to demonstrate the truth of Qoheleth's assertion that *everything* is in constant motion and that this activity takes place within certain narrow limits defined by the deity.

---

18. Whybray, *Ecclesiastes*, p. 41. Cf. Podechard (*L'Ecclésiaste*, pp. 237-38) who takes the panting as referring to the sun's desire to continue on its course *despite* its monotonus nature.

19. Barton, *Ecclesiastes*, p. 70; Gordis, *Koheleth*, pp. 205-206; Murphy, *Ecclesiastes*, pp. 5-6; Seow, *Ecclesiastes*, p. 107.

20. Crenshaw, *Ecclesiastes*, pp. 64-65.

21. Whybray, *Ecclesiastes*, pp. 41-42.

5. Ecclesiastes 1.7

The idea behind the statement that 'all the rivers flow to the sea, but the sea is never full' is usually linked by commentators with the saying of Aristophanes that 'the sea, though all the rivers flow to it, does not increase in volume' (*The Clouds* 1294).[22] Indeed, the thrust of this verse seems to be very similar to that of 1.4, in which a generation passes into the earth as its successor emerges. Just as the earth 'stands forever' (i.e. sees no net increase or loss), so the sea never fills as a result of the waters that flow into it.

The MT of the latter part of this verse is, however, ambiguous. One could translate the Hebrew אֶל מְקוֹם שֶׁהַנְּחָלִים הֹלְכִים שָׁם הֵם שָׁבִים לָלֶכֶת 'to [or "at"] the place from which the rivers flow, there they flow again', or 'to the place from which the rivers flow, there they return to flow'. The former takes the participle שָׁבִים (from a verb meaning 'return') as complementary to לָלֶכֶת ('to go') (rather than as denoting an entirely separate action), and emphasizes the repetitive nature of the waters' movement. The latter emphasizes its cyclical nature. Either reading accords with the intent of the passage as a whole as I imagine it, although I favour a cyclical understanding of the waters' movement on the basis of the apparently cyclical nature of the 'generations' spoken of in 1.4.[23] This is also the understanding of the LXX, which translates εἰς τόν τόπον οὗ οἱ χείμαρροι πορεύονται, ἐκεῖ αὐτοὶ ἐπιστρέφουσι τοῦ πορευθῆναι ('to the place [from] where the rivers came there they return to go').[24]

In summary then, Qoheleth has now outlined the cyclical nature of the earth, the sun (fire), the wind (air) and now the waters. The picture

22. Plumptre, *Ecclesiastes*, p. 106; Hertzberg, *Prediger*, p. 61; Gordis, *Koheleth*, p. 206; Lauha, *Kohelet*, p. 35; Crenshaw, *Ecclesiastes*, p. 65.

23. The first rendering ('again') may also imply a cessation of activity on the part of the waters. The exegesis offered here at least has the benefit that this source of possible confusion is removed.

24. The Vulgate ('ad locum, unde exeunt flumina, revertuntur ut iterum fluant' ['to the place from which the rivers came, they return to flow again']) hedges its bets by translating the crucial participle שָׁבִים twice: once as 'revertuntur' 'return', and once as 'iterum' 'again, a second time'. Rashi interprets along the same lines as the LXX, speaking of the rivers as flowing back from the sea to their original springs through subterranean tunnels. Ibn Ezra explains that the waters evaporate from the sea and return to their original springs in the form of rain.

painted is of a creation always in motion, never at rest. If commentators such as Murphy and Seow are correct in seeing the term שָׁאַף ('pant') applied to the sun in 1.5 in its negative sense of panting from exertion or exhaustion, then one might even be able to describe creation as never being 'at ease'. As such, it forms an excellent parallel with the situation in which humanity find themselves in Ecclesiastes.

6. *Ecclesiastes 1.8*

The focus of the poem now switches back to humanity, though there is considerable ambiguity evident in the MT of v. 8a: לֹא יוּכַל אִישׁ לְדַבֵּר כָּל הַדְּבָרִים יְגֵעִים ('all things are weary: a man cannot speak') and this has led to widely differing translations and interpretations by modern commentators. Among the problems to be faced is that of the meaning of הַדְּבָרִים, which could mean either 'things' or 'words', and its relationship with לְדַבֵּר ('to speak'). Then there is the question of the meaning of יְגֵעִים, which has been translated as an adjective 'wearisome', 'weary', or as a participle 'labouring'. The general confusion of latter-day exegetes is mirrored by that of the Versions. The Vulgate translates 'cunctae res difficiles: non potest homo explicare sermone' ('all things are difficult: nobody can explain them with words'), while the LXX's literal translation, which renders דברים with λόγοι ('words, things') offers no assistance.

The argument of those commentators who translate הַדְּבָרִים as 'words' in preference to the alternative 'things' is twofold. First, it is stated that elsewhere in Ecclesiastes, the plural of דבר always means 'words' (1.1; 5.2 [ET 3]; 6.11; 7.21; 9.17; 10.12-14; 12.10 [×2]). Second the proximity of the verbal form לְדַבֵּר ('to speak') is also said to militate against a possible reference to 'things'.[25] However, such a position relies on the assumption that Qoheleth is absolutely consistent in his use of language and also ignores the possibility that he may be indulging in a play on words in v. 8a/8b. As Whybray points out, the term דברים in v. 8a as well as being picked up by the use of לְדַבֵּר, meaning 'to speak' in v. 8b, is also echoed by the use of the singular דבר to mean 'thing' in v. 10. Ultimately, the way that the term דברים is translated must depend upon the conclusions reached about the meaning of the rest of the verse.

---

25. Seow, *Ecclesiastes*, p. 109.

Many commentators translate the term יְגֵעִים 'wearisome' so also the NEB and NRSV). This path has been followed most recently by Seow with his translation 'wearying'.[26] However, in other locations in which the adjective appears (Deut. 25.18; 2 Sam. 17.2), it apparently means 'weary', 'weak', either through lack of sustenance or through over-exertion. There is no evidence of which I am aware, either in biblical or postbiblical Hebrew, that the adjective can express the idea of *causing* weariness.[27] An alternative view, that יְגֵעִים here means 'weary', has been advanced, among others, by Fox.[28] With this suggestion, it is the sense more than anything else that raises questions: what might Qoheleth mean by the statement that 'all things/words are weary'? Fox understands the adjective to refer to 'words' (הדברים) which are 'weary' in the sense of being too feeble to describe existence accurately (v. 8b), but this may be an overreading of the text.

As Seow observes, the root meaning of יגע is a dual one. The verb can mean not only 'to be weary', but also 'to toil, labour' (cf. Job 9.29; Isa. 49.4). Since the adjective יְגֵעִים is very rare, both Lohfink and Whybray have suggested that the sense of יְגֵעִים here may be 'toiling, labouring'.[29] Accordingly, one may translate 'all things are toiling, a man cannot speak'. The term יְגֵעִים would then be understood to refer to the constant activity of the elements described in vv. 4-7 which prevents human beings from accurately describing existence—'a man cannot speak'. This harmonizes well with the statements that 'the eyes are not sated with seeing, nor the ears full from hearing', which most commentators take to mean that human beings are unable to register or to comprehend the full scale of this activity precisely because it is ceaseless. Just as the sea is never 'full' (מלא) from the rivers which flow into it, so human perception is never 'full' (מלא) from the information

---

26. Seow, *Ecclesiastes*, p. 109. Cf. Crenshaw, *Ecclesiastes*, p. 61; Murphy, *Ecclesiastes*, pp. 5-6.

27. Seow's argument (*Ecclesiastes*, p. 109) that we have here a unique usage of a stative participle meaning 'weary, wearying' does not solve the problem. The dual sense which he suggests (including the idea of causation in the latter) he derives from analogy with the Hebrew statives מלא ('being full, filling') and ירא ('being afraid, fearing'). Yet it is notable that the second of these examples does not contain the idea of 'causing (another) to be afraid' as he would wish. The dual sense of מלא may therefore be exceptional.

28. Fox, *Contradictions*, p. 171.

29. Lohfink, *Kohelet*, p. 22; Whybray, 'Ecclesiastes 1.5-7', p. 107.

it receives.[30] Here too, a concrete link is established between the ceaseless toil of nature and that of humanity.

3. *Conclusion*

The passage of which Eccl. 1.3-8 forms a part has aptly been termed the 'prologue' to the book of Ecclesiastes, for it is here that Qoheleth sets the scene for the rest of his work. The rhetorical question with which it opens ('What profit is there for human beings in all their labour at which they labour...?') is set firmly in the context of a restless creation in which all things engage in unending and laborious activity. The sun, the wind, the rivers, the 'generations' which emerge from, and return to, the earth combine to maintain existence on an even keel. Existence, and by extension God, 'profits' from the activity of the elements: the elements themselves do not. Human beings also form a part of the world and have a role in the unfolding of its history—well might one ask if any more benefit accrues to human beings than to the elements themselves from all this labour that is carried out.

A darker dimension is added to Qoheleth's question by the observation that not only do the elements perform their activities unceasingly, they do so along predetermined paths. The waters flow to the sea in their channels, the sun travels across the sky from east to west. The wind blows in a north–south–north circle. Even the 'generations' of 1.4 begin and end with the same thing. By implication the course of humanity, both as a whole and on an individual level, is mapped out. Human beings cannot escape the harsh fact of 'toil' nor have any control over how that toil is carried out.

If there is no 'profit' to be derived from the sentence of hard labour, one may at least attempt to discover what aspects of that labour are good, or at any rate, better than others. This is the real question that forms the basis of Qoheleth's investigation into existence (2.3), though the answer is as unpalatable (3.12; 8.15) as that implicit in the rhetorical question of 1.3. As will be argued in Chapter 6 of the present work, even those aspects of existence that may be termed 'good' are controlled by the deity—God controls not only the distribution of wealth, but even the individual's ability to appreciate and use that wealth.

---

30. The idea that the constant movement of a body prevents an accurate description of it has latterly found expression in the twentieth century.

Chapter 4

'A TIME TO GIVE BIRTH, A TIME TO DIE':
A REREADING OF ECCLESIASTES 3.1-15

1. *Introduction*

Ecclesiastes 3.1-15 is a key text for our understanding of Qoheleth's thought. Unfortunately, as we have seen, it lends itself to a variety of interpretations. Until very recently commentators were divided into two camps as to the intent of this passage. While some see the text as enumerating a variety of 'ideal' times for human activities which human beings are unable to, or prevented from, achieving,[1] others have argued that Qoheleth is advancing the thesis of determinism.[2] Despite objections that several passages in Ecclesiastes presuppose a degree of free will, the reasonably wide acceptance that the deterministic under-standing of this passage enjoys is partly due to the fact that the first two actions cited in 3.2. עת ללדת ועת למות, translated by RSV, NRSV, NEB, NAB and many commentators 'a time to be born, a time to die', are not generally recognized as being under human control.[3]

An alternative reading has been offered by Joseph Blenkinsopp, who has presented a series of arguments which call into question the legiti-macy of this deterministic reading. His thesis is that Eccl. 3.2-8 repre-sents a quotation from a Stoicizing Jewish sage to which Qoheleth prefaces a title (3.1) and a commentary refuting the content of this quotation (3.9-15).[4] The observation that 3.2-8 may be an extended quotation is not new,[5] and previous commentators have also suggested

1.   Plumptre, *Ecclesiastes*, pp. 126-31; Whybray, *Ecclesiastes*, p. 67.
2.   Delitzsch, *Ecclesiastes*, p. 255; Gordis, *Koheleth*, p. 229; Murphy, *Eccles-iastes*, p. 33.
3.   Delitzsch, *Ecclesiastes*, p. 256; Zimmerli, *Prediger*, p. 162; Scott, *Proverbs Ecclesiastes*, pp. 220-21; Fox, *Contradictions*, pp. 190, 192.
4.   Blenkinsopp, 'Ecclesiastes 3.1-15', pp. 55-64.
5.   A.G. Wright, '"For everything there is a season": The Structure and

that it expresses the Stoic ideal of living according to nature.[6] Where Blenkinsopp diverges from earlier interpretations of this passage is in the suggestion that Qoheleth specifically argues against the content of this passage in 3.9-15.[7] It is to this question there that attention shall first be directed.

2. *Text and Context*

The argument that 3.2-8 is most likely a quotation, rather than original to Qoheleth, rests on two foundations. The first is that the language of this passage finds little or no echo in the rest of the book of Ecclesiastes. The second is that the idea of the passage does not reflect Qoheleth's thinking elsewhere in Ecclesiastes.[8] The former issue is one with which it is relatively simple to deal. The second is more difficult: there is no consensus as to the intent of 3.2-8. Its relationship (or not) to the rest of Qoheleth's work is therefore entirely dependent on how the individual commentator reads the passage.

Blenkinsopp does not state outright his reasons for rejecting the idea that 3.2-8 advances a deterministic thesis. It cannot be that he rejects determinism in Ecclesiastes generally, for he argues that Qoheleth puts forward this idea in 3.9-15 to counter the (indeterministic) content of 3.2-8.[9] The problem appears to lie in the extent to which reading 3.2-8 deterministically would subordinate human free will to the control of the deity.[10] Thus Blenkinsopp—like many commentators—accepts a form of determinism in which God predisposes events to happen, while

Meaning of the Fourteen Opposites (Ecclesiastes 3, 2-8)', in J. Doré *et al.* (eds.), *De la Tôrah au Messie: Mélanges Henri Cazelles* (Paris: J. Gabalda, 1981), pp. 321-28; Whybray, *Ecclesiastes*, pp. 69-70; Murphy, *Ecclesiastes*, p. 33.

6.	Tyler, *Ecclesiastes*, p. 13; Gammie, 'Stoicism and Anti-Stoicism in Qoheleth', p. 175.

7.	Whybray (*Ecclesiastes*, pp. 69-70, 72) comes close to suggesting that Qoheleth argues against the content of 3.2-8 in 3.9-15 when he hypothesizes that Qoheleth reinterprets the passage which he has just quoted. Cf. also W.J. Fuerst, *The Books of Ruth, Esther, Ecclesiastes, the Song of Songs, Lamentations* (Cambridge: Cambridge University Press, 1975), p. 113.

8.	Whybray, *Ecclesiastes*, p. 70; Blenkinsopp, 'Ecclesiastes 3.1-15', p. 57.

9.	Blenkinsopp, 'Ecclesiastes 3.1-15', pp. 61-63.

10.	This also seems evident in the work of Gammie ('Stoicism and Anti-Stoicism in Qoheleth', p. 175), for he understands some actions as illustrative of Stoic determinism, and others as illustrative of free will.

leaving humanity free to make the choice of how they respond to these events (a philosophy not without precedent in the work of Chrysippus). However, before moving on to the thought of this passage and its relation to the rest of Ecclesiastes, let us consider the language of 3.2-8.

1. *The Language of Ecclesiastes 3.2-8*

Despite the argument that neither the thought nor the language of 3.2-8 is characteristic of Ecclesiastes, there are significant cross-overs between this passage and the rest of the book. Purely on a lexical basis one can point to the fact that the word עֵת, 'appointed time', while it occurs 29 times in 3.2-8, is used a further 11 times outside this passage (3.11, 17; 7.17; 8.5, 6, 9; 9.8, 11, 12 [×2]; 10.17). The use of the term חֵפֶץ ('business', 'purpose') in 3.1, which although not strictly part of the passage according to Blenkinsopp, nevertheless summarizes Qoheleth's understanding of it, finds its echo in the seven uses of √חפץ in 3.17; 5.3, 7; 8.3, 6; 12.1, 10. Although four of these citations occur in a different context of desire or pleasure (and as such translated in the LXX by the verb θέλω [8.3] or the related noun θέλημα [5.3; 12.1, 10]),[11] the usages in 3.17; 5.7; 8.6 retain the same sense as that in 3.1.[12] Indeed in 3.17 and 8.6 Qoheleth repeats a variation of the basic phrase in 3.1 that 'there is an appointed time for every purpose' (עֵת לְכָל חֵפֶץ). While not all of the actions in 3.2-8 feature elsewhere in the book of Ecclesiastes, a significant proportion do. The verb ילד ('give birth') occurs four times outside our passage (4.14; 5.13; 6.3; 7.1) while the verb מות ('die') occurs eight times (2.16; 4.2 [×2]; 7.17; 9.3, 4, 5 [×2] and the noun six times (3.19 [×2]; 7.1, 26; 8.8; 10.1). The verb נטע ('plant') occurs outside this passage three times (2.4, 5; 12.11), while the verbs פרץ ('tear down') occurs in 10.8 and בנה ('build up') in 2.4; 9.14. More significantly, √שׂחק ('laugh') is used four times outside this passage (2.2; 7.3, 6; 10.19). The verbs ספוד (mourn') occur in 12.5 and בנוס ('gather') in 2.8, 26, while the verbs חבק ('embrace') occur in 4.5 and רחק ('be far') in 12.6. The verb בקשׁ ('seek') is more frequent in Ecclesiastes with six occurrences outwith this passage (3.15; 7.25, 28, 29; 8.17; 12.10) and verbal forms of √אבד ('lose', 'perish', 'destroy') occurring five times (5.13; 7.7, 15; 9.6, 18). The verb שׁמר ('keep') is

---

11. W. Staples, 'The meaning of *ḥepeṣ* in Ecclesiastes', *JNES* 24 (1965), pp. 110-12.

12. Blenkinsopp himself points out this fact ('Ecclesiastes 3.1-15', p. 60).

repeated eight times outside this passage (4.17; 5.7, 12; 8.2, 5; 11.4; 12.3, 13). The verb דבר ('speak') occurs in 1.8, 16; 3.7; 7.21 with the derived noun דבר ('word') occurring a total of 24 times. The verb אהב ('love') occurs in 5.9 [×2]; 9.9 and its derived noun אהבה ('love') in 9.1, 6, while its opposite שׂנא ('hate') occurs twice (2.17, 18) with its derived noun also in 9.1, 6. Finally, the noun מלחמה ('war') occurs twice outside this passage (8.8; 9.11).

2. *The Ideas of Ecclesiastes 3.2-8*

There seems little reason not to suppose on a lexical basis that Qoheleth might have written this passage. While none of the terms contained therein are unique to Qoheleth, he nevertheless uses most of them on a regular basis throughout Ecclesiastes. However, Blenkinsopp's arguments concerning the meaning of 3.2-8 also demand closer examination. Blenkinsopp rightly points out the fact that the infinitive in עת ללדת in 3.2 is qal and therefore has an active sense (i.e. it should be best translated 'a time to give birth'). Where Qoheleth does speak of 'being born', he follows standard Hebrew usage with a niphal form, as in 7.1 ויום המות מיום הולדו, 'the day of death (is better) than the day of birth'.[13] This translation of 3.2 may perhaps be supported by the LXX's ambiguous καιρὸς τοῦ τεκεῖν ('a time of birth').[14] Such is certainly the case with the Targum's עידן בחיר למילד בנין ועידן בחיר לקטלא בנין לקטלותהון מסרבין באבנין ומרגזין על מימר דיניא ('A time chosen to bear sons and a time chosen to kill rebellious and blaspheming sons, to kill them with stones by order of the judges') and the Peshitta's ܘܙܒܢܐ ܠܡܐܠܕ ('a time to bear'), although the Vulgate's 'tempus nascendi' ('a time to be born') has attempted to harmonize with עת למות by rendering the phrase in a passive sense.

Since the phrase עת ללדת, is active and to be translated 'a time to give birth', this, claims Blenkinsopp, leaves the expression, עת למות 'a time to die', as the only one of 28 human actions or events not under human control. The context of the passage therefore demands an interpretation of למות ('to die') in which human beings choose to die, and

---

13. Blenkinsopp, 'Ecclesiastes 3.1-15', pp. 56-57. Cf. Tyler, *Ecclesiastes*, p. 124; Podechard, *L'Ecclésiaste*, pp. 286-87; Glasser, *Qohelet*, pp. 58-59; Crenshaw, *Ecclesiastes*, pp. 91, 93; Murphy, *Ecclesiastes*, pp. 28-29.

14. The Arabic version of Ecclesiastes, dependent on the LXX, translates *waqt lilwilāda* ('a time for childbearing').

so may be explained as an exhortation to suicide in line with contemporary Stoic thought.

It is true that there seems to have been no prohibition in Jewish law against suicide.[15] One could therefore understand עת למות as referring to the rational, planned suicide of the Stoic sage. Can its opposite, however, giving birth, really be said to be an activity under human control? Blenkinsopp's statement that 'it...makes sense to speak of deciding to have a child and choosing the best time to do it'[16] essentially understands 3.2 as a text extolling the virtues not only of euthanasia, but also of of family planning: yet, children are never depicted in the Hebrew Bible as anything other than a blessing.[17] On a strictly literal level, moreover, the time at which one gives birth once pregnant is something over which the individual has no control.[18] Qoheleth indeed speaks of the 'untimely birth' (הנפל—6.3) in a passage that vividly illustrates the inability of human beings to find happiness by their own efforts.

Whether Stoic or no, it would in fact be rather strange if a Jewish sage claimed that human beings had control over either birth or death. Not only do these two actions encompass the whole of human life,[19] they are also the two single actions that an ordinary Jew could accept without hesitation to be in the hands of God rather than those of humanity.

As an illustration of this, God is often said in the Hebrew Bible to 'give' or to 'add' a son (Gen. 17.16; 29.33; 30.6, 24; 1 Kgs 3.6; 5.7; Isa. 9.6), cf. Gen. 4.1; Judg. 13.3; 2 Kgs 4.16; Isa. 7.14. Moreover, God is said to enable or prevent the bearing of children by opening or closing the womb (Gen. 20.18; 29.31; 30.22; 1 Sam. 1.5), indeed the role of God was essential in the creation of new life since he formed it in the womb and brought it forth from there (Job 10.18; 31.15; Isa. 44.2; 66.8). Qoheleth himself in Eccl. 11.5 compares the 'way of the spirit' and the formation of the foetus in the womb to 'the works of God who makes everything'. Conversely, Qoheleth also speaks in Eccl. 12.7 of

---

15. A.J. Droge, 'Suicide', *ABD*, VI, pp. 227-30. The idea that למות may refer to suicide is mentioned but rejected by Plumptre (*Ecclesiastes*, p. 127).

16. Blenkinsopp, 'Ecclesiastes 3.1-15', p. 60.

17. J.A. Grassi, 'Child, Children' *ABD*, I, pp. 904-905.

18. Tyler (*Ecclesiastes*, p. 124) took עת ללדת to refer to the nine-month period of gestation in human beings, indicative of the general law of Nature rather than of a determinism that applies to individuals.

19. Crenshaw, *Ecclesiastes*, p. 93; Murphy, *Ecclesiastes*, p. 33.

God's role at the moment of death when 'the spirit returns to God who gave it'. Human beings are arbiters neither of the time of conception, nor or birth: these mysteries are firmly in the control of God.

Likewise, the qal of מות ('die') is often used of death inflicted by God in the Hebrew Bible (albeit as a penalty for disobedience or sin): Gen. 3.3; 20.3, 19; Exod. 11.5; 12.33; 28.35; 30.22; Lev. 8.35; 10.2, 6, 7, 9; Num. 3.4; 4.19, 20; 14.35; Deut. 5.22; 18.16; Josh. 10.11; Judg. 6.23, and so on. The specific expression מות ימות ('surely die') occurs in Gen. 2.17; 3.4; 20.7; Num. 26.65; Judg. 13.21, 22; 2 Sam. 12.14, and so on. Naturally these may be argued to be exceptions, examples in which God cuts short life for a specific act on the part of the sinner. One might also argue on this basis that God has very little to do with determining the time of death under normal circumstances, and more-over that none of the texts cited above have very much to do with the wisdom tradition of which Qoheleth was a part. However, the deter-mination of the time of one's death by God is a question expressly con-sidered by the wisdom tradition: for while those who follow the path of the simple are promised an early death, those who follow the dictates of wisdom are said simultaneously to enjoy 'length of days, long life and peace' (Prov. 3.2) and 'favour and good understanding in the sight of the Lord' (Prov. 3.4). Likewise, personified Wisdom is said to offer 'length of days in her right hand, and in her left hand riches and honour' (Prov. 3.16) and states that 'whoever finds me finds life' (Prov. 8.35). Implicit in Eccl. 7.17 is the idea that it is God who determines the time (עת) of one's death, and God who can change this time if he so wills. For the Israelite therefore, there was no theoretical problem in accepting a limited form of determinism, so long as it was emphasized that this determinism was God-driven rather than simply an impersonal irrational force. The appeal of Stoicism for some thinking Jews lay pre-cisely in the fact that it identified God (i.e. Zeus) and the deterministic mechanism controlling the universe as one and the same.[20]

The location of these two actions, birth and death, at the head of the list in 3.2-8 seems therefore rather to be intended as a preparation for what comes after. In other words, acceptance that birth and death are in the hands of God paves the way for the acceptance of the idea that all other events and actions on earth are likewise in the hands of God. This is further underlined by the last pair of opposites, 'a time of war, a time

20. H.A. Fischel, 'Stoicism', *EncJud*, XV, p. 410.

of peace' (3.8) which have also attracted attention from commentators.[21] No human action whatsoever is implied here: Qoheleth does not claim that there is 'a time *to make* war, a time *to make* peace'. Again, these are states which any Jew would have accepted without question to be within God's power—Yahweh brings war or peace on Israel (2 Kgs 24.2; 1 Chron. 5.22; 22.9; Hag. 2.9). The predetermined actions and emotions in human life which might be more questionable to a Jew are sandwiched between these two absolutes. They serve as the sugar coating to the bitter pill of determinism.

3. The Thought of Ecclesiastes 3.9-15

What is the relationship between 3.1-8 and the thought of 3.9-15 immediately following? Having effectively argued against a deterministic reading of the former, Blenkinsopp suggests that 3.9-15 is intended to refute the thesis of 3.2-8 that everything has its appropriate time, in accordance with which human beings can act.[22] In many ways, this suggestion is similar to the work of commentators such as Tyler and Lohfink, who have argued that Qoheleth makes use of the Stoic diatribe.[23] The similarity with the work of Whybray, who has suggested that some portions of Ecclesiastes contain quotations which Qoheleth subsequently refutes, is even more pronounced.[24] To this extent, the thought of 3.9-15 will now be considered with reference to the preceding section.

a. Ecclesiastes 3.9-10
Generally speaking, commentators seem puzzled by Qoheleth's introductory question in 3.9, 'What profit has the worker at that wherein he labours?' Several suggestions as to the interpretation of this verse in the light of 3.1-8 have been offered. Murphy argues that the rhetorical question, essentially a re-statement of 1.3, judges human activity as

---

21. Jastrow (*A Gentle Cynic*, pp. 209-10 n. 40) in fact deletes all of 3.3-8. However, Delitzsch sees as significant the fact that the list of activities ends in 'peace' (*Ecclesiastes*, p. 259), and Crenshaw (*Ecclesiastes*, p. 96) suggests that the change in syntax and structure in 3.8 allows the poem to come to a forceful conclusion.

22. Blenkinsopp, 'Ecclesiastes 3.1-15', pp. 59, 61.

23. Tyler, *Ecclesiastes*, p. 48; Lohfink, *Kohelet*, p. 10.

24. Whybray, *Ecclesiastes* (OTG; Sheffield: JSOT Press, 1989), pp. 35-40. This view was also to some extent advanced by Gordis (*Koheleth*, pp. 95-108).

profitless because it cannot change what God has determined.[25] This is possible from the immediate context, but why should Qoheleth advocate that God's work be *changed*? Qoheleth's ambitions seem directed rather at *finding* 'the work of God/the work which is done under the sun' (3.11; 8.17). Conversely, Whybray (followed by Blenkinsopp) suggests that activity is profitless because human beings are unable to act at the appropriate moment that God has determined for each work.[26] One could certainly argue that this would make human activity profitless for God, but whether it is so for human beings is less clear: implicit in Qoheleth's question in 1.3; 3.9 is the idea that there is no profit for humanity in any activity. This is despite the fact that some actions (e.g. joy/toil, 2.26; love, 9.9) are explicitly stated to be determined by God (and hence would occur at the 'appropriate time' according to Whybray and Blenkinsopp's understanding of 3.2-8).

Crenshaw's interpretation is that human activity is profitless because each opposite in 3.2-8 cancels the other out: labour thus produces nothing in the long term.[27] One could perhaps argue this for humanity as a whole, but not for the individual. Thus, Delitzsch's suggestion seems best to fit the context: Qoheleth's claim is that activity is without profit for human beings because everything is determined by God as 3.1-8 implies.[28]

This viewpoint may be illustrated with the hypothetical case of a slave working on the estate of a large landowner. The slave is not an autonomous being in his own right, but a tool, an extension of the master's will. The actions of the slave are entirely determined by the will of this master and he works not for himself but for another. Well might this slave ask himself 'what benefit do I get from all my work?'

Such is the situation in which humanity finds itself in a world where all human activity is determined by an inscrutable deity: this interpretation is supported moreover in 3.10, in which Qoheleth states: 'I have seen the toil (עָנְיָן) which *God has given to humanity* to be occupied with'. The overall עָנְיָן in life in 3.10 is reflected by the times and seasons determined by God for every human action, thought and

25. Murphy, *Ecclesiastes*, p. 34.

26. Whybray, *Ecclesiastes* [NCBC], pp. 72-73; Blenkinsopp, 'Ecclesiastes 3.1-15', p. 61. Cf. Plumptre (*Ecclesiastes*, p. 131) and Podechard (*L'Ecclésiaste*, p. 291).

27. Crenshaw, *Ecclesiastes*, p. 96.

28. Delitzsch, *Ecclesiastes*, p. 259. Followed to some extent by Barton (*Ecclesiastes*, p. 101).

emotion in 3.1-8—but Qoheleth has not merely *seen* this divinely determined toil, he has shown it to the reader.

b. *Ecclesiastes 3.11*

The exegesis of 3.11 has already been discussed in some depth in Chapter 2 of this book. The theme of determinism evident in 3.1-8 and continued in 3.9-10 supports the reading given therein, that the phrase 'he (i.e. God) has made everything beautiful in its time' refers to the irresistible nature of the times determined by God. To put it another way: human beings have no choice or control over the actions which they perform, but are simply drawn to act when and how God wills.[29]

Murphy, following Podechard, is most likely correct in his assessment of the phrase, 'God has put העלם ('eternity') in their (humanity's) minds' as referring to God's placing of an *eternity of times* in human minds.[30] This too ties the verse in with the deterministic context of 3.1-8, for העלם is the whole of which each individual עת ('time') is a part: thus Qoheleth envisions God programming humanity with all the actions which they will perform in their lives. Since it is this עלם ('eternity') that controls human action, the action of placing it in the human mind thereby ensures that 'humankind may not find out the work of God from beginning to end'.

Probably for reasons of space, Blenkinsopp gives less consideration to this verse, although I would argue that whether one regards it as positive or negative commentary on 3.2-8, it remains crucial to any interpretation of the catalogue of seasons. Apparently, the expression יפה בעתו ('beautiful in its time') is understood in the sense 'appropriate to its time': that is, while God makes everything happen, the proper fulfillment of the activities listed in 3.2-8 (and presumably the success of the overall divine plan for the world) are dependent solely on humanity's ability to determine these times and to act in accordance with them. Yet no clear explanation is given for 3.11b which ought to provide further evidence for this view: human beings, according to Blenkinsopp, lack the knowledge to align their actions with the divine activity (understanding העלם as 'ignorance'?).[31] Yet what of God's role and its implications? If the divine plan requires human beings to act in accordance with the 'times' which he has set, why does he

---

29. Fox, *Contradictions*, p. 193.
30. Murphy, *Ecclesiastes*, p. 34; Podechard, *L'Ecclésiaste*, p. 295.
31. Blenkinsopp, 'Ecclesiastes 3.1-15', pp. 59, 61.

deprive human beings of the necessary knowledge to do so (for it is, after all, God who places הָעֹלָם in human minds)? Another difficulty is that Qohelet clearly uses the phrase לְעֹלָם in 3.14 in the sense of 'eternal', potentially undermining Blenkinsopp's understanding of the meaning of this term in 3.11.

c. *Ecclesiastes 3.12-13*
A full discussion of the implications of Qoheleth's recommendation to joy may be found in Chapter 6 of the present work. For now, however, it is worth giving consideration to these verses in the light of Qoheleth's advocacy of a deterministic God. First, Qoheleth's comment in 3.12, 'I know that there is no good in them (בָּם) except to rejoice and to experience good in life', demands attention. Most commentators follow BHS here and emend בָּם to בָּאָדָם (translating: 'I know that there is no good for humankind but to rejoice...') in order to provide an antecedent for the pronominal suffix on חַיָּיו.[32] This ability to enjoy life is determined by the deity, for it is termed by Qoheleth in 3.13 'the gift of God' (מַתַּת אֱלֹהִים) that one may 'eat and drink and experience good in all one's labour (עֲמָלוֹ)'.[33] Again, the term עֲמָלוֹ picks up on the participial form עָמֵל in Qoheleth's rhetorical question in 3.9. There is no profit (יִתְרוֹן) in labour, but there is some good (טוֹב).[34] This, however, is entirely subject the the goodwill of the deity.

d. *Ecclesiastes 3.14-15*
The conclusions which Qoheleth draws from the fact of determinism in 3.12-13 (that the only good activities are to eat, drink and enjoy life, but that even this much is dependent on the deity) are heralded by his use of

32. Among those who emend are Podechard (*L'Ecclésiaste*, pp. 296-97); Zimmerli (*Prediger*, p. 163), Fox (*Contradictions*, p. 194). Others explain by referring the plural suffix back to בָּאָדָם in the preceding verse (Murphy, *Ecclesiastes*, p. 30; Whybray, *Ecclesiastes* [NCBC], p. 74). Hertzberg (*Prediger*, p. 86) retains MT without comment. However, the suffix on בָּם could be taken to refer to the divinely determined actions listed in 3.2-8. Thus, Qoheleth would be commenting that the only good actions among the 'all' of 3.1 which God determines are 'to rejoice' (לִשְׂמוֹחַ) and similarly, 'to fare well' (לַעֲשׂוֹת טוֹב) (note the infinitives, which pick up on and extend the range of those of 3.2-8; Tyler, *Ecclesiastes*, p. 126).

33. Glasser, *Qohelet*, p. 65; Whybray, 'Preacher of Joy' [NCBC], pp. 89-90.

34. Whybray (*Ecclesiastes*, p. 74) lays particular emphasis on the threefold repetition of the term טוֹב in 3.12-13.

the phrase כי ידעתי ('I know that…'). In 3.14, Qoheleth makes another
point introduced by this phrase: 'I know that all which God does is
eternal: there is no adding to it, nor is there any taking away from it'.
Murphy notes the unusual nature of Qoheleth's comment on the
immutability of the divine deed as opposed to the divine word here,[35]
but Qoheleth does not mean that the results of God's actions last
forever. Nor does לעלם mean that God's actions cannot be changed by
human beings (though Qoheleth would certainly agree that God's
actions are unchangeable).[36] The text states that human beings cannot
add to or *take away* from what God does. In the context of determinism
this would mean that human beings cannot add to God's work by acting
under their own initiative, nor subtract from it by refusing to perform
the actions which God has allotted them. By making all human activity
dependent on himself, God ensures respect from humanity (שיראו
מלפניו).[37]

This deterministic reading of 3.14 is in fact supported by Blenkinsopp.[38] Yet if one cannot add to or take away from God's work, what
are we to make of the all-embracing advocacy of human free will that
underlies Qoheleth's supposed quotation of 3.2-8? His reading of 3.11
underlines the ability of human beings to make the divine plan go awry
(albeit unintentionally), since they are unable through lack of knowledge to fulfill their part in the divine plan: how then can God's work be
'eternal' (or indeed, find any expression whatsoever)?

The idea that Qoheleth offers a deterministic commentary on the text
of 3.2-8 finds further support in the next verse: 'What is has already
been, and what is to be already is. God seeks out the pursued'. Human
beings are unable to change the course of events in the world by their
own initiative: all is controlled by God. Whatever the meaning of the
difficult phrase והאלהים יבקש את נרדף ('God seeks out the pursued')
(and most commentators take it as illustrative of God's control over
history as a whole), the section 3.14-15 would appear to reiterate the

---

35. Murphy, *Ecclesiastes*, p. 35.

36. Delitzsch, *Ecclesiastes*, p. 263; Crenshaw, *Ecclesiastes*, p. 99.

37. This understanding is not far removed from that of Glasser (*Qohelet*, p. 65)
who suggests the meaning 'définitif' for לעלם. Similar is Fox (*Contradictions*,
p. 195), who says that Qoheleth means to express the idea that 'it is always the case
that what happens is only what God has made happen'.

38. Blenkinsopp, 'Ecclesiastes 3.1-15', p. 62.

deterministic theme that is evident in the catalogue of times and seasons and the commentary which Qoheleth offers on it.[39]

e. *Concluding remarks on Ecclesiastes 3.9-15*
Thus far, this chapter has sought to demonstrate that 3.1-15 can be read as a unity, with determinism the central linking theme between the two subsections 3.1-8 and 3.9-15, of which it is composed. Yet the fact that 3.1-15 *can* be read in this way does not necessarily mean that it *should* be read thus, or that Qoheleth's intent was that it should be read thus.

Blenkinsopp's reading of 3.1-15, while cleverly argued, also creates complications. The simplest solution, that 3.1-8 reflects a deterministic worldview severely limiting human free will, and that Qoheleth offers a positive commentary upon this in 3.9-15, offers a logical development of thought in the passage. Considerations arising from an examination of the wider context of Qoheleth's thought in Ecclesiastes also support this interpretation.

3. *The Wider Context*

Neither Blenkinsopp nor Whybray rely for their understanding of Eccl. 3.1-15 entirely on internal evidence from the passage itself, they also rely on the wider context of Qoheleth's thought. This section will therefore consider whether this extra evidence truly supports the thesis that Qoheleth engages in a dialogue in 3.1-15 about human attempts 'to live according to nature', or whether it supports the thesis that 3.1-8 is expressive of God's imposition of his 'times' on humanity.

1. *Time and Judgment (Ecclesiastes 3.17; 8.5-6)*

Blenkinsopp in fact argues that the whole of 3.9-22 serves as Qoheleth's commentary on the catalogue of times and seasons but restricts his article to an examination of the passage 3.9-15.[40] This response has been similarly restricted so far, but it is at this point that Qoheleth's connection between 'time' (עֵת) and judgment (√שׁפט) (3.17; 8.5-6)

---

39. E.g. McNeile, *Ecclesiastes*, p. 63; Barton, *Ecclesiastes*, pp. 102-103; Gordis, *Koheleth*, pp. 233-34. Cf. R.B. Salters ('A Note on the Exegesis of Ecclesiastes 3 15b', *ZAW* 88 [1976], pp. 419-20) for the history of interpretation of this difficult passage.
40. Blenkinsopp, 'Ecclesiastes 3.1-15', p. 57.

will come into consideration. Blenkinsopp briefly considers both passages in which the phrase occurs: on 3.17, he remarks 'the allusion in 3.17 to the time appointed for every matter and work, in this case the punishment of the wicked, suggests that vv. 16-22 are also part of the commentary on the poem'.[41]

There is good reason for Blenkinsopp's claim here. The text of 3.17 states:

אמרתי אני בלבי את צדיק ואת הרשע ישפט האלהים כי עת לכל חפץ
ועל כל מעשה שם

I said to myself, 'God will judge the righteous and the wicked, for there is a time for every business and for every work there'.

Of particular interest are two aspects of this passage.

First, the phrase עת לכל חפץ ועל כל מעשה שם ('a time for every business and for every work there') in 3.17 clearly echoes the comment לכל זמן ועת לכל חפץ תחת השמים ('to everything there is a season, a time for every purpose under heaven') which Qoheleth made earlier in 3.1 (accepted by Blenkinsopp as a title outlining Qoheleth's understanding of the times and seasons in 3.2-8).[42] Second, the fact that 'there is an (appointed) time for every business' is given as a reason for Qoheleth's statement that *God* will judge the righteous and the wicked.

This creates a serious problem for any commentator who understands the catalogue of times and seasons as an expression of the Wisdom belief in an 'ideal' time for human action. For if it is God who acts at the 'appointed time' in 3.17, surely it is also God whose action (through human beings) is being catalogued in 3.1-8.[43] Moreover, it is 'the work of God' which is the putative subject of human investigation in 3.11.

Ecclesiastes 8.5-6 is also considered briefly in this context: here Qoheleth links the two concepts of 'time' and 'judgment' more overtly. Blenkinsopp adopts the position that in 8.5, the phrase עת ומשפט ידע לב חכם ('a wise mind knows time and judgment') refers to the ability of the wise man to tailor his actions to act at the appropriate time. In a courtly context, such as we find in 8.2-6, this may appear a not unreasonable understanding.[44] However, Blenkinsopp has suggested

41. Blenkinsopp, 'Ecclesiastes 3.1-15', p. 57.
42. Blenkinsopp, 'Ecclesiastes 3.1-15', p. 60.
43. Murphy, *Ecclesiastes*, p. 36.
44. Cf. Gordis, *Koheleth*, p. 289.

in 3.9-15 that human beings are unable to act in accordance with 'time'.[45] Thus, one must argue that the wise mind in 8.5 is an exception to the general rule, or that it is simply another of those contradictions which some commentators see in Qoheleth's work.

However, in Chapter 2, I have argued that Qoheleth introduces this section in 8.2 with a reference to the special status of the king with respect to God: Qoheleth adjures loyalty to the king on the basis of 'the oath of God' (which I take to be the oath the God has sworn concerning kingship).[46] This passage, and the relationship between king and God, will be considered in more detail in Chapter 7 of this work. However, if one understands the king as God's subordinate, as 8.2 would appear to suggest, then one can explain the statement: 'a wise mind knows time and judgment' as a recognition of the fact that the king is placed there by God and that to obey the king's will is ultimately to obey that of God. Thus, the wise mind recognizes 'time' and God's will behind it when it occurs, rather than being able to recognize the 'time' to act appropriately.[47] This reading has the added advantage that it harmonizes with the context of 3.1-15, if one also understands this deterministically.

In the same context, it is significant that Qoheleth again echoes the thought of 3.1 in his statement in 8.6: כי לכל חפץ יש עת ומשפט כי רעת האדם רבה עליו ('Because to every purpose there is time and judgment, the misery of humankind is great'). A variation of the same formula, as we have seen, is found in 3.17: 'God shall judge the righteous and the wicked because there is a time for every purpose (עת לכל חפץ) and concerning every work there'.[48] In that passage, it referred to God's action at the 'appointed time'. Here too, it must mean the same, for in 8.7 additional reasons are given for humankind's sorry situation: 'for he does not know what will happen, for who can tell him when it will happen?'

---

45. Blenkinsopp, 'Ecclesiastes 3.1-15', p. 59.

46. Hertzberg, *Prediger*, p. 143; Tyler, *Ecclesiastes*, p. 101.

47. Hertzberg (*Prediger*, p. 144), Ginsberg (*Qohelet*, p. 106) and Fox (*Contradictions*, p. 247) following the LXX, all understand עת ומשפט as a hendiadys equivalent to עת משפט, 'time of judgment' although 'judgment' is understood by Fox in the traditional sense of God judging the human evil which the despotic ruler of 8.2-5 is said to represent.

48. Lauha, *Kohelet*, pp. 149-50; Fox, *Contradictions*, p. 247.

If 'time' refers to an ideal moment for action (which human beings are unable to acheive), then 8.6 would mean 'human beings are wretched because they are unable to act at the correct time'. There is, however, no causal connection between this reading and the fact that human beings are ignorant of the future. Though human beings may fail to act at the correct time, they retain some control over their own destiny. Only by understanding 'time' as referring to divinely imposed action (i.e. determinism) can one retain the causal link between 8.6 and 8.7 (i.e. human beings are wretched because all their actions are controlled by the deity [8.6]; as a result they have no control over their own future, nor do they even know what will happen to them).[49]

Thus, from both 3.17 and 8.5-6, two things may be inferred: (1) that Qoheleth agrees with his statement in 3.1 outlining the theme of 3.2-8 (contrary to what one would expect if he were arguing against it) and (2), that עת is, or can be, linked with God's judgment. Thus, evidence not only from the immediate context of 3.1-15, but also from the wider context in Ecclesiastes refutes Blenkinsopp's thesis that Qoheleth is engaged in a dialogue in this text.

2. *Concluding Remarks: The Question of Free Will*

The problem with understanding Ecclesiastes as a deterministic text is that Qoheleth presupposes a certain amount of free will in life.[50] As I suggested earlier in this chapter, it is most likely this fact that underlies non-deterministic readings of 3.2-8. However, even commentators such as Blenkinsopp and Whybray understand Qoheleth as advocating in Ecclesiastes a mixure of necessity and free will; it is simply that this necessity is understood to be limited. Occurrences in life are 'pre-disposed' rather than 'preordained'. Yet, what if it is free will rather than necessity that is restricted? Does Qoheleth have any kind of system that explains how human free will can exist and what are the things over which humanity has control? If it can be shown that Qoheleth does indeed have a rational system of free will that fits in with the deterministic world view in Ecclesiastes, this will do much to relieve the tensions that exist in our current understanding of Qoheleth's work.

---

49. Murphy (*Ecclesiastes*, p. 84) avoids the problem by translating כי in 8.6 adversatively and understanding 8.6b-7 as an attack on the 'traditional' wisdom of 8.5-6a.

50. Podechard, *L'Ecclésiaste*, p. 192.

This problem will be considered in more depth in Chapter 7. For now, however, the evidence would appear to support the idea that Qoheleth views events in life as largely determined by God, and that though there may be some instances in which human beings have a degree of control over their destinies, these are seemingly limited. There is after all, 'a time for everything; an appointed time for every purpose under heaven'.

Chapter 5

'A TIME TO LOVE, A TIME TO HATE': THE DIVINE DETERMINATION OF EMOTION IN ECCLESIASTES

1. *Introduction*

In the catalogue of seasons in Eccl. 3.1-8, Qoheleth appears to speak not only of human activity being under the control of the deterministic deity, but even of the same being true of human thought and feeling. Nevertheless, commentators remain sceptical as to whether Qoheleth can indeed be considered a 'hard' determinist. Seow's reading of 3.1-8, for example, is that:

> the occasions are not those that human beings plan, nor are they contingent on human decisions... These are occasions in which people find themselves, and they can only respond to them.[1]

Seow in other words understands Ecclesiastes to be a deterministic work, but one that expounds a 'determinism of circumstances' and presupposes that the responses to the situations that arise in the life of the individual are theirs to make. Yet the passage 3.1-8 contains a mixture of action and feeling—activities *and* responses to events—God's control, 3.1 implies, is total. Others, as we have seen, have adopted the view that Qoheleth is expressing a more truly deterministic worldview, while stopping short of claiming that God directly determines the inner world of his human subjects. This chapter will focus on this inner world of humanity by looking at Qoheleth's portrayal of two of the opposing emotions which are mentioned in the catalogue of seasons: love and hate.

Qoheleth's attitude toward women has troubled modern commentators in that he appears to take diametrically opposing views of that sex in the two passages in which they are mentioned in Ecclesiastes.

---

1. Seow, *Ecclesiastes*, p. 171.

Traditionally, Qoheleth's assessment of women in Eccl. 9.9 has been viewed as a positive one.[2] Yet most commentators also argue that the depiction of women in 7.26, 28 is partially or wholly misogynistic.[3] A few scholars have attempted to harmonize the two passages by arguing that Qoheleth refers in 7.26, 28 only to a 'certain type of woman' against whom the sages warned, typified by some of the 'outsider' feminine figures who appear in the book of Proverbs (Prov. 2.16-19; 5.3-14, 20-23; 6.24-26; 9.13-18),[4] or have suggested that Qoheleth quotes a negative view of women in 7.26 and then argues against it.[5] The difficulties in the interpretation of the figure of the woman in 7.26, 28 are made still greater by the fact that there exists no real consensus on the locations of the beginning and end of the section in which she appears. Gordis and Murphy, for example, have argued that 7.23-24 are not connected with the verses that follow it.[6] However, there seems to be good reason for thinking that the passage involving the Woman extends from 7.23-29: 7.25 reiterates a variety of verbs which appear in 7.23, and contextual continuity is provided by the repeated use of the verbs בקשׁ ('seek') and מצא ('find out').[7]

2. Delitzsch, *Ecclesiastes*, pp. 363-64; Plumptre, *Ecclesiastes*, p. 188.

3. Fox, *Contradictions*, p. 238. A. Barucq, *Ecclésiaste* (Paris: Beauchesne, 1968), p. 137.

4. Barton, *Ecclesiastes*, p. 147; Crenshaw, *Ecclesiastes*, p. 146.

5. Lohfink's close analysis has been challenged on several counts: the meaning 'bitter' (rather than 'stronger') for מר in 7.26 seems assured from 1 Sam. 15.32. Nor do the sages, though undoubtedly androcentric, have been misogynistic in the way that Lohfink envisions. The comparison of the mortality of woman with the occasional immortality of man in 7.28 presents contextual problems in the light of Qoheleth's statements elsewhere (1.11; 2.16; 6.4) (N. Lohfink, 'War Kohelet ein Frauenfeind? Ein Versuch, die Logik und den Gegenstand von Koh. 7:23–8:1a herauszufinden' in M. Gilbert [ed.], *La Sagesse de l'Ancien Testament* [BETL, 51; Gembloux: Duculot; Leuven: Leuven University Press, 1979], pp. 259-87). Murphy translates and interprets 7.28 as Qoheleth's refutation of a traditional saying that women are worse than men (*Ecclesiastes*, pp. 75-77). I feel that Murphy is right to view this passage within the wider context of 9.9 but is the affirmation of the saying that women are worse than men really the thesis that Qoheleth has set out to prove ('that which I sought continually')?

6. A few scholars maintain that 7.23-24 is to be related back to the section beginning in 7.15 (Gordis, *Koheleth*, pp. 280-82; Murphy, *Ecclesiastes*, pp. 71-72).

7. Whybray, *Ecclesiastes* [NCBC], p. 123; M.V. Fox and B. Porten, 'Unsought Discoveries: Qohelet 7:23–8:1a', *HS* 19 (1978), pp. 26-38 (26). The question of

2. *A Time to Love: Translations*

(7.23) I have tested all this by wisdom; I said, 'I shall be wise', but it was far from me. (24) That which is far off and very deep, who can find it out? (25) My heart and I turned to know, to search, and to seek out wisdom and the sum, and to know [the wickedness of folly and] foolishness and madness.[8] (26) And I find more bitter than death Woman, whose heart is snares and nets, whose hands are bonds; whoever God favours will escape her, but the 'sinner' will caught by her. (27) 'Look, this I found', says Qoheleth, 'One to one to find the sum (28) That which[9] I sought continually I have not found: one man in a thousand I found, but a woman in all these I did not find. (29) Only see what I found—that God made humankind upright, but they have sought many sums'.

(9.9) Experience life with the woman you love, all the days of the life of your vanity which he has given you under the sun, all the days of your vanity: for that is your portion in this life and in your labour which you take under the sun.

3. *Text and Context*

1. *Ecclesiastes 7.26*

In Eccl. 7.23-29, Qoheleth describes his search for Wisdom. Specifically, he seeks to acquire knowledge of 'wisdom and the sum... wickedness and folly, foolishness and madness' (7.25). Qoheleth says more about his search for the חשבון, 'sum' (7.27, 29), yet he also makes reference to a mysterious woman (7.26, 28). Whybray observes the 'unexpected introduction' of this subject in 7.26 and goes on to remark:

---

whether this section continues into 8.1 is not considered here since its inclusion or otherwise does not significantly affect the outcome of this investigation.

8.   I follow the LXX and Syriac versions in my reconstruction of 7.25 and delete רשע כסל as a secondary gloss.

9.   I follow the translation of Crenshaw here (*Ecclesiastes*, pp. 144, 147) but relate אשר back to חשבון in 7.27. Fox's argument for the emendation of אשר to אשה although valid orthographically, depends on his assertion that Qohelet does discover a חשבון in 7.28. If so, it can surely not be the same one which he intends in 7.25.

> If this verse is in fact part of the section which begins in 7.23 and not the beginning of an entirely new section, it can only be understood as being intended to be in some sense a particular illustration of some point which has been made in 7.23-25.[10]

That such is indeed the case is accepted by most commentators: 7.23-25 and 26-29 share a common vocabulary and conceptualization. Qoheleth continually uses the language of seeking and finding, the verbs בקשׁ ('seek') occurring three times (7.25, 28, 29) and מצא ('find') eight times (7.24, 26, 27 [×2], 28 [×3], 29). The verb תור ('search') also occurs (7.25). Qoheleth denies the ability of any person to 'find out' (מצא—7.24) wisdom and the sum, but he does 'find' (מצא—7.26) that woman is 'more bitter than death'.[11] Qoheleth's heart (לב—7.25), the intellectual part of his character which is engaged in the search, makes a discovery about the equivalent part (לב) of the opposite sex, that it is 'snares and nets'.[12]

Fox seems to echo the scholarly consensus when he paraphrases the thought of 7.26 in the context of the preceding verses: '"See where my painstaking research led me: to the knowledge that woman is a menace!"'[13] By this reading, Qoheleth's grandiose search for wisdom ends in banality. It is not difficult to see why such an understanding of

10. Whybray, *Ecclesiastes*, p. 125.

11. Dahood appeals to the use of √מרר in Aramaic and Ugaritic to posit the meaning 'stronger' in this verse, a meaning also evident in Ezek. 3.14 ('Qoheleth and Recent Discoveries', pp. 308-309). The meaning 'bitter' is, however, assured in 1 Sam. 15.32, the only other occurrence in the Hebrew Bible of the terms מר and מות together.

12. Delitzsch understands היא in the expression אשר היא מצודה as a copula, hence: 'who is a snare, whose heart is a net...' (*Ecclesiastes*, pp. 331-32), followed by Crenshaw (*Ecclesiastes*, p. 146). I have followed the Masoretes' understanding of this expression, although no material difference to the argument of this chapter is made if either is adopted.

13. Fox, *Contradictions*, p. 242. Lohfink and Baltzer are almost alone in attempting to exonerate Qoheleth completely from charges of misogyny. A summary of Lohfink's position may be found in his commentary (*Kohelet*, pp. 57-59). Cf. K. Baltzer, 'Women and War in Qohelet 7:23–8:1a', *HTR* 80 (1987), pp. 127-32. Athalya Brenner devotes a brief paragraph to Qoheleth's treatment of the subject of women in a feminist study on Israelite wisdom literature, but the position taken is strongly negative (Athalya Brenner, 'Some Observations on Figurations of Woman in Wisdom Literature', in A. Brenner [ed.], *A Feminist Companion to Wisdom Literature* [The Feminist Companion to the Bible, 9; Sheffield: Sheffield Academic Press, 1995], pp. 50-66 [59-60]).

the text might appeal to a commentator with a fine sense of irony, and yet several questions remain unanswered. Why is woman a menace? Why does Qoheleth personally find her 'more bitter than death'? Does the woman, as Whybray has suggested, illustrate some point made in 7.23-25, and if so, how?

It is perhaps significant that while Qoheleth goes on to speak in more detail in 7.27-29 about 'the sum' which he mentions in 7.25, he appears to say nothing more about the 'wickedness and folly, foolishness and madness' that he mentions in the same verse. The Hebrew phraseology of this clause (רשע כסל והסכלות הוללות) in fact finds several echoes in the search that Qoheleth undertakes in the so called 'Royal Experiment' of 1.12–2.26 in addition to the verbs נסה ('test'), and תור ('search'), which are shared only by these passages (נסה occurs in 2.1; 7.23 and תור in 1.13; 2.3; 7.25). These two passages are the only places in which the term (ה)קהלת ('[the] Qoheleth') appears in the body of the book (1.13; 7.27) as opposed to the prologue or epilogue (1.1, 2; 12.8, 9, 10). The terms סכלות ('foolishness') and הוללות ('madness') occur in close proximity elsewhere only in 1.17; 2.12,[14] while in the same passage the related term מהולל ('mad') occurs in 2.2 and סכלות on its own in 2.3, 13. In the Royal Experiment, Qoheleth describes his personal quest for knowledge of the world around him, specifically to 'see what was good for human beings to do under the heavens the few days of their lives' (2.3). In the context of this search, Qoheleth specifically describes laughter as 'madness' (2.2) and the surrender of self to pleasure as 'foolishness' (2.3).

I follow Whybray's argument that the text of the final clause of 7.25 is corrupt and that at least one of the words רשע כסל והסכלות הוללות is not part of the original text.[15] However, there seems no reason to doubt the authenticity of סכלות ('foolishness') and הוללות ('madness'). Both are part of Qoheleth's vocabulary, for he outlines the limits of his search in 7.25 in a way similar to his statement in 1.17: ואתנה לבי לדעת חכמה ודעת הללות ושכלות, 'I applied my mind to know wisdom and to know madness and foolishness'.[16]

---

14. Although both occur in 10.13 describing the speech of a fool, they are not joined in the same catchphrase which is evident in 1.17; 2.12; 7.25.

15. Whybray, *Ecclesiastes* [NCBC], p. 124.

16. I follow the Masoretic punctuation of 1.17 and read ודעת as an infinitive (so also RSV). The versions understand as an object of לדעת but this creates an awkward tautology.

If anything is dubious in 7.25b, it is the phrase רשע כסל ('wicked-ness and folly'). Qoheleth fails to mention 'wickedness' (רשע) any-where in the Royal Experiment (the abstract noun is used elsewhere only in 3.16; 7.17). The noun כסל is otherwise absent in Ecclesiastes (the abstract noun 'folly' is represented by סכל in 10.6). Hence, it may well be that רשע כסל is an exegetical gloss inserted to link 7.25 with the 'wicked' woman in 7.26. If it were deleted, לדעת ('to know') in 7.25b would have two direct objects (which should read סכלות והוללות ['foolishness and madness'] on the basis of 1.17; 2.12) to balance חכמה וחשבון as the two direct objects of לדעת in 7.25a. The whole of 7.25 would then essentially be a restatement of Qoheleth's intent which he sets out in 1.17.

Although רשע כסל is represented in all the versions (so that one would have to assume the gloss to have been added before Ecclesiastes was translated), the LXX and Peshitta bear out part of this reconstruc-tion. The former reads, καὶ τοῦ γνῶναι ἀσεβοῦς ἀφροσύνην καὶ σκληρίαν καὶ περιφοράν, presupposing a Hebrew text of כסל ולדעת רשע וסכלות והוללות. The latter's ܘܠܡܕܥ ܪܘܫܥܐ ܘܣܟܠܘܬܐ ܘܫܛܝܘܬܐ ܘܚܪܥܘܬܐ, presupposes the same Hebrew text underlying the rendering of the LXX, but understands כסל as if it were כסיל.

Because of its Aquilan character, the LXX of Ecclesiastes can be useful in textual reconstruction. The evidence of the LXX supports the deletion of the definite article from סכלות ('foolishness') and the LXX, Peshitta and Targum all support the addition of the conjunction to הוללות ('madness'). The Hebrew text underlying all of these also lends some credence to the hypothesis that רשע כסל ('wickedness and folly') and a conjunction may have been added before an original סכלות והוללות ('foolishness and madness') for all of them are witness to a strange text in which the verb ידע is followed by a genitive con-struction, itself followed by the two direct objects which we should expect to find according to 1.17. The deletion of the conjunction from הוללות which underlies the Vulgate's rendering: 'impietatem stulti et errorem imprudentium', and the MT may be understood as subsequent attempts to make sense of this earlier Hebrew text by rendering the four nouns as double accusatives after a verb of cognition.

In addition to these considerations, further evidence supports the deletion of רשע כסל from 7.25, for the terms in which Qoheleth describes the woman of 7.26 and her male victims preclude an under-standing of either as 'wicked'.

a. *Qoheleth's vocabulary of entrapment*

Three words suggesting entrapment are associated with the woman in Eccl. 7.26. The woman's intellectual/emotional side (לֵב) is characterized by the terms מְצוֹדִים ('snares') and חֲרָמִים ('nets'). Her physical side (יָד) by the term אֲסוּרִים ('bonds'). Qoheleth speaks using very similar entrapment vocabulary in 9.12. There, humankind are portrayed as fishes caught (יֶאֱחָזִ/שֶׁקֹּי) in the fisherman's net (מְצוֹדָה), or birds in that of the fowler (פַּח). In the latter passage, the hunter is divine, rather than human: Murphy correctly points out the parallel between the 'evil time' (עֵת רָע) mentioned in 9.12 and the catalogue of times which are determined by God in 3.1-8.[17]

Some of these words are relatively rare in the Hebrew Bible, and an examination of the contexts in which they occur elsewhere yields interesting results.

The term מְצוֹדָה 'net, prey' occurs four times in the Hebrew Bible outside the book of Ecclesiastes (Ps. 66.11; Ezek. 12.13; 13.21; 17.20). In three of these occasions (Ps. 66.11; Ezek. 12.13; 17.20), it has its primary meaning of 'net'. In all three examples, the usage is a figurative one, illustrative of Yahweh's judgment. On the one occasion when it means 'prey' (Ezek. 13.21), it refers to the people of Judah as the prey of a foreign power through the acquiescence of Yahweh: again, it is a reflection of divine judgment.

The term מָצוֹד 'net' occurs only twice outside Ecclesiastes (Prov. 12.12; Job 19.6). Unfortunately, the text of the former is dubious, and its use there cannot be verified, but in Job 19.6, the context is once again of Yahweh as Job's hunter. It would appear from the examples which we find, that outside Ecclesiastes, both terms are used in a context in which God is the hunter of the (sinful) person.

The term חֵרֶם which appears in Eccl. 7.26 refers to a fisherman's dragnet (as opposed to a מִכְמֹרֶת or 'casting net' which is spread on the surface of the water—Isa. 19.8). Outside Ecclesiastes, the term חֵרֶם appears only in the prophets (Ezek. 26.5, 14; 32.3; 47.10; Mic. 7.2; Hab. 1.15, 16, 17).

Of the eight times which this term is used outside Ecclesiastes, only one occurrence uses חֵרֶם in a figurative sense of a weapon used by evil people to ensnare each other (Mic. 7.2). Even here, it has been suggested that חֵרֶם may be derived from √חרם (I) and mean

---

17. Murphy, *Ecclesiastes*, p. 94.

'destruction'.[18] Three other occurrences use חרם in the phrase משׁטוח
לחרמים/משׁטח חרמים 'place for the spreading of nets (to dry)' either
as an image of divine judgment (Ezek. 26.5, 14) or blessing (Ezek.
47.10). The remaining four (Ezek. 32.3; Hab. 1.15-17) concern the use
of the חרם itself as a figure of divine judgment. G. Giesen comments
concerning this usage that 'the "divine" net in the hand of Yahweh, or
used by others at his behest is a symbol of power and sovereignty'.[19] In
Ezek. 32.3 the term is illustrative of Yahweh's power over Pharoah,
who is depicted as a crocodile hauled out of the water in Yahweh's
חרם. In Hab. 1.15-17, Yahweh has allowed the Babylonians to become
so mighty that they can catch other nations like fish. In this example,
the Babylonians effectively act as God's viceregents, punishing the sins
of the surrounding nations, including Judah.

The term אסור ('fetter', 'bond') is a more neutral one, generally used
in a literal rather than figurative sense. In Judg. 15.14 the plural is used
of the fetters binding Samson, and in Jer. 37.15 in the phrase בית
האסור 'prison'. However, √אסר can sometimes be used of divine
chastisement (Job 36.13; Ezek. 3.25; Ps. 149.8). The qal passive participle is also found in Eccl. 4.14.

b. *Woman as divine agent*

In 9.12, Qoheleth describes the times (עת) which go to make up
existence in terms of a fisherman or fowler catching human beings in
his nets. The terms in which the heart of the woman is described in 7.26
suggest that she is likewise the agent of a deterministic force. Where
מצודה ('snare') occurs in 9.12 for God's nets which harvest human
beings in order to impose the destiny that God has willed for them, the
related term, מצוד, describes the nets with which the woman ensnares
men. As we have seen, both are predominantly used outside
Ecclesiastes in the context of a divine, or divinely appointed, hunter
catching sinful human beings. The same applies to the term חרם, and
although אסור may be a more neutral term, the root from which it
comes, as we have seen, can occasionally be used in this sense. If 3.1-
15 is understood as a deterministic text as well as 9.12, the depiction of
the woman as representative of an inescapable divine force would be
consonant with Qoheleth's statement that there is 'a time to love' (3.8).

---

18. A.S. Van der Woude, *Micah* (Nijkerk: Callenback, 1976), p. 244.
19. G. Giesen, 'חרם (II)', *TDOT*, V, pp. 200-203 (202).

Although Qoheleth's reaction to the woman in 7.26 is strongly negative, she cannot be termed 'wicked', since she performs God's will. Her
role as an instrument of divine judgment on humanity is emphasized in
7.26: 'those who are good before God will escape from her; the sinner
will be caught by her'. Unlike the traditional portrait of the feminine
outsider in the book of Proverbs (2.16-19; 5.3-6; 7.5-23; 9.13-18), the
'sin' of her victim lies not in the act of following her (the woman of
7.26 appears to be morally neutral). Rather, it is preexistent in the man
who encounters her. Moreover, the victim is unable to exercise free will
in the face of the woman's power. He is entirely dependent on God as
to whether he is caught or whether he escapes.

The dragnets (חרמים) with which the woman is associated suggest
the efficiency of the woman at the task allotted to her. Unlike Israelite
Wisdom's negative portraits of the feminine outsider, it is not the occasional stray who succumbs to her allure, but whole shoals of the sinful.
In the previous section, Qoheleth comments that 'there is not a just man
on earth that does good and does not sin' (יעשה טוב ולא יחטא—
7.20), preparing us for Qoheleth's statement that one 'who is good
before God' (טוב לפני האלהים) will escape her, while she will
ensnare 'the sinner' (חוטא). The ubiquity of sin among men (as suggested by 7.20 and implicit in 7.29) as well as the scale of operations
evident from her dragnets (חרמים) forces the conclusion that the image
of the woman is intended universally: it is for this reason that 7.26
should not be translated, 'More bitter than death is the [sort of] woman
who...' as a foil to Qoheleth's apparently positive statement in 9.9.
Rather, she seems representative of her gender and the role in God's
creation which Qoheleth envisions for it.

In Ecclesiastes, √חטא ('sin') occurs eight times (2.26; 5.5; 7.20, 26;
8.12; 9.2, 18; 10.4). From these examples, it is evident that Qoheleth
very often uses terms derived from this root not so much to denote a
simple moral transgression, but rather the act of displeasing God in
some form, which may not be obvious to the doer of this action.[20] The
majority of commentators hold that this is true particularly of 2.26, in
which the participle חוטא ('sinner') occurs in opposition to the phrase
טוב לפני האלהים, 'good before God'.[21] This opposition between חוטא
and טוב לפני האלהים occurs elsewhere in Ecclesiastes only in 7.26 in
the context of those who are fated to fall victim to the woman and those

---

20. This idea is particularly evident in 4.17 (ET 5.1).
21. For a detailed treatment of this subject, cf. Gordis, *Koheleth*, pp. 227-28.

whom God will allow to escape her. This forces the conclusion not that the woman's victims are immoral, but that they have displeased God.[22] The woman's victims therefore cannot be designated en masse as 'wicked' (although some may be).

c. *The purpose of the woman*

If the woman's victim is free from moral guilt, we must ask the purpose of the woman's appearance. Possibly she is a symbol of the arbitrary nature of the deity's intervention in life (as in 9.11-12). This is not, however, illustrative of any point in 7.23-25.

Whatever the reasons for incurring God's displeasure, it would appear that the חוטא ('sinner') is punished with a life tightly circumscribed by God. His fate is '...toil (עְנְיָן): to gather and to heap up to give to one who is good before God' (2.26). Love (3.8) is also a form of עְנְיָן doled out by God (3.10), one of the times apparently allotted 'so that nobody may find out the work of God from beginning to end' (3.11). This appears to bear out 2.26, where we are told that God gives wisdom to those who are טוב לפני האלהים ('good before God'), denying it to the חוטא. The woman may therefore have a role in preventing the sinner from discovering 'the work of God' (exactly the kind of information which Qoheleth seeks [7.13; 8.17]). When speaking of the pleasures (including women) associated with the kingly lifestyle in the Royal Experiment, the author of Ecclesiastes stresses that he maintained his hold on wisdom (2.3, 9). Qoheleth supposes such pleasures as the woman embodies as antithetical to wisdom (they are 'folly and madness' [1.17; 2.3, 12; cf. 7.25]).[23]

Qoheleth's viewpoint in his assessment of the woman is that of the sage, the seeker after wisdom. Escape from the woman may therefore be a mark of divine favour. Though one who falls victim to 'time' (עת) may not find the work of God, he may find contentment. Qoheleth's advice to the 'sinner'—the vast majority, if not all of his audience, is to accept the decision of God with equanimity. It must be emphasized that Qoheleth's assessment of the woman as 'more bitter than death' is a

22. Murphy, *Ecclesiastes*, p. 76; Crenshaw, *Ecclesiastes*, p. 146; Whybray, *Ecclesiastes*, p. 125.

23. Crenshaw argues that שחק in 2.2 refers only to lighter side of joy: 'Qohelet dismisses frivolity as incompatible with intelligence and psychological stability' (*Ecclesiastes*, p. 77), but the same might be said of all joy, for Qoheleth dwells on the sadness of the sage in 1.18; 7.4.

personal one (מוצא אני, '*I* find…'). It is not so for her quarry. The reason for Qoheleth's *personal* assessment of the woman as 'more bitter than death' has never been satisfactorily explained: presumably God has permitted the sage's escape, so why so harsh a judgment? A possible solution to this problem will be offered presently (pp. 111-12).

2. *Ecclesiastes 9.9*

There is no conflict between Qoheleth's view of the woman in 7.26 and 9.9. In the latter passage, Qoheleth states:

> Experience life with the woman you love all the days of the life of your vanity, which he has given you under the sun, all the days of your vanity: for that is your portion in this life, and in the labour which you take under the sun.

Qoheleth sees typical life with the woman as reflective of the overall 'vanity' of life. Yet he also advises his (male) audience to 'experience life' with her. Man's love of Woman is unavoidable: no choice is suggested here as to how Man feels about her (as indeed there is none in 7.26), although Man can perhaps embrace his fate enthusiastically or not. God's hand in the matter of love between the sexes, illustrated by the imagery of the divine nets in 7.26, is reflected in the fact that Woman is called the 'portion' of Man in life.[24] For Qoheleth, love is part of 'the work which is done under the sun'. It is potentially a positive thing for the one who experiences it: 9.9 suggests that Woman may be a source of companionship and support through life. The gift which God gives is associated with הבל ('vanity') however, like the less pleasant one which he gives to the חוטא in 2.26. Qoheleth seeks that which is not הבל, explaining why he considers escape from the woman in 7.26 a mark of divine favour.

Qoheleth's view of Woman is at once restricting and liberating. Like Man, she is a being controlled by the deity. Yet she is depicted as an extremely powerful, almost semi-divine figure. Her weapons are allocated to her by God, and Man has no defence in the face of them. God

---

24. Such an interpretation is supported by the Oriental Ketib in 9.9 which reads היא חלקך 'she is your portion' for הוא חלקך 'it is your portion'. However, הוא probably refers to (joyful) life with the woman: thus, Murphy, who remarks, 'the usual irony is present; one is to accept this "portion," but without forgetting the perspective of "vain life" and its "toil"' (*Ecclesiastes*, p. 93).

may pull the strings from heaven, but on earth, it is Woman who is the master.

3. *Ecclesiastes 7.27-28*

a. *Humanity and the sum*

As noted previously, it is the entrapment imagery of 7.26 more than any other single factor in this passage that has led scholars to conclude that the woman associated with it is an archetype of wickedness. However, if I am correct in thinking that this imagery can be understood in a morally neutral sense, this must call into question traditional interpretations of the passage. Much therefore hinges on the interpretation of 7.27-28, particularly the values assigned to the terms מצא ('find [?trustworthy])', and חשבון ('sum, account').

In 7.27, Qoheleth describes the counting process by which he hoped to discover this 'sum'. The term חשבון is in fact identified with Wisdom in 7.25, but a possible connection between humanity (Man and Woman) and the חשבון is underlined by the repetition of the verb מצא in Qoheleth's statement that 'one man in a thousand have I found, but a woman in all those have I not found' (7.28).

This repetition may be significant. Qoheleth speaks of failing to 'find' the חשבון (described as 'that which I sought continually'), and then, in what appears to be an explanation of his statement, remarks on his inability to 'find' human beings. The human connection is reinforced by the appearance of the חשבון in 7.25 among the human qualities of 'wisdom...foolishness and madness' which define the internal state of all human beings and their external actions.[25] This human element is further suggested by its parallel usage to wisdom (חכמה), knowledge (דעת) and work (מעשה) in 9.10. Qoheleth considers that the חשבון may be discovered by an investigation into humanity, their motivations and their deeds—this is also implied by Qoheleth's statement that he intended 'acquainting my heart with wisdom...to lay hold on folly, till I might see what was that good for humankind which they should do under the heavens...' (2.3).

---

25. Crenshaw states: 'Coupled with wisdom, *ḥešbôn* constitutes the substance of human thought, the sum total of all knowledge' (*Ecclesiastes*, p. 145). Whybray follows a similar course in his understanding of it as 'the sum of things' (*Ecclesiastes*, p. 124).

Very often, the term מצא in 7.28 is interpreted elliptically to mean 'find trustworthy' (i.e. 'one man in a thousand I found trustworthy, but a woman in all these I did not find to be so'). On this tendency among scholars, Murphy rightly comments that 'it is the context (vv. 26 and 29) which justifies the assumption that the specific meaning deals with moral conduct'.[26] However, if the context provided by 7.26 is of Woman acting as a divine agent not against men who have committed a distinct moral transgression, but who have 'displeased God' in some indefinable way, the justification for a moral understanding of the 'finding' of human beings in 7.28 becomes more tenuous, and the possibility of an alternative interpretation opens up.

b. *The language of seeking and finding*
In speaking of the חשבון Qoheleth never uses the verb חשב ('think', 'reckon') Instead, the verbs בקש ('seek') (7.25, 28, 29) and מצא ('find out') (7.24, 26, 27 [×2], 28 [×3], 29; 9.10) occur. The other significant object of these verbs as concerns Qoheleth's search is 'the work of God'/'the work which is done under the sun' (3.11; 8.17).

In Chapter 2 of this work, I argued for the positions of Gordis, Fox and Murphy that 'the work of God' and 'the work which is done under the sun' eesentially refer to one and the same thing.[27] Qoheleth sees (ראה) 'all the work of God' in the course of his investigation (8.17) and recommends his followers to do likewise (7.13), but this work is impossible to 'find out' (מצא—3.11) or 'know' (ידע—11.5). Likewise, Qoheleth and others can see (ראה—1.14; 2.17; 4.3) 'the work which is done under the sun', but Qoheleth denies the ability of humankind to 'find out' (מצא—8.17) this work.

Thus, both 'the work which is done under the sun' and 'the work of God' appear to be the objects of Qoheleth's search, along with the חשבון. Perhaps all three are not to be identified exactly, though that is certainly the implication of Whybray's definition of the חשבון as 'the whole of that which is'. Nevertheless, it does seem reasonable to suppose that finding the חשבון must be linked fairly intimately with the

---

26. Whybray is alone in insisting that the verse 'does not state what it is that the speaker has sought, and which he has, or has not, found' (*Ecclesiastes*, p. 127). Cf. Murphy, *Ecclesiastes*, p. 77.

27. Gordis, *Koheleth*, pp. 298-99; Fox, *Contradictions*, p. 175; Murphy, *Ecclesiastes*, p. 13.

other declared objects of Qoheleth's search. Indeed, Murphy's comment that 3.14 'whatsoever God does, it shall be forever: nothing can be added to it, nor anything taken from it' is about 'the immutability of the divine *deed*, not word' and is thus to some extent divorced from possible antecedents in Deut. 4.1-2 and 13.1 would appear to support the idea that Qoheleth might have envisioned 'the work of God' as a חשבון.[28] Qoheleth's intent, however, is not to alter it but to count it.

In the context of his search, whether he chooses to denote the object as 'the work which is done under the sun', 'the work of God' or 'the sum', Qoheleth uses the terms בקשׁ and מצא in the sense of 'seek to know', and 'find out about' respectively.[29] This is reflected in the parallel usage of the verbs בקשׁ and ידע in 7.25 and of בקשׁ/מצא and ידע in 8.17. When Qohelet speaks of 'seeking' and 'finding', he never uses it in a moral context.

In 7.28, Qoheleth speaks of 'finding' a man, but not 'finding' a woman on his quest for knowledge about 'the sum'. Qoheleth seeks knowledge of the world around him, and specifically what is 'good for people to do under the sun' (2.3) by finding 'the work which is done under the sun'. In order to do this, he considers by turns the cases of other individuals in order to build up his worldview, drawing appropriate conclusions with which to illuminate his thinking. Thus, having experienced the life of a king (2.12), he examines the situation of 'the man whose labour is in wisdom and in knowledge and equity' who may leave his wealth to an unworthy person (2.21); he considers the oppressed as a group (4.1); the solitary driven individual with no-one to inherit the fruits of his toil (4.8); the young man who attains rank but is ultimately despised (4.13-16); the man who loses his money in an unlucky venture so that he cannot leave it to his son (5.12-17 [ET 13-18); the man who is given riches and the ability to enjoy them (5.19 [ET 20]); the man who is given riches but no ability to enjoy life, although he has every advantage including children and longevity (6.2-6). He cites the case of the righteous man who dies young and the wicked man who has an extended life span (7.15), the man who 'rules over another to his own hurt' (8.9), the poor wise man who is despised despite his wisdom (9.13-18), and the situation in which servants appear to have

---

28. Murphy, *Ecclesiastes*, p. 35.

29. Cf. Whybray's understanding of the verb מצא as 'find out' (*Ecclesiastes* [NCBC], p. 74); Crenshaw's translation 'fathom' (*Ecclesiastes*, pp. 91, 153), or that of Gordis, 'discover' (*Koheleth*, pp. 156, 186).

greater status than their masters (10.7). These examples which he gives are 'real life' cases which he examines in the course of his quest for 'wisdom and the sum' (7.25). From these examples he attempts to discover an underlying pattern that might tell him 'that which is good for people to do under heaven the few days of their lives' (2.3). Thus, the 'finding' of people is intimately linked with the enquiry into the חשׁבון: it is the only way in which Qoheleth, who cannot take for granted those beliefs touted as certainties by the sages, can hope to comprehend the nature of existence.[30]

Just as Qoheleth 'sees' (ראה) 'the work of God' or 'the work which is done under the sun', he 'sees' these people who make up his world-view. Just as he fails to 'find' (מצא) his object, whether this be termed 'the sum', 'the work of God' or 'the work which is done under the sun', he fails to 'find' human beings. Essentially, Qoheleth uses the term 'see' for the consideration of events and people: 'find' has to do with the acquisition of knowledge from this process. Yet human actions are tainted by the irrational (2.3; 9.3) and the behaviour of human beings leaves Qoheleth bewildered (2.2, 15; 4.4, 8; 5.10 [ET 11]; 6.7; 9.16; 10.7). Because of this, the humanity may be as unfindable as 'the sum'.

c. *Woman and the sum*
Qoheleth's attempt to discover the חשׁבון is based on his examination of humanity as a whole, their motivations and actions as defined by wisdom and folly: those characteristics of humanity, in other words, which reside in the mind (לב) of the individuals which he considers. This search is conducted by Qoheleth's application of his own mind (לב) to certain features of existence. The term לב is used with a first person suffix 18 times in Ecclesiastes (1.13, 16 [×2], 17; 2.1, 2.3 [×2], 10 [×2], 15 [×2], 20; 3.17, 18; 7.25; 8.9, 16; 9.1). Once again, there is a concentration of usages in the Royal Experiment (12 uses), finding an echo in 7.25. Yet Qoheleth by this means also considers and reaches conclusions about the hearts and minds (לב/לבב) of other people, both individually and as groups (2.22, 23; 3.11; 5.19 [ET 20]; 7.4 [×2], 7; 8.5, 11; 9.3 [×2]; 10.2 [×2], 3).

---

30. Such cases may be 'hypothetical' or 'an example from daily observation' (Crenshaw, *Ecclesiastes*, p. 110), but even if the former, Qoheleth could not men-tally reproduce all possible scenarios which may occur in a human existence. Such hypotheticals would also still have to be based on some form of knowledge gained from observation.

Qoheleth reaches a conclusion about the לב of Woman in 7.26; the counterpart to Qoheleth's heart with which he embarks on his quest for 'the sum'. It is a mass of traps (חרמים/מצודים) ready to close on the unwary. Those who are caught by the woman may obtain the chance for a closer investigation, but as far as Qoheleth is concerned, the best that the sage can hope for is not that the male individual may 'find' the woman: that way lies entrapment. Rather, God's favour lies in escape and the hope that God may grant the sage 'wisdom, knowledge and joy'.

Qoheleth's statement therefore, that 'a woman…I did not find' works on two levels. On the one hand it suggests his objectivity and that he retained his wisdom (as in 2.3, 9), but on the other, it signals failure to know the sum totality of human motivation and action which is denoted by the חשבון or 'the work which is done under the sun'. If failure to find the חשבון is explained by Qoheleth's inability to 'find' men and women, we must assume both to be necessary for a successful resolution of his search.

Essentially, Qoheleth finds himself in what might be called a 'Catch 22' situation. Even were he able to 'find' more than a miniscule proportion of the male population, the finding of even one woman, equipped as she is with her divine weaponry, would mean the end of the search for the חשבון. In Qoheleth's classic consideration of Sheol in 9.10, he states: 'Whatever your hand finds to do, do mightily, for there is no work (מעשה), no sum (חשבון), no knowledge (דעת), no wisdom (חכמה) in Sheol where you are going'. Woman has prevented Qoheleth's object, stated in 7.25 to be 'to know (לדעת)…wisdom and the sum (חכמה וחשבון)', and described in 8.17 as 'the work (מעשה) which is done under the sun'. Because of the woman of 7.26, Qoheleth experiences a form of death-in-life, a grim foretaste of Sheol. Little wonder then that he can say on a personal level '*I* find more bitter than death… Woman'. The dead are aware of nothing (9.5): Qoheleth lives on with the experience of failure and no expectation of better things after death.

Whether the individual is trapped or allowed to escape by God, the integrity of the חשבון remains intact. Qoheleth's earlier assertion that '(Humankind) cannot contend with one stronger than them' (6.10) is proved correct. Woman forms a divine defence against attempts to find such knowledge as Qoheleth seeks. God may give 'wisdom, knowledge and joy' to the one who escapes the woman but this is not the same thing as the 'the sum' which Qoheleth wishes to attain.

4. *Ecclesiastes 7.29*

The meaning of 7.29 remains obscure, and commentators have attempted to deal with it in a variety of ways. Bearing in mind the apparently co-extensive nature of the חשבון with 'the work which is done under the sun' and 'the work of God', Qoheleth's experience in seeking the first has allowed him to conclude something about what God has done: it is that 'God made (עשה) humankind pleasing but they have sought many חשבנות.

The MT's, חשבנות has the general idea of 'intrigues'. It is difficult to see how such a meaning fits in with the rest of the passage. Crenshaw remarks 'Qohelet's search for the sum...has failed, but humankind's search for many devices or intrigues...has succeeded admirably'.[31] Yet it is not the verb מצא ('find out') but בקש ('seek') which is used, suggesting that humankind have failed in their search for חשבנות ('sums'). Fox, following Ginsberg, appears to see the object of humankind's searching as essentially the plural of חשבון, and accordingly translates 'sums': 'the entire book of Qohelet, in fact, tells of his search for *ḥiššᵉbonot'*.[32] I think the instinct of both is correct: they are supported by other commentators who have argued at least for a double meaning for חשבנות which takes into account the context of Qoheleth's search for the חשבון.[33]

I would therefore repoint the MT's חִשְׁבֹנוֹת as חֶשְׁבֹּנוֹת. At this point, however, another difficulty arises. Fox's argument that Qoheleth searches for חשבנות meets with a problem because there is only one חשבון mentioned by Qoheleth. However, if I am on the right lines in suggesting that the חשבון is ultimately made up of the thoughts and actions of humanity (i.e. 'the work which is done under the sun'), it may be that Qoheleth considered it to be capable of change. When people die, they go to the place where there is no חשבון and have no further part in 'the work which is done under the sun'. When people are born, they become part of the חשבון. 'The work which is done under the sun' may thus be different at one point in history than another. If the

31. Crenshaw, *Ecclesiastes*, p. 148.

32. Ginsberg (*Qohelet*, p. 103). Fox points to the use of the key term בקש in 7.29 as in 7.25, 28 (*Contradictions*, p. 243). I do, however, disagree with Fox's assertion that ישר means 'simple, intellectually direct'. The argument of Whybray, who points to the idiom 'to be ישר in God's sight' in the sense of 'to be pleasing to God' seems to better fit the context (*Ecclesiastes*, p. 127).

33. Lohfink, *Kohelet*, pp. 58-59; Zimmerli, *Prediger*, pp. 209-10.

חשבון is, as Whybray suggests, 'that which is', there may be חשבנות רבים ('many sums') stretching back into the past: 'those which were'. More likely, if we take into account such texts as 1.4-11 and 3.15, it may be the same חשבון repeated many times. That something similar may be meant by Qoheleth might be the case is suggested by the third person plural perfect form בקשו in 7.29—Qoheleth is saying that he is merely the latest in a long line of seekers after a חשבון.

4. *Summary of Qoheleth's Thought*

In 7.25, Qoheleth considers humanity and their actions as defined by the terms 'wisdom and the sum...foolishness and madness'. His failure in this endeavour is signalled by the introduction of Woman, the divine agent protecting the חשבון. Elsewhere, Qoheleth describes how 'the work of God' is protected by the allocation of עת and עניך. Love is both of these: the one who displeases God is caught by the woman and once caught there is no escape (9.9). Only God can determine the fate of the male individual with respect to this woman.

We may assume that Qoheleth did escape the woman, but her existence nevertheless has serious consequences for Qoheleth's search. Not only does she protect 'the work of God' from the sinner; she ensures that the counting process (of people, their motivations and actions) by which Qoheleth hoped to find the חשבון (7.27), which appears to be linked with 'the work of God'/'the work which is done under the sun', is doomed to failure. Qoheleth finds only a small proportion of Mankind whose actions make up the חשבון. He is unable to find Womankind (7.28), for she is too dangerous to approach—God's favour is demonstrated not in finding Woman but in escaping her (7.26). Qoheleth's conclusion (7.29) ironically plays on this hunt for 'the work of God'. He finds that that God did not intend humankind to search for the חשבון but that, like himself, they have done so throughout history.

5. *A Time to Hate: Translations*

(2.17) So I hated life, for the work which is done under the sun is troublesome to me, for everything is absurd and shepherding the wind. (18) And I hated all my toil at which I had toiled under the sun, which I shall leave to the person who will come after me.

(9.1) All this I laid to heart, examining it all, how the righteous and the wise and their deeds are in the hand of God; no-one knows either love or hate. Everything that confronts them (2) is absurd, since the same fate comes to all; to the righteous and to the wicked, to the good and to the bad, to the clean and to the unclean, to him that sacrifices and to him that does not sacrifice. As is the good, so is the sinner and he who swears (falsely) as he who fears an oath. (3) There is an evil that is done under the sun, for one fate happens to all, and also the human mind is full of evil; madness is in their minds while they live, and afterwards—to the dead. (4) For him who is joined to the living there is hope, for a living dog is better off than a dead lion. (5) For the living know that they will die, but the dead know nothing. Nor do they have any further reward, for the memory of them is forgotten. (6) Their love, their hate, and their envy have already perished, and they will never have any further portion in anything that is done under the sun.

6. *Text and Context*

1. *Ecclesiastes 2.17-18*

a. *Hatred of life and toil*

Outside the catalogue of seasons in 3.1-8, the √שׂנא ('hate') appears four times in the book of Ecclesiastes (2.17, 18; 9.1, 6). Its appearance in the former alongside √אהב ('love') might lead the reader to expect that Qoheleth will depict the emotion of hatred elsewhere as equally under divine control. This is not immediately apparent in the first two usages of this root in 2.17-18, however. There Qoheleth states:

> So *I hated life*, because the work which is done under the sun is burdensome to me...and *I hated all my labour* that I had done under the sun, because I should leave it to the person who shall be after me.

Qoheleth says that his 'hatred' has two separate objects, and is born of two things. First, the reason for his hatred of life is explained by the statement that 'the work that is done under the sun is burdensome to me' (רע עלי המעשׂה שׁנעשׂה תחת השׁמשׁ). The significance of this phrase 'the work which is done under the sun' has already been discussed in Chapter 2. There it was noted that it appeared to be co-extensive with the phrase 'the work of God' (מעשׂה האלהים), and was indicative of a deterministic view of life. The work of God, and the work that is done under the sun are identified by Qoheleth as one and the same because the deterministic God performs his works through the activity of humanity. In 1.13, he expounds upon the related phrase, 'all that is done under the heavens' (כל אשׁר נעשׂה תחת השׁמים), describing this 'all' as '(the) burdensome task God has given humanity to be occupied with' (ענין רע נתן אלהים לבני האדם לענות בו). In the light of this, Qoheleth's statement in 2.17 that human activity is 'burdensome' may be understood to convey the meaning either that Qoheleth's own toil, which forms a part of the larger deterministic whole, has become irksome, or more likely that Qoheleth's awareness of the fact that human activity is determined, that it is carried out on behalf of the deity, has made him hate not *his* life, but life or existence in toto. This distinction is supported by 4.1-3, in which Qoheleth considers 'the evil/burdensome work that is done under the sun' (v. 3), and congratulates the dead or unborn rather than the living because they are not present to view existence.

The reason for Qoheleth's hatred of his עמל ('toil', or the products thereof), in 2.18 is different.[34] In this passage, it arises because he will have to leave his possessions to a successor after his death without regard to their merit. At stake for Qoheleth is the issue of natural justice: he has, he feels, worked hard for his wealth. Why should it pass to someone who has not worked for it, or who may waste it? More important still for Qoheleth is the fact that he has no control himself over where his wealth will go when he is dead. Not only do people have no control over their own lives, those few material benefits over which they do acquire some form of control in life are distributed to others arbitrarily after death (cf. 2.26).

While this may bespeak a deterministic view of life—or, at the very least, a worldview in which humans have no control over circumstances—it cannot be said that Qoheleth speaks of his 'hatred' as being directly under divine control. The divine determination of emotion is not a significant aspect of this particular passage.

2. *Ecclesiastes 9.1-2*

a. *Hatred as a determined emotion*
The importance of 'love' (אהב) as a determined emotion has already been discussed in relation to Ecclesiastes 9, in which Qoheleth exhorts

---

34. The term עמל in Ecclesiastes typically refers to 'toil, labour'; here it is a metonym for 'wealth acquired by labour', hence 'goods': a rendering which is borne out by Qoheleth's disquiet that one day he should have to relinquish them to an heir. So Hitzig, *Prediger*, p. 142; Delitzsch, *Ecclesiastes*, pp. 248-49; Podechard, *L'Ecclésiaste*, p. 276. Cf. Rashbam, who explains עמלי as 'my riches' (ואת עושרי) (S. Japhet and R.B. Salters, *Rashbam on Qoheleth* [Jerusalem: Magnes Press, 1985], pp. 110-11).

the reader to 'experience life with the woman you love' (9.9) and envisions the 'times' that define the life of the individual as a series of snares and traps into which human beings unwittingly blunder (9.12). The opposing emotion 'hate' (שֹנא) also plays a key role in the development of Qoheleth's thought in this chapter, however (it appears in 9.1, 6, both times in opposition to אהב). Both occurrences lend weight to the suggestion that hate, like love, lies outside the sphere of human control.

b. *Textual problems*
Before proceeding further, it should be noted that two possible textual problems have been observed with the MT of Eccl. 9.1-2a. The Hebrew text reads:

כי את כל זה נתתי אל לבי ולבור את כל זה אשר הצדיקים והחכמים
ועבדיהם ביד האלהים גם אהבה גם שנאה אין יודע האדם הכל לפניהם:
הכל כאשר לכל מקרה אחד

> All this I laid to heart, examining it all, how the righteous and the wise and their deeds are in the hand of God; no-one knows either love or hate. Everything that confronts them is absurd, since the same fate comes to all.

First, the phrase ולבור את כל זה (Lit: 'and to examine all this') appears awkward after the finite verb נתתי ('I laid' [lit. 'I gave']). Accordingly, Fox, following the LXX, Peshitta, Syro-Hexapla and Coptic, reads ולבי ראה את כל זה ('and my heart saw all this'). The arguments that Fox advances in favour of this suggestion, that confusion between ר/ו is a relatively common scribal error, and that the missing ה in the MT can be explained as omission by parablepsis, are sound, though his assertion that the MT is 'syntactically impossible' is perhaps an overstatement.[35] Gordis, for example, retains the MT, arguing that לבור ('to examine') may be understood as an infinitive construct which continues a finite verb (GKC §114p), and there is a tendency at present for commentators to accept the text as it stands.[36]

---

35. Fox, *Contradictions*, p. 256.

36. A further issue is the form of לבור, which appears to be a qal infinitive construct of the √בור, otherwise unattested in Hebrew. Rashi explains the form as a derivation of ברר, a position which has been echoed by most modern commentators (Gordis, *Koheleth*, p. 299; Crenshaw, *Ecclesiastes*, p. 159; Murphy, *Ecclesiastes*, pp. 88-89). More recently, Seow has taken a different route, suggesting that a derivation from √בור may be appropriate. One of the meanings of

Second, many commentators perceive a difficulty with the phraseology and meaning of the final words of v. 1 and the beginning of v. 2, גַּם אַהֲבָה גַּם שִׂנְאָה אֵין יוֹדֵעַ הָאָדָם הַכֹּל לִפְנֵיהֶם: הַכֹּל כַּאֲשֶׁר לַכֹּל מִקְרֶה אֶחָד. Translated literally, the MT reads 'nobody knows either love or hate: all is before them. All as to all is one fate'. Qoheleth's precise meaning here is obscure, and many commentators (and the NRSV) posit that the verse division between vv. 1 and 2 should precede כַּאֲשֶׁר ('as, because') and that the first word of v. 2 should be emended from הַכֹּל ('all') to הֶבֶל ('absurd') ('No-one knows either love or hate. Everything that confronts them is absurd'). The emendation is a minor one, and finds support in the LXX, Symmachus, Vulgate and Peshitta.[37] Moreover, a clear parallel to the thought of this verse may also be seen in 2.15, 17 where the observation that the wise man meets the same fate as the fool leads to the conclusion not simply that this state of affairs is absurd (הֶבֶל—v. 15), but even that 'all is absurd' (הַכֹּל הֶבֶל—v. 17).

c. *The meaning of the text*

In view of the difficulties associated with the MT of 9.1-2a, it is little wonder that there exists no real consensus among modern scholars as to the translation or meaning of this text. Tyler, for example, argued that Qoheleth's meaning is that the destinies of the just and the wise are entirely in the hands of God, and that no human being can be sure of how God is disposed towards them.[38] By this reading, existence is seen by Qoheleth as partially deterministic: God controls the outcome of

its Arabic cognate is 'to examine, try, prove', and a verb *bâru* 'to become certain, proved' (D-Stem: 'to establish sth. as true, to find') exists in Akkadian (*Ecclesiastes*, p. 297). Seow's reading is an attractive one and is preferred here.

37. Fox, *Contradictions*, p. 257. Not all commentators have had recourse to emendation, however. Crenshaw (*Ecclesiastes*, pp. 158, 160), for example, follows Gordis (*Koheleth*, pp. 186, 299-300) and translates הַכֹּל כַּאֲשֶׁר לַכֹּל 'everything is the same for everybody' referring to the phrase אֶהְיֶה אֲשֶׁר אֶהְיֶה 'I shall be what I shall be' in Exod. 3.14. I nevertheless follow Fox in view of the weight of the versional and contextual evidence.

38. Tyler, *Ecclesiastes*, p. 143; Plumptre, *Ecclesiastes*, p. 184; Podechard, *L'Ecclésiaste*, p. 409; Lohfink, *Kohelet*, p. 65; Fox, *Contradictions*, pp. 256-57; Murphy, *Ecclesiastes*, p. 90. This was also the position of several earlier commentators, for example Rashi, Isaiah da Trani and Sforno. R. Kroeber (*Der Prediger* [Berlin: Akademie-Verlag, 1963], pp. 54-55) cites a parallel in the Instruction of Ptahhotep: 'He whom God loves is a hearkener, (but) he whom God hates cannot hear' (*ANET*, p. 414).

human endeavours, rather than human action itself.[39] Yet, as Crenshaw observes, Qoheleth does not just claim that people are in God's power; 'their works' (עבדיהם) are also said to be under divine control.

This statement can be explained in two different but related ways: (1) either it refers to the idea that God helps the wise and the righteous in their endeavours (i.e. what they think they accomplish by their own ability is in fact down to divine aid), or (2) it refers to the inability of such people to do anything without God's approval of their actions.[40]

In this context, the use of the term עבדיהם proves significant. Both the Targumist and Rashi had difficulty with this expression and read it as עבדיהם ('their slaves'), taking it to refer to the 'disciples' (Targ. תלמידיהון; Rashi: תלמידיהם) which the righteous and wise might be expected to accumulate. The pointing of the MT (supported by the Versions), however, indicates that we are dealing with the plural form of a noun עֲבָד, an Aramaism derived from the √עבד ('work, serve'). For Fox, the use of עבדיהם is to all intents and purposes equivalent to the Hebrew מעשׂה ('work'), which occurs throughout the book, and comments:

> It is difficult to understand why an author composing in Hebrew would use a common word, ma'ăśeh, numerous times, then once choose a unique Aramaism (unattested, as far as I can ascertain, in Hebrew literature before or after Ecclesiastes) that expresses no more than the Hebrew equivalent does.[41]

Fox's point is an important one, and it is worth asking whether Qoheleth did not have some particular idea which he wanted to express with the term עבדיהם; one which could not be expressed with the expected

---

39. Murphy's statement here, 'For [Qoheleth] "the hand of God"...merely designates divine power, from which there is no escape' (Ecclesiastes, p. 90) is ambiguous, but is probably intended to convey the same meaning as Crenshaw.

40. Crenshaw, Ecclesiastes, p. 159. On a slightly different tack, Fox (Contradictions, pp. 256-57) explains: 'Of course, all people are under God's control. But the righteous and the wise might be thought to have greater power over their fate than most because (conventional wisdom teaches) the behavior of the righteous brings the expected blessings, whereas the fate of the wicked is (to them) a surprise...'

41. This fact had earlier been used by Zimmermann to argue for an Aramaic original of Ecclesiastes, and Fox (Contradictions) makes clear the fact that he has some sympathy for such a theory, at least at this point.

מעשה. This, I would argue, is in fact the case. If, as some commentators suggest, 9.1 is read as being expressive of a deterministic worldview in which God controls the activity of human beings (here, specifically, those of the righteous and the wise), the term עבדיהם may be expressive not simply of 'work' or 'activity' in a neutral sense, but 'work for on behalf of' a third party, as in Middle Hebrew.[42] Thus, the choice of the term עבד rather than מעשה in this instance would be intended to highlight God's control over human beings.

What, then, is one to make of the phrase 'nobody knows either love or hate...'? Does this mean that human beings do not know how the deity is disposed towards them, or, alternatively, does it suggest that human beings do not have control over their own emotions?[43] In favour of the first position, Qoheleth elsewhere observes that wisdom and/or righteousness are frequently unmet by their just rewards (e.g. 'there are righteous people who are treated as if they had behaved wickedly, and there are wicked people who are treated as if they had behaved righteously' [8.14, cf. 4.13-16; 9.13-16]). One could perhaps argue that this forms a suitable starting point for the theme of death, the 'one fate that happens to all' (9.2), which pervades the first part of this chapter.

However, the context provided by 9.5-6, which contain several important echoes of the chapter, suggests otherwise. In 9.1, Qoheleth states: גם אהבה גם שנאה אין יודע האדם ('nobody knows either love or hate'). The theme of knowledge initiated in this verse is continued in 9.5 with the statement: כי החיים יודעים שימתו והמתים אינם יודעים מאומה ('the living know that they will die, but the dead know nothing'), and Qoheleth goes on to explain the lack of knowledge that characterizes the dead in 9.6: גם אהבתם גם שנאתם גם קנאם כבר אבדה ('both their love and their hate and their jealousy have already perished').

A comparison between 9.1 and 9.6 demonstrates that the latter repeats the structure גם...גם ('both...and...') with the nouns אהבה ('love') and שנאה ('hate') as the subjects of the sentence found in the former. However, the pronominal suffix on these nouns in 9.6 has המתים ('the dead') as their referent. The theme of knowledge, or lack

---

42. Cf. Jastrow, *Dictionary*, p. 1034.

43. Hitzig, *Prediger*, p. 188; Delitzsch, *Ecclesiastes*, p. 355; Hertzberg, *Prediger*, p. 155; Lauha, *Kohelet*, p. 166. The Targum and the eighteenth-century *Metzudath David* by Yehiel Altschuler also take this stance.

thereof on the part of humanity, also features in 9.5. Where humanity in 9.1 were said not to know love or hate (אֵין יוֹדֵעַ—particle of non-existence + qal participle), it is likewise stated in 9.5 that while the living can know of only one thing—their mortality—human beings know nothing (אֵינָם יוֹדְעִים מְאוּמָה—particle of non-existence + qal participle + adverb) after their death. It is human beings who 'do not know' their own love or hate in 9.5-6; this suggests that the love or hate described in 9.1 is likewise that felt by human beings rather than the deity.

What then are we to make of 9.1? The thrust of 9.5-6 would seem to be that the dead are incapable of feeling, sensing, or otherwise experiencing any emotion or activity. They 'know nothing'. The negative use of the verb יָדַע ('know') here, it should be noted, does not suggest that the dead *do not know how* to do certain things, but that they *are incapable* of such activity. Similar uses of the verb יָדַע to denote the ability to perform a certain function rather than the know-how to do so may be seen in Prov 29.7: יֹדֵעַ צַדִּיק דִּין דַּלִּים רָשָׁע לֹא יָבִין דָּעַת. One may translate this statement, 'the righteous man knows justice for the poor, but the wicked man does not understand knowledge', though the thought would be somewhat obscure. However, if the knowledge mentioned here is taken to refer to the ability to do something, one could arrive at a more lucid translation, 'the righteous man *is capable of* justice towards the poor, but the wicked man *is utterly incapable*'. One may perhaps detect a similar usage in Eccl. 4.13 'Better a poor youth—and wise, then an old king—and foolish, who is incapable of being/does not know how to be admonished' (לֹא יָדַע לְהִזָּהֵר). In a similar way, the statement that human beings 'know neither love or hate' could be taken to mean that humanity are unable to feel even the most basic emotions on their own account. Rather, they are instigated by the deity.

Such a reading of the text is, admittedly, a radical one, but it does find support in Qoheleth's statement that 'the righteous and the wise and their works are in the hand of God' (בְּיַד הָאֱלֹהִים). As noted earlier, the phrase 'to be in the hand of someone'. means to be in their power.[44] If one accepts that the good and their deeds are under divine control, as some of Qoheleth's contemporaries might have done, this belief could be used as evidence that divine control operated at an even more fundamental level in human life.

44. Cf. P.R. Ackroyd, 'יָד', *TDOT*, V, pp. 409-10.

Without claiming any direct influence at this stage, it is worth noting that Cleanthes, the second leader of the Stoic school, proposed a model for human existence similar in many ways to that of Qoheleth, when he observed that 'no deed is done on earth, God, without your offices... save what bad men do in their folly' (*Hymn to Zeus* 1.537). For the third century Stoic, God could take the credit for the deeds of the good, and yet deny responsibility for the actions of the wicked. Qoheleth claims essentially the same thing when he asserts that the activities of 'the righteous and wise' are under divine control. As we shall see in Chapter 7 of this work, the author of Ecclesiastes also sought to defend God from accusations that a deterministic deity must bear direct responsibility for human wickedness.

A final but crucial piece of evidence in favour of the suggestion that hatred, like love, is a predetermined emotion, is that the absence of love, hatred, and envy in the dead is equated with the absence for them of any 'portion in all that is done under the sun'. The significance of the term חֵלֶק in the book of Ecclesiastes, as observed in Chapter 2 of this work, is that it seems to refer to the limited good allotted to humanity by the deity—particularly the ability to find pleasure in life or otherwise engage emotionally with existence. Love, hatred, joy—all are human-ity's 'portion'. The fact that such emotions are said to form part of the 'all' that is done in 9.6, and in the catalogue of seasons (3.1-8), is also significant. If even human thought and feeling forms part of 'the work of God', then the deity must be involved in even the most intimate aspects of the individual's life.

7. Conclusion

In 3.1, Qoheleth claimed that God's deterministic control extended over every aspect of existence. As we have seen in previous chapters, this applies equally to the workings of the cosmos (1.3-8), and to human activity (3.2-8). Yet God also controls, whether directly or indirectly, human thought and feeling. For Qoheleth, the woman of 7.26-29 serves as a symbol of the way that human emotions are determined by God. It is not for nothing that she is depicted as a quasi-divine huntress. To love her is part of man's 'portion' in life (9.9). The determined nature of human emotion is underlined further in Eccl. 9.1 which speaks of humanity's inability to control even the fundamental aspects of their own lives. According to Qoheleth, the corollary of determinism is that one must derive what pleasure one can from what life throws up. However, even here, one may do so only if 'God has already approved your works' (9.7). Appropriately, it is to the theme of human joy that we turn in the next chapter of this work.

Chapter 6

'A TIME TO WEEP, A TIME TO LAUGH':
QOHELETH AND HUMAN JOY

1. *Introduction*

It would be fair to say that the joyful imperative is the one positive conclusion that Qoheleth reaches during his investigation into 'what was
that good for humankind, that they should do under the heaven all the
days of their life' (2.3). Yet Qoheleth initially discounts pleasure and its
material trappings as a legitimate good for human beings (2.1-2, 11).[1] It
is, more than anything else, the predetermined nature of life which
forces Qoheleth to revise his initial conclusions about the value of
pleasure. Thus, Qoheleth frequently makes use of the phrase אֵין טוֹב
'there is nothing better' to qualify his recommendations to enjoy the
material benefits that life can offer (2.24; 3.12, 22; 8.15).[2]

Whybray considers the immediate contexts of the passages in which
Qoheleth affirms pleasure as a positive good (2.24-26; 3.10-15, 22b;
5.17-19; 8.14-15; 9.7-10; 11.7–12.1).[3] From these passages, several
things become clear. The first, and most notable is that the opportunity
and the ability to take pleasure in the material benefits of life is a gift
granted by God himself. The verb נָתַן ('give' [2.26; 5.17-18; 8.15; 9.9])
and the derived noun מַתָּת (3.13; 5.18) occur with some frequency in

---

1.   Delitzsch, *Ecclesiastes*, pp. 233-34, 243; Murphy, in particular, stresses that
Qoheleth's experiment is not with mindless joy, but with 'the good life' (*Ecclesiastes*, pp. 17-18). Whybray explains Qoheleth's failure to find satisfaction in this
experiment to the fact that he seeks it independently: joy can come only at the time
which God determines for it (*Ecclesiastes*, p. 52). A very similar view is adopted by
Hertzberg (*Prediger*, pp. 81-82).
2.   Murphy, *Ecclesiastes*, pp. 26, 39, 53.
3.   Whybray, 'Preacher of Joy', p. 88. This pattern is followed in the main by
S. de Jong ('A Book on Labour: The Structuring Principles and the Main Theme of
the Book of Qohelet', *JSOT* 54 [1992], pp. 107-16 [110]).

these passages.[4] Yet Qoheleth also offers other reasons that are essentially related to this one: that one's lot in life is unchangeable and must be accepted (2.26; 3.14, 22b; 5.18; 9.9),[5] that life is fleeting and must therefore be made the most of (5.17b; 9.9b; 11.9; 12.1b),[6] and similarly that the present must be enjoyed because future events are concealed from human beings (3.11, 22b; 8.14).[7]

Although it is doubtful that Qoheleth regards all of these things as 'positive incentives' rather than 'depressing considerations', the essential points of Whybray's analysis of Qoheleth's attitude to pleasure are sound.[8] In Qoheleth's view, God does indeed play a pivotal role in the allocation of pleasure. This in itself is indicative to some extent of a deterministic understanding of life on Qoheleth's part. The question is whether pleasure, as Johnston and Whybray suggest, really can be considered solely as being within 'the gift of God'.[9]

2. Human Efforts to Attain Joy

Qoheleth's philosophy of life is notable in that human attempts to achieve contentment appear from the very beginning to be doomed to failure. In 4.8, he remarks on the case of the individual, without a companion, who labours purely for himself: 'there is no end of all his labour, nor does he ask, "For whom am I labouring and depriving myself of good things?"' Such a person is symptomatic of the general dissatisfaction of humanity with the material benefits of life (a dissatisfaction which Qoheleth himself has, ironically, experienced).[10] The

4.   Whybray, 'Preacher of Joy', p. 88.

5.   Johnston states: 'Man's pleasure depends on God's good pleasure, and the divine action cannot be neatly categorized or programmed by man' ('Confessions of a Workaholic', p. 25). Cf. S. de Jong ('God in the Book of Qohelet: A Reappraisal of Qohelet's Place in Old Testament Theology', *VT* 47 [1997], pp. 154-67 [163]), who states likewise that 'the enjoyment of life has to be given by God'.

6.   Glasser, *Qohelet*, p. 168; Barton, *Ecclesiastes*, pp. 184-85.

7.   Gordis, *Koheleth*, p. 238. Crenshaw sees the expression ('after him') as referring to what happens to oneself after death (*Ecclesiastes*, p. 105).

8.   Whybray, 'Preacher of Joy', p. 88.

9.   Whybray, 'Preacher of Joy', p. 89; *idem, Ecclesiastes*, p. 52; Johnston, 'Confessions of a Workaholic', p. 25; Crenshaw, *Ecclesiastes*, p. 90; Murphy, *Ecclesiastes*, p. lx.

10.   Jastrow (*A Gentle Cynic*, p. 214 n. 62) perhaps goes too far in seeing an autobiographical touch in 4.8, but Qoheleth has in a sense experienced the disappointments of wealth in 2.11.

theme of acquisitiveness and the concomitant disillusionment with that which is acquired is one that is close to Qoheleth's heart, for he dwells on it in an extended passage (5.9-16 [ET 10-17]).[11] In 5.9-11 he states:

> He that loves money shall not be satisfied with money, nor he that loves abundance with increase: this is also vanity. When goods increase, their consumers increase but what good is there to their owners except to look at them with their eyes? The sleep of a labouring man is sweet, whether he eats little or much: but the rich man's abundance will not allow him to sleep.

The paradox of toiling ceaselessly to achieve a series of goals, each in turn proving to be unsatisfying, is highlighted in the introduction to the book in 1.4-8. There, as we have seen, Qoheleth uses a series of analogies from the natural world: the unceasing circular motion of the sun (depicted as a weary runner), wind and rivers. The labour of the human observer of these phenomena is also suggested in this passage: 'the eyes are not sated with seeing, nor the ears full from hearing' (1.8), that is that just as these items are in perpetual motion, so this results in a continual stream of information to our senses.[12] Every one of these natural phenomena follows a predetermined path: the implication for Qoheleth's view of human labour is clear. Humankind, on both a collective and individual level, also follows a predetermined path. This idea is implicit in the cycle of death and birth for humanity as a whole in 1.3.[13]

The idea of toil driven by dissatisfaction is also evident in 4.4, 'Again, I considered all travail, and every right work, that for this a man is envied of his neighbour'—Qoheleth's comment here recognizes the importance of rivalry and competition in human society but also contains the implication that competition leads to a vicious circle in which the individual drives himself without knowing the reason why, or without having an adequate reason for so doing.[14] As we shall see presently, a successful outcome to one's labour and the ability to make use of the

---

11. Devine (*Confessions*, p. 100) detects a note of 'sympathy with the rich' here.

12. Fox, *Contradictions*, p. 69.

13. E. Levine, 'The Humor in Qohelet', *ZAW* 109 (1997), pp. 71-83 (78-79). By way of contrast, G.S. Ogden ('The Interpretation of רוח in Ecclesiastes 1.4', *JSOT* 34 [1986], pp. 91-92), followed by Whybray ('Ecclesiastes 1.5-7', pp. 105-107) argues that רוח refers to the cycles of the natural phenomena in 1.4-8.

14. D.C. Rudman, 'A Contextual Reading of Ecclesiastes 4:13-16', *JBL* 116 (1997), pp. 57-73 (58).

material benefits therefrom is entirely dependent on the good will of the deity.

3. God's Role in the Allocation of Joy

Qoheleth appears to recognize that it is necessary for human beings to achieve some kind of balance if they are to have any hope of contentment. Thus, he avers, 'better is one hand full with quietness than two hands full with toil and chasing the wind' (4.8), and in a similar vein he comments, 'better is the sight of the eyes than the wandering of desire' (6.9).[15] How is such an equilibrium to be achieved? This question is closely linked with the double-sided nature of God's gifts to humankind: on the one hand, God gives joy—the ability to 'experience the benefits in one's labour', and on the other, toil—a sentence of hard labour without mitigating benefits. In order to illustrate this, the relevant parts of the seven passages which Whybray considers as central to understanding Qoheleth's view of human joy will be considered in this section.

1. Ecclesiastes 2.24-26

The text reads:

> There is nothing better for a man than that he should eat and drink, and that he should let himself enjoy the good in his labour. This also I saw, that it was from the hand of God... For God gives to the one who pleases him wisdom, and knowledge and joy: but to the one who displeases him he gives toil, to gather and to heap up, in order that he may give to the one who pleases God.

Qoheleth generally finds it difficult to reconcile pleasure to wisdom, preferring to associate it with folly or madness (2.2, 3; 7.1-6). By contrast, wisdom is frequently associated with distress (1.18; 2.23; 7.1-6). Uniquely in the book of Ecclesiastes, pleasure is paralleled with wisdom in 2.26. In this context, it is significant that both lie within the 'gift of God'. Only God, it seems, can find a way of resolving the essential incompatibility between these two concepts and allow them to be present in a single individual.[16]

---

15. Gordis also points out Qoheleth's expression of the limited nature of joy here, i.e., that it lacks any 'absolute value' in the grand scheme of things (*Koheleth*, pp. 261-62).

16. In this context, it is worthy of note that Loader (J.A. Loader, *Polar*

The fact that it is God, and God alone, who grants both wisdom and joy to the individual points of itself to a deterministic agenda on Qoheleth's part. Yet, Qoheleth's explanation in 2.26 of how God acts to bring this state of affairs about is more significant still: God gives to the 'sinner', that is to one who displeases him, עִנְיָן ('toil', 'business', 'affliction'). It is the fate of this unfortunate individual 'to gather and to heap up' material wealth, to give to 'one who pleases God'. God thus determines the course of one's life whether one is favoured or not: everyone it would seem is subject to some degree of divine interference.[17]

On another level, the fact of עִנְיָן being within God's gift means that divine interference in human actions is not momentary but continuous. In 1.13, the expression 'all things which are done under heaven' is described as the עִנְיַן רָע ('evil business') which God has given (נָתַן) to humankind in general. In 3.10, the term עִנְיָן is used in conjunction with the concept of 'God's gift' to humankind with reference to list of divinely appointed actions in 3.2-8.[18] God's responsibility for all human action is, as we have seen in Chapter 2 of this work, reflected in Qoheleth's parallel usage of 'the work of God' with 'the work which is done under the sun'.

Structures in the Book of Qohelet [BZAW, 152; Berlin: W. de Gruyter, 1979], pp. 38, 41-42) argues that one should read וּמִי יָחוּשׁ חוּץ מִמֶּנּוּ in 2.25, partially supported by some manuscripts, the Peshitta and Coptic version (cf. Barton, *Ecclesiastes*, p. 97; Zimmerli, *Prediger*, p. 164; Hertzberg, *Prediger*, p. 81) He goes on to translate 2.25 'for who can eat and who can *think* without him?' There is a strong contextual case for this reading, which would certainly be a supreme exposition of determinism on Qoheleth's part. Whitley (*Koheleth*, pp. 28-29) is sympathetic to this reading but rightly cautious in the light of the fact that the secondary meaning 'to worry/consider' for חוּשׁ occurs only in later Rabbinic Hebrew and Mandaic.

17. Cf. Fox's remark (*Contradictions*, p. 188) that the complaint implicit in 2.26 has its basis in 'God's all-determining will'.

18. Murphy (*Ecclesiastes*, p. 34) links עִנְיָן in 1.13 with a divinely appointed task of making sense out of existence but is less clear as to its frame of reference in 3.10, stating simply that it is 'applied to the problem of determinate times' in 3.1-8. It cannot mean that human beings are given the 'toil' of making sense of these determinate times, since God acts in 3.11 to prevent human beings from 'finding out' the work of God. Thus, the 'toil' is that of carrying out these divinely determined actions. This occupies human beings to such an extent that they are unable to act under their own initiative to find out God's plan (3.11).

Returning once more to the theme of pleasure in this passage, Whybray's words, though quoted already by the present author, remain significant:

> man should 'eat and drink and find enjoyment in his toil'; but this is possible only when it comes 'from the hand of God'. God may give joy and pleasure; man can never achieve it for himself, however hard he may try.[19]

The phrase יד האלהים ('the hand of God') occurs again in 9.1 alongside √נתן and there too is indicative of Qoheleth's deterministic worldview.

2. *Ecclesiastes 3.1-12*

The depiction of joy or pleasure as 'the gift of God' is in line with the predetermined nature of life evident in 3.1-8, in which Qoheleth speaks of the times (עת) for all activities and feelings mapped out for humankind by the deity. Many commentators, as we have seen, continue to regard this as a deterministic text, and so it may appear odd that √שמח does not appear among the actions listed therein for which there is a divinely appointed time.

Whybray's thoughts on this passage are somewhat ambiguous. Despite his comment that 'God may give joy and pleasure, man can never achieve it for himself',[20] the exegesis of this passage offered in his commentary follows the line that the 'times' of 3.1-8 are ideal times, unknowable to human beings, for various actions.[21]

Although √שמח may not be mentioned in this passage, the idea that pleasure is one of the predetermined aspects of human life is borne out by the appearance of √שחק in the list of times in this passage, for Qoheleth states that there is 'a time to weep, a time to laugh' (3.4). Moreover, the title with which Qoheleth prefaces his list of actions states that 'to *everything* there is a season, and an appointed time to *every business* under heaven'. The universality of this passage is stressed by most commentators.[22]

---

19. Whybray, 'Preacher of Joy', p. 89. Cf. Glasser, *Qohelet*, p. 53.
20. Whybray, 'Preacher of Joy', p. 88.
21. Whybray, *Ecclesiastes* [NCBC], p. 66.
22. E.g. Delitzsch, *Ecclesiastes*, pp. 254-55. Barton (*Ecclesiastes*, p. 98) also makes a link with ch. 1 in this context and suggests the idea not only of all human action being carried out but all action also being repeated periodically.

The text of 3.12-13 itself reads:

> I know that there is no good for humankind but to rejoice and to fare
> well during one's life, and also that everyone should eat and drink and
> experience good in all one's toil: it is a gift of God.

In the face of the fact of divine control over our actions asserted in
3.1-11, Qoheleth's conclusion is as one might expect, 'I know that *there
is no good for humankind but to rejoice* (אין טוב בם כי אם לשמוח)...it
is the *gift of God* (מתת אלהים)' (3.12-13). In Chapter 4 of this work, I
suggested that 'good' refers to the fact that it is an action over which
the individual has some form of control, a suggestion borne out to some
extent by the fact that enjoyment of life depends on being granted
'authorization' (שלטון) from God to do so. Even this 'authorization' is
distributed according to 'time', however (8.9). Paradoxically, even for
those things that are apparently within our power, we are dependent
upon God. It is therefore the opportunity for pleasure that is determined
by God rather than the feeling itself (or perhaps one could say that the
feeling is determined indirectly, by means of the authorization): in any
case, the idea that humanity's ability to find joy is determined by the
deity is expressed in 3.13 by the phrase 'it is the gift of God'.[23]

3. *Ecclesiastes 3.22*

The next significant passage in which the same advice occurs is 3.22:

> So I understood that there is nothing better than that a man should
> rejoice in his own works, for that is his portion (חלקו), for who shall
> bring him to see what shall be after him?

Qoheleth's use of the term חלק ('portion'), has already been a subject of study in Chapter 2. There it was concluded that one's 'portion'
in life was mainly associated with the realm of human emotions: joy
(2.10; 3.22; 5.17 [ET 18]), love (9.9) or love, hate and envy (9.6).[24] This
conception of 'portion' was also notable, however, in that God was also
depicted as the giver or allotter of one's portion in life (5.18). As Fox
points out, the refusal to take one's portion can be construed as a refusal

---

23. Loader (*Polar Structures*, p. 105) notes however, 'The conclusion drawn...
is laden with tension because enjoyment comes from God. Enjoy, but remember
that God's gift could just as well have been different (another *'et* can come)'.

24. This aspect of the concept of portion is illustrated by Fox's helpful study
(*Contradictions*, pp. 57-59, 258).

to submit to God's will (9.9).[25] God's control over human emotions is another pointer towards Qoheleth's deterministic view of existence.

In this context the term חלק is once again indicative of God's role in the allocation of pleasure. Yet there is also another aspect to this verse: one's portion is to 'rejoice in *one's own* works'. In 3.11, Qoheleth remarks that God acts as he does in order that 'no one might find out the work of God', and in 8.17, he states that 'no one can find out the work which is done under the sun'. Implicit in Qoheleth's words in 3.22 is the counsel that that human beings should rejoice individually in their own actions and leave those within God's sphere to God himself ('who shall bring him to see what shall be after him?').[26]

4. *Ecclesiastes 5.17–6.2*

Qoheleth's commentary on the dissatisfaction experienced by the avaricious man considers the situation of the man whose wealth is lost in an unlucky venture (5.12-13). Material wealth, it seems, may be lost as quickly as it is gained. This emphasizes the lack of control that human beings have over their destiny in much the same way as 9.11. By itself, this remark need not be suggestive of determinism, however.

There are, however, a number of other significant features in the subsection 5.17-19 which do betray a deterministic outlook on life. The text in question states:

> Behold that which I have seen: it is good and comely for one to eat and drink, and to experience the benefits of all one's labour which one takes under the sun all the days of his life, which God has given [נתן] him: for it is his portion [חלק]. Every man also to whom God has given riches and wealth, and has given him authority to use it, and to take his portion, and to rejoice in his labour; this is the gift of God.

---

25. Fox, *Contradictions*, p. 59.

26. Podechard (*L'Ecclésiaste*, pp. 317-19), Gordis (*Koheleth*, p. 238), Loader (*Polar Structures*, p. 106) and Fox (*Contradictions*, p. 199) argue that this phrase, repeated in 6.12, refers to the individual's future in his own lifetime. This is the position taken in this book, but whether it is understood as referring to this or to foreknowledge of one's personal circumstances after death (Delitzsch, *Ecclesiastes*, p. 272; Whybray, *Ecclesiastes* [NCBC], p. 81), or of events on earth after one's death (Murphy, *Ecclesiastes*, p. 37) or both of the latter (Barton, *Ecclesiastes*, p. 110; Crenshaw, *Ecclesiastes*, p. 105), the implication is the same: human knowledge is restricted to one's actions in the present. Concerning the future in any capacity, there is only ignorance.

The imperative to pleasure is based not only on the fact that the ability to enjoy pleasure in a specific instance is a gift of God (2.26), but also here because life itself is a gift. Qoheleth has come a long way from his initial reaction on discovering the absence of true meaning to human existence. In 2.17, he 'hates life'. Here he accepts that it is a gift to be made the most of. More significantly still, however, the ability 'to eat and to drink and to experience the benefit in one's labour' is termed the 'portion' of the worker.

God's purpose in allocating pleasure seems apparent in 5.19 for, speaking of the individual whom God favours, Qoheleth comments, 'he shall not much remember the days of his life, for God occupies him by the joy of his heart (בשמחת לבו)'. Like the process of labour, joy prevents humankind from dwelling on the futility of his existence. Joy, and indeed, woman occupy the intellectual/emotional side of one's character (לב) occupied just as labour does the physical side.[27] The לב is the part of Qoheleth which attempts to grasp the underlying nature of existence during the royal experiment (1.17), but the לב also 'rejoices' in his labour or the products thereof (2.10). It is only when Qoheleth turns and takes a second, closer look at his achievements that he sees their הבל ('vanity'/'absurdity'), and begins to seek something more substantial.[28] God's reason for allotting the gift of joy to certain individuals may not be disinterested.

Yet joy is not a universal gift. Qoheleth also speaks of certain people who have every material advantage in life but who for one reason or another, find themselves unable to make use of these benefits. This is illustrated in 6.1-2:

---

27. Gordis argues against the idea that joy 'deaden's man's sensibility to the brevity of life' (*Koheleth*, pp. 255-56) and derives מענה from ענה (I) 'to answer' (cf. Jastrow, *A Gentle Cynic*, p. 219 n. 88), although this interpretation is behind the translations of the LXX, Peshitta and Vulgate. However, the basis for this, that 'Koheleth regards joy not as a narcotic, but as a fulfillment of the will of God' (Gordis) fails to take into account the possibility that joy's narcotic quality may reflect God's will. Fox argues against Gordis's position effectively on linguistic grounds (*Contradictions*, p. 218).

28. Whybray (*Ecclesiastes* [NCBC], pp. 55-56) argues that joy is 'vanity' in the royal experiment because it is achieved independently by Qoheleth without divine assistance (thus it is opposed to the 'gift of God'). Yet Qoheleth achieves both wisdom and knowledge and joy in the course of his investigations (cf. 2.26). Even when it is clearly part of the divine gift, as in 9.9, joy is still 'vanity', for 'all is vanity' (1.2; 12.8).

> There is an evil which I have seen under the sun, and it is common among men: a man to whom God has given riches, wealth and honour, so that he wants nothing for himself of all that he desires, but God does not give him the authority to use it and a stranger eats of it: this is vanity and an evil sickness.

This passage clearly shows the importance of God not only in the allocation of the initial gift of material benefits to the individual, but also in the opportunity to enjoy it. It is God who is the giver of 'riches, wealth and honour': the individual does not acquire them for himself.[29] It is also God, however, who gives or withholds 'authorization' (שׁלטו—5.18 [ET 19]; 6.2) to use the material goods which one acquires during one's toil. Seow has correctly pointed out the legalistic overtones of Qoheleth's use of שׁלטו.[30] God is portrayed by this means as an absolute ruler who controls every action of his subjects. He may allow human beings to enjoy the material things for which they have worked so hard, or, alternatively, he may not. For every worker who enjoys the fruits of their labour, there is another who loses what has been gained (2.26) or who remains trapped in the bondage of labour (6.1-2). God bears ultimate responsibility not just for happiness, but also for its absence, since it is he who controls its distribution among humanity. This is the dark side to Whybray's benevolent deity. In depicting God's apparent arbitrariness in the choice of his favourites (2.26; 5.17; 6.2), Qoheleth may perhaps intend a parallel to the despotic rulers of his own time.[31]

5. *Ecclesiastes 8.15*

God's role in the allocation of joy is also implicit in 8.15 in which Qoheleth states:

---

29. Crenshaw (*Ecclesiastes*, p. 125) remarks concerning this concept of divine gift, 'This knowledge that life's pleasures cannot be earned through diligence and good conduct undercuts the fundamental premise of wisdom thinking… In Qoheleth's affirmations about God, the notion of divine gift loses its comforting quality. The gift comes without rhyme and reason; it falls on individuals indiscriminately. Those who do not receive it can do nothing to change their condition'. At the same time, though divine gifts may be unpredictable, Qoheleth does not suggest that they are random.

30. Seow, 'Socioeconomic Context', pp. 176-81; 'Linguistic Evidence', pp. 653-54.

31. This assessment holds true whether one dates Ecclesiastes to the Persian or Greek periods.

> So I praised joy, for a man has no better thing under the sun than to eat, and to drink, and to be merry: for that shall remain with him of his labour during his life, which God gives him under the sun.

Qoheleth, as Whybray notes, goes further in this passage than in his previous commendations of joy by praising (שׁבח) it as a positive benefit.[32] His thought has developed somewhat since 4.2 in which the same verb occurs when he stated, 'So I praised (שׁבח) the dead more than the living'. The reasoning for taking this opportunity is not so much that God has given (נתן) life to humankind, but that he has given a relatively short span of life.[33] This life, in Qoheleth's view is to be made the most of, but the fact that pleasure is a second best option for all Qoheleth's recommendation is well illustrated by Qoheleth's use of the formula אין טוב...כי אם ('there is no good...except').[34]

Although God's role in the allocation of pleasure is not emphasized in this text as in others, the rationale behind finding enjoyment is suggestive of God's role as the one who gives and takes away life. By extension, this implies joy as part of the divine plan for human beings. This is particularly evident in the next passage to be considered.

6. *Ecclesiastes 9.7-9*

The text of 9.7-9 is a crucial one for understanding how Qoheleth's recommendation to joy fits in with his deterministic worldview:

> Go, eat your bread with joy and drink your wine with a happy heart, for God has already approved your actions. Let your clothes be always white and let your head lack no ointment. Experience life with the woman you love all the days of your vain life which he has given you under the sun, all the days of your vanity, for that is your portion in this life, and in your labour which you undertake under the sun.

---

32. Whybray, 'Preacher of Joy', p. 87.

33. Cf. Whybray (*Ecclesiastes* [NCBC], p. 102) on the relationship between the brevity of life and the possibility of joy: 'Qoheleth does not disguise this limitation of man's enjoyment: it is precisely this limitation which adds point to the advice to enjoy life as much as possible'.

34. G.S. Ogden ('Qoheleth's Use of the "Nothing is Better" Form', *JBL* 98 [1979], pp. 341-50) notes the function as a partial response to the generally negative answer required to the question מה יתרון לאדם but also links it strongly to deterministic thought: the only good for the individual is to follow along the path that God has willed for him.

The imperative to joy in 9.7-9 is a remarkably strong one. It is particularly significant for understanding God's role in the allocation of joy to the individual because Qoheleth bases his advice on the fact that 'God has already approved your works' (את האלהים רצה כבר מעשיך). The precise meaning of this phrase is a matter of some debate among commentators. The verb רצה ('to accept') used in this verse is elsewhere used of the pleasure that God takes in sacrifices (Deut. 33.11; Amos 5.22, and so on). The idea for Murphy is therefore that this divine pleasure means 'the mysterious approval and gifts freely bestowed by God' (cf. 2.26). Presumably, this would mean, as with Whybray, that the fact that God has given human beings the opportunity to take pleasure in life means that God has in general approved the taking of pleasure.[35]

This, however, is not precisely what the text says. As I suggested in the previous chapter, the statement that 'God has already approved your works' would appear to suggest that the choices which the individual makes and the resulting actions are known in advance by God (how else could one's actions be 'already approved'?). Qoheleth's use of the more general term 'your works' (את מעשיך) as opposed to a more specific reference such as 'these works', 'pleasure' or the like, which one should perhaps expect, is suggestive that he understands such actions as simply one part of the overall activity that God has willed for humanity.[36]

In the wider context, such a reading is in line with the deterministic worldview advanced by Qoheleth in Ecclesiastes 9 as a whole. Thus, Qoheleth states in 9.1: 'the righteous and the wise and their works are in God's power [lit: "the hand of God"] (cf. 2.24): no one knows either love or hatred by all which is before them'.[37] God's sphere of deterministic control is delineated here as 'the righteous and the wise

---

35. Murphy, *Ecclesiastes*, p. 92; Whybray, *Ecclesiastes*, p. 144. So also Barton, *Ecclesiastes*, p. 162; Fox, *Contradictions*, p. 259.

36. Most commentators such as Podechard (*L'Ecclésiaste*, p. 414), however, understand the term מעשיך in the specific (but still deterministic) sense: 'Qoh. estime que si le travail d'un homme lui a procuré quelques facilités de jouir, c'est une marque certaine que Dieu veut qu'il jouisse en effet, car Dieu seul donne les biens et le pouvoir d'en profiter...' ('Qoheleth reckons that if a man's work provides him with the means to rejoice, it is a sure sign that God wants him to rejoice, for only God gives the wherewithal and the ability to make use of it'.)

37. G.S. Ogden ('Qoheleth IX 1-6', *VT* 32 [1982], pp. 158-69 [160]) notes the appearance of the phrase in 2.24 but understands 9.1 in a non-deterministic sense. God determines the 'outcome' of an action rather than the action itself.

and their deeds (עבדיהם)', thus prefiguring the statement that 'God has already approved your works' (מעשיך) in 9.7.[38]

The same deterministic atmosphere is evident in 9.11-12. The divine nets and snares of 9.12 and their relevance for determinism have already been discussed in Chapter 5 of this work. This is reinforced by the occurrence of the phrase עת ופגע ('time and event') in 9.10 as the controlling factor in the outcome of human endeavour. As has been argued in Chapter 2, this passage is similarly indicative of Qoheleth's deterministic outlook on existence.

In the context of these passages, the statement in 9.7 that 'God has already approved your works' is an affirmation of the necessity of deriving pleasure from life in the light of Qoheleth's deterministic view of the same. The rationale given for Qoheleth's advice is that one may as well enjoy life to the full because God has already decided what we are to do. Qoheleth's use of the 'nothing is better' formula in the context of joy takes on a deeper significance therefore. For Qoheleth's avowed aim is to find out 'what was that good that men should do under the heavens'. Since all is predetermined, such a search loses its raison d'être—and Qoheleth can conclude that there is nothing better than to 'sit back and enjoy the ride'.

This reading of 9.7 is lent further support by the appearance of Woman in 9.9. Again, I have argued that Woman acts as a divine agent in Qoheleth's worldview. The entrapment vocabulary with which she is associated in 7.26 make her a universal force from which escape is possible only through the assistance of God. This is reflected in 9.9 in which Qoheleth advises his reader to 'experience life with Woman whom you love'. No choice is given over whether Woman is loved: this is taken for granted by Qoheleth.

Thus, the passage 9.7-9 reflects the wider context of Ecclesiastes 9 in which it is placed but also establishes links with several other deterministic passages in the book. Once again, God's role in the allocation of human joy is amply illustrated by Qoheleth.

---

38. Delitzsch (*Ecclesiastes*, pp. 354-55) interprets 9.1 in this overtly deterministic way extending even the emotions of human love and hatred to God's control. The fact that it is the wise whose actions are under God's control links neatly with 9.7 for Qoheleth advises the wise disciple, whose actions are thus divinely 'approved'. The same position is also held by Galling (*Prediger*, p. 113) and Loader (*Polar Structures*, p. 102).

7. Ecclesiastes 11.8–12.7

The next and final section in which joy is recommended, indeed commanded, by Qohelet is found in 11.8–12.7. For the purposes of making detailed comment, 11.8-10 is reproduced below:

> But if a man live many years and rejoice in them all, yet let him remember the days of darkness, for they shall be many. All that comes is vanity. Rejoice, young man, in your youth and walk in the ways of your heart and in the sight of your eyes *but know that for all these things God will bring you into judgment*. So remove sorrow from your heart, and put away evil from your flesh, for childhood and youth are vanity.

Part of the rationale for the enjoyment of life stems from the consciousness of the finality of death. but Qoheleth also makes another statement: that God will 'bring into judgment' the young man, holding him accountable for the actions that Qoheleth recommends. Yet recommend them Qoheleth does, both before and after this warning of divine judgment. What can be meant by this sentence 'Know that for all these God will bring you into judgment'?

In Chapter 2, it was argued that the term מֶשְׁפָּט is expressive of one aspect of God's determination of all events. Yet this particular passage depicts God judging human beings for following Qoheleth's advice concerning the enjoyment of life. Life itself and the ability to enjoy life are clearly stated elsewhere to be the gift of God (2.26; 5.18 [ET 19]; 8.15; 9.9; 12.7). Can the idea of God's judgment in this passage be reconciled with Qoheleth's advice to make use of this opportunity here and elsewhere?

Gordis attempted to resolve the difficulties posed by the appearance of this sentence in such a context by arguing that God will judge the youth according to the way in which he has used the opportunities for joy granted to him.[39] Others have pointed out that the idea of divine judgment is not a concept alien to Qoheleth, and therefore that even if such a judgment implies a negative attitude towards human pleasure on the part of the deity it is compatible with Qoheleth's thought.[40] More

---

39. Gordis, *Koheleth*, p. 336.

40. The case for retaining 11.9b is propounded by G. Wildeboer, 'Der Prediger', in K. Budde (ed.), *Die fünf Megillot* (KHAT, 7; Freiburg: J.C.B. Mohr, 1898), p. 161; Gordis, *Koheleth*, p. 336; Jones, *Proverbs and Ecclesiastes*, p. 341; G.S. Ogden, 'Qoheleth IX 7–XII 8: Qoheleth's Summons to Enjoyment and Reflection',

typically, however, the statement is seen as a gloss.[41]

The structure of the passage 11.9–12.8 as a whole is as follows:[42]

11.8	If a man lives many years	Time Phrase
	let him *rejoice*	Theme A
	and *remember*	Theme B
	the days of darkness will be many	Time Phrase
	all that comes is *hebel* (vanity)	Conclusion
11.9-10	*Rejoice*	Theme A
	(in your youth)…in the days of your youth	Time Phrase
	for youth…is *hebel* (vanity)	Conclusion
12.1	*Remember*	Theme B
	in the days of your youth	Time Phrase
	before…	
12.2	before…	
12.6	before…	
12.8	*habel habalim* (vanity of vanities)	conclusion
	…all is *hebel*(vanity)	

The same applies to the first stanza of this passage (11.9-10). If the sentence in question, וְדַע כִּי עַל כָּל אֵלֶּה יְבִיאֲךָ הָאֱלֹהִים בַּמִּשְׁפָּט 'Know that for all these, God will bring you into judgment', is deleted from 11.9b, the structure of this short passage can clearly be seen:

שְׂמַח בָּחוּר בְּיַלְדוּתֶךָ   וִיטִיבְךָ לִבְּךָ בִּימֵי בְחוּרוֹתֶיךָ

וְהַלֵּךְ בְּדַרְכֵי לִבְּךָ   וּבְמַרְאֵי עֵינֶיךָ

וְהָסֵר כַּעַס מִלִּבֶּךָ   וְהַעֲבֵר רָעָה מִבְּשָׂרֶךָ

כִּי הַיַּלְדוּת וְהַשַּׁחֲרוּת הָבֶל

VT 34 (1984), pp. 27-38 (31-32); Fox, *Contradictions*, p. 279; D.C. Fredericks, 'Life's Storms and Structural Unity in Qoheleth 11.1–12.8', *JSOT* 52 (1991), pp. 95-114 (101); Murphy, *Ecclesiastes*, p. 117.

41. Siegfried, *Prediger*, p. 73, followed by McNeile, *Ecclesiastes*, p. 26; Barton, *Ecclesiastes*, p. 185; Podechard, *L'Ecclésiaste*, p. 452; Jastrow, *A Gentle Cynic*, p. 238; Zimmerli, *Prediger*, p. 242; Scott, *Proverbs and Ecclesiastes*, p. 254; Galling, *Prediger*, p. 120; Salters, 'The Book of Ecclesiastes', p. 227; Crenshaw, *Ecclesiastes*, p. 184.

42. This scheme is derived from G.S. Ogden (*Qoheleth* [Readings: A New Biblical Commentary; Sheffield: JSOT Press, 1987], pp. 193-94), based upon the study of H. Witzenrath (*Süss ist das Licht…: Eine literaturwissenschaftliche Untersuchung zu Kohelet 11:7–12:7* [MUSKTF. ATSAT, 11; S. Ottilien: Eos, 1979).

Rejoice, young man in your youth	Let your heart cheer you in the days of your youth
Walk in the ways of your heart	And in the sight of your eyes
Remove sorrow from your heart	Put away evil from your flesh

For youth and dark hairs are vanity

The first line introduces the overall theme of enjoying youth; the term ילדות ('youth') in the first half is balanced by בחורות ('youth') in the second half, while the succession of imperatives dominate the passage as a whole (שׂמח, 'rejoice'; יטיב, 'let cheer' [jussive]; הלך, 'walk'; הסר, 'remove'; העבר, 'put away'). Of itself, this would not point to 11.9b being a gloss, for it too uses an imperative, דע ['know']. Significantly, however, it appears between the second and third lines of this passage which appear to form a couplet. Line 2a and 3a give advice with respect to the intellectual/psychological side of the young man's life 'your heart': these are, however, balanced by the physical dimension to life in 2b and 3b as expressed by the terms 'your eyes'/'your flesh'. That there is a close relationship in structure and thought between the second and third lines of the passage above is clearly suggested by its structure, yet the phrase ודע כי על כל אלה יביאך האלהים במשפט ('but know that for all these things, God will bring you into judgment') is interposed between them in the MT, breaking up both the rhythm and the thought of the passage.

This consideration alone might give grounds for suspicion that Qoheleth himself was not responsible for 11.9b. Yet commentators deny the authenticity of this phrase on other grounds: the similarity between על כל אלה יביאך האלהים במשפט in 11.9b and a corresponding expression, את כל מעשה האלהים יבא במשפט על כל נעלם in 12.14 is striking, and has led many to suppose that the addition of 11.9b has resulted from the influence of the second epiloguist. That is, an attempt has been made to interpret the extended passage 11.7–12.7 in the light of the pious comment of the second epiloguist in 12.14. This may also underly the MT's reading of בוראיך 'your creator'.[43]

---

43. I emend to בורך 'your grave', with Scott (*Proverbs Ecclesiastes*, p. 253). This best fits the context as delineated by the overall structure of 11.8–12.8. 12.1 should be a recapitulation of Theme B, i.e., a reminder to remember the brevity of life (cf. 11.8). It is possible to retain the MT's בוראיך 'your Creator' if this is understood as an oblique reference to God's role in giving and taking away life (cf. 12.7): this view is advanced by Fox (*Contradictions*, p. 300) and Murphy (*Ecclesiastes*, p. 117). The alternative, of emending to בארך 'your well', and understanding this as a reference to Woman (cf. Prov. 5.15—so Crenshaw,

While it is true that Qoheleth speaks of judgment elsewhere in Ecclesiastes, it is the context of this particular occurrence that gives cause for suspicion. In 3.17, Qoheleth mentions that God will judge the righteous and wicked as a natural follow up to his observations about the lack of human justice. The fact that this remark is made in the context of there being 'a time there for every purpose and every work', recalling his original statement in 3.1 gives it a ring of authenticity. The fact that it is God who is the subject of the verb reinforces the idea that these times refer to the appointed times for divine activity, or to human activities which are determined by God.

Likewise, the terms מִשְׁפָּט ('judgment') and עֵת ('time') are associated in 8.5, 6, in which Qoheleth speaks of the sage's ability to detect God's activity in the events that occur on earth and also humanity's distressing situation resulting from the divine control of such events. Again, there is a clear echo of 3.1, 17, in the phraseology of 8.6: 'because *to every business there is time and judgment*, therefore the misery of man is great' (כִּי לְכָל חֵפֶץ יֵשׁ עֵת וּמִשְׁפָּט כִּי רָעַת הָאָדָם רַבָּה עָלָיו).[44] This use of the term מִשְׁפָּט ('judgment') finds no parallel in 11.9. On the basis of this, and the other evidence adduced, it should therefore be considered as a gloss.

This consideration of the passage 11.8–12.8 has so far sought to demonstrate that God does not seek to judge those who make use of the material benefits they derive from life. The receipt of and ability to use these benefits are part of the gift of God and to that extent are determined by God. Nevertheless, the emphasis in this passage is on human rather than divine activity as the succession of imperatives in 11.9–12.1 suggests. This does not detract from Qoheleth's essentially deterministic worldview, for as I will argue in Chapter 7, the ability to act for oneself depends on God's authorization (√שׁלט) to do so, and even this limited area of free will is dependent on 'time'.

4. Conclusion

Although a certain amount of human free will is presupposed in the taking of pleasure, indicated by the legalistic use of √שׁלט to suggest God's acquiescence in such actions, and by the imperative forms that

---

Ecclesiastes, pp. 181, 184-85), fits neither the context, nor is it in keeping with the structure of the passage.

44. Fox, *Contradictions*, p. 247.

Qoheleth uses in his exhortations to the reader to enjoy life (cf. esp. 9.7-10; 11.9-10), the fact remains that human beings according to Qoheleth's worldview are entirely dependent on God for the finding of pleasure.[45]

First of all, humanity is reliant on God for the material goods from which pleasure may be derived (2.26; 5.18 [ET 19]; 6.2). Qoheleth speaks of pleasure in terms of eating and drinking (2.24; 3.13; 5.17 [ET 18]; 8.15; 9.7). It is also closely associated with material wealth (2.1-11; 5.17-19 [ET 18-20]; 10.19). Only God can provide these things: human efforts to acquire them are doomed to failure. Second, and more significantly, human beings are dependent on God for the *ability* to make use of the material wealth that they acquire (5.18 [ET 19]; 6.2). This is a fundamentally new idea in the Hebrew Bible. For whereas God is shown to bestow riches on the sage in Proverbs, the implications of God being responsible for the ability of the individual to make a choice as to whether such wealth is used points more strongly to a deterministic outlook on life.

It is perhaps too fine a distinction to make as to whether God 'gives' joy per se (2.26), thereby imposing it on human beings, or whether he is responsible simply for giving the ability to find joy in life (5.18 [ET 19]). Qoheleth seems to have viewed the two as identical. What is certain, however, is that the acquiescence of the deity is absolutely essential to human attempts to find happiness. Conversely, the absence of happiness is also attributable to the deity, who distributes his gifts in an inscrutable and apparently arbitrary fashion. One may acquire wealth, but not necessarily be permitted by God to enjoy it (2.26; 6.2). One may have many children and live to a great age and still find no pleasure in life. Such partial gift-giving may appear worse than no gift at all—as if the deity were playing a bad joke on the hapless recipient. Certainly, Qoheleth himself is affected by his contemplation of the unfortunate who does not find favour with God, and condemns his circumstances as 'an evil disease' (6.2). In this area, as in others, God's control over human life is absolute.

---

45. Crenshaw, *Old Testament Wisdom*, p. 136.

Chapter 7

QOHELETH AND THE PROBLEM OF FREE WILL

1. *Introduction*

In a recent study of the language of the book of Ecclesiastes, Seow has linked Qoheleth's usage of √שׁלט ('have power over') (particularly in 2.19; 5.18 [ET 19]; 6.2; 7.19) with those of Aramaic legal documents dating from the Persian period.[1] In such texts, the root frequently has a specialized legal/economic meaning, usually referring to the legal rights that an individual may be granted to impose taxes or to dispose of goods or slaves,[2] and a similar idea may indeed be discerned behind some of Qoheleth's uses of the root. However, Seow has cited this as evidence for a fourth century (or earlier) setting for the book, arguing that the technical sense of √שׁלט is no longer evident in texts dating from a time later than the Persian period—in contexts where one might have expected previously to find √שׁלט, one finds √רשׁה ('have power over', 'permit/be permitted') instead. This chapter will examine some of Seow's conclusions with regard to the date of the book, before considering some of the implications of the appearance of this specialized sense of the root in Ecclesiastes.

The legal/economic sense of √שׁלט is attested in Aramaic from the fifth century BCE onwards. As the Persian period progresses, this specialized application becomes more commonplace until the Hellenistic period when, in the words of Gropp, '...the meaning of *šalliṭ* is *increasingly restricted* [my italics] to the political sphere, with the

1.   Seow, 'Linguistic Evidence', pp. 653-54.
2.   Three apparent technical usages of √שׁלט also occur in biblical texts from the Persian period (Ezra 4.20; 7.24; Neh. 5.15). A list of extrabiblical occurences may be found in D.M. Gropp ('The Origin and Development of the Aramaic *Šalliṭ* Clause', *JNES* 52 [1993], pp. 31-36 [34 nn. 28, 29]) with additional citations by Seow ('Linguistic Evidence', p. 653 nn. 57, 59).

meaning "to rule, have dominion"; "ruler, commander"'.[3] It is important to note that Gropp does *not* claim that the technical sense of √שלט
fades completely either during or after the Hellenistic period. In fact, as
will be demonstrated presently, this specialized usage can be shown to
occur right up to the Mediaeval period and beyond.

2. *The* √שלט *in the Persian Period*

Seow presents a persuasive case on socioeconomic and linguistic
grounds for a *possible* Persian dating of Ecclesiastes, yet almost none of
the evidence that he produces can be said to rule out the possibility that
Qoheleth is a child of the Hellenistic period.[4] Seow's assertion that
Qoheleth uses √שלט in the same technical sense that is found in the
Persian period, and that this root is replaced in legal contexts during
and after the third century by √רשה, therefore takes on a heightened
significance.

Alongside occurrences in the books of Ezra and Nehemiah (Ezra
4.20; 7.24; Neh. 5.15), the legal sense of √שלט is attested in the Persian
period in the Aramaic Papyri from Elephantine (fifth century BCE)[5] and
in the Samaria Papyri (fourth century BCE).[6] Significantly, the latter
documents are dated to the very end of the Persian period; it would
seem reasonable to assume therefore that √שלט might retain a legal
sense at least into the early Hellenistic era. Unfortunately, the lingua
franca of this period for most legal documents was Greek and not

3.   Gropp, '*Šallīṭ* Clause', pp. 34-36.
4.   Seow, 'Socioeconomic Context', pp. 159-95.
5.   See Gropp ('*Šallīṭ* Clause', p. 31 n. 2) for a full bibliography. Among the
more recent material cited is E.Y. Kutscher, 'New Aramaic Texts', *JAOS* 74
(1954), pp. 233-48 (239); R. Yaron, 'Aramaic Marriage Contracts from Elephantine', *JSS* 3 (1958), pp. 9-10; 'Aramaic Deeds of Conveyance', *Bib* 41 (1960),
pp. 248-71; Y. Muffs, *Studies in the Aramaic Legal Papyri from Elephantine*
(Studia et Documenta ad Iura Orientis Antiqui Pertinenta, 8; Leiden: E.J. Brill,
1969), pp. 6 nn. 23 and 24, 39 n. 3, 41 n. 2, 134, 151 n. 3, 152-53, 176-78, 204, 206,
208.
6.   F.M. Cross, 'Samaria Papyrus 1: An Aramaic Slave Conveyance of 335
B.C.E. Found in the Wadi ed-Daliyeh', in *Nahman Avigad Volume* (ErIsr, 18;
Jerusalem, 1985), pp. 7-17; *idem*, 'A Report on the Samaria Papyri', in J.A.
Emerton (ed.), *Congress Volume, Jerusalem, 1986* (VTSup, 40; Leiden: E.J. Brill,
1988), pp. 17-26; Gropp also considers the use of √שלט in the Samaria papyri in
some detail ('*Šallīṭ* Clause', p. 32).

Aramaic.[7] It is correspondingly difficult to prove that the use of the technical sense of √שלט *in legal contracts* was discontinued in favour of √רשה before the mid-to-late third century date assigned to Ecclesiastes by most commentators.

3. The √שלט in the Hellenistic Period

1. The Book of Daniel

A close examination of the relevant texts in Daniel reveals several clear examples of the technical usage of √שלט. In 2.38, Daniel tells Nebuchadnezzar:

> Wheresoever humankind dwells, the beasts of the field and the birds of the heavens has *He* (i.e. God) *placed in your power and has given you right of disposal* (יהב בידך והשלטך) over them all.

One does not exercise *political* power over animals, but one may be granted *proprietorship*. The metaphor demands that √שלט be understood in its legal/economic sense. A parallel is made between the everyday world of business transactions and kingship, as if God had signed a deed giving Nebuchadnezzar an estate complete with its livestock, or the hunting and trapping rights over the whole earth.

In the same context, Rabinowitz has drawn attention to parallels between the legal terminology of papyrus Brooklyn 12 and the text of Dan. 4.14 (ET 17), 22 (ET 25), 29 (ET 32) stating that the formula used in the latter 'was adopted from the phraseology of the legal document which was current in his day'.[8] In these particular examples, the phrase in question reads: די שליט עליא במלכות אנושא ולמן די יצבא יתננה ('that the Most High rules in the kingdom of humankind, and gives it to whomsoever he will'). The context makes it clear that the term שליט ('rule') in these locations refers not merely to 'a generalized power' but

7.   J.J. Rabinowitz (*Jewish Law: Its Influence on the Development of Legal Institutions* [New York: Bloch, 1956], pp. 124-40), studying the Greek legal papyri from the Hellenistic period, appears to show that the successor to the classic Aramaic *šallīṭ* clause was an equivalent Greek *kyrieia* clause.

8.   Rabinowitz, *Jewish Law*, pp. 128-29 (cf. also pp. 131-33 for a similar usage of legal terminology in Dan. 4.31-32 [ET 34-35]). The full text of the document may be found in E.G. Kraeling, *The Brooklyn Museum Aramaic Papyri: New Documents of the Fifth Century B.C. from the Jewish Colony at Elephantine* (New Haven: Yale University Press, 1953), pp. 268-69.

to a legal 'right of disposal'. A modified version of this legal formula also occurs in Dan. 5.21.

2. *The Book of Ben Sira*

In his article on the legal use of √שלט, Gropp defines a *šallîṭ* clause as '...stating some legal right(s) in general terms which must be further specified by context. This specification is most unambiguously achieved by means of one or more complementary infinitives.'[9] This specific construction of √שלט + infinitive occurs not only in Eccl. 5.18 (ET 19); 6.2; 8.9, but also in Sir. 9.13. The expression, 'Keep far from a man with the power to kill (שלטון להרג), and you will not be worried by the fear of death...' seems to be a technical usage of the root: Ben Sira warns not against being the companion of a man psychologically able to kill, nor of a man with the money to hire assassins. Rather he warns against working for a powerful man with the *legal right* to put people to death if they displease him (cf. Prov. 23.1-2 for a similar thought).

Although √רשה ('permit') occurs in Sir. 3.22, the use of this root is by no means characteristic only of the Hellenistic period. The term רשיון ('permission') is attested in Ezra 3.7 (in which book √שלט, as we have seen, also retains its technical sense). Thus, there is no reason to think that √רשה is being used in Ben Sira in preference to the technical sense of √שלט. Humanity's access to different types of wisdom is the topic of discussion in this particular text, so that שהורשית ('has been permitted') in Sir. 3.22 cannot reasonably be construed in the sense of 'right of disposal'. The term נסתרות ('that which is hidden') to which it is in opposition, conveys not illegality, but impossibility. Hence, it would appear that √שלט retains its technical sense into the second century, and that √רשה in Ben Sira has much the same general meaning as in the Persian period.

3. *Later Texts*

While evidence from later writings shows that √רשה may sometimes be used in place of √שלט in legal contexts, the validity of these sources in dating Ecclesiastes to the Persian period is limited. The Murabbaʿat and Naḥal Ḥever documents, for example, date from the early second

---

9. Gropp, 'Šallîṭ Clause', p. 34, citing Muffs (*Studies in the Aramaic Legal Papyri*, p. 41 n. 2).

century CE. Likewise, the Nabataean tomb inscriptions utilizing √רשה are of late date, coming mainly from the first century CE.[10]

Significantly, the economic/legal sense of √שלט seems never to have died out entirely: a Syriac bill of sale dated 243 CE containing an elaborate *šallīṭ* clause remains extant.[11] This technical usage also appears in the Talmud. For example, *j. Naz.* 4.53b speaks of a woman having right of disposal over her husband's property (במשלמת על נכסיו ['(a case) in which she is guardian over his property']). Similarly, *j. Ket.* 9.33a concerns a woman authorized to manage her husband's property during his lifetime (נכסים שנשתלטה בהן). Both use √שלט in its legal/economic sense, specifically in the context of property (נכסים, 'property'), as in Eccl. 5.18 (ET 19) and 6.2, where people may be given authorization (√שלט) to make use of 'wealth and property' (ונכסים עשר).[12] Mediaeval Jewish deeds of conveyance also makes use of the *šallīṭ* clause, as Rabinowitz has demonstrated.[13]

4. Consequences for the Dating of Ecclesiastes

Qoheleth's use of the technical sense of √שלט finds several parallels in documents from the fifth and fourth centuries BCE, but this meaning of the root evidently survived throughout the Hellenistic period and well into the Christian era. Indeed, one might well argue that the figurative use of √שלט in Daniel, where the God issues property grants to favoured human subjects, has more in common with the thought of Qoheleth than does the purely literal usage of this root in the legal papyri of the Persian period, or in Ezra–Nehemiah. Qoheleth's use of √שלט cannot be used as evidence against a Hellenistic background, even if it does not preclude an earlier dating.

5. The Book of Ecclesiastes: Text and Context

Many commentators have argued that the catalogue of times in 3.1-8 represent Qoheleth's expression of the divinely determined nature not

10. The relevant literature is cited in full by Gropp ('*Šallīṭ* Clause', p. 34 nn. 28, 29).

11. J.A. Goldstein, 'The Syriac Bill of Sale from Dura-Europos', *JNES* 25 (1966), pp. 11-12.

12. Cf. the Yiddish proverb: 'The miser has no right of disposal (שליטה) over his possessions' cited by Gordis, *Koheleth*, p. 255.

13. Rabinowitz, *Jewish Law*, p. 132.

merely of human actions, but even of human thought and feeling.[14] A clear parallel therefore exists between Qoheleth and the Stoic school, who reformulated the work of earlier Greek philosophy in order to combine the concept of determinism with that of free will.[15] A similar outlook on the nature of existence, however, is not conclusive proof of cross fertilization. In fact, commentators have been hard pressed to find convincing evidence of specific Greek influence, preferring to ascribe similarities between Qoheleth and various Greek philosophies to a general Hellenistic *Zeitgeist*.[16]

Although Delitzsch saw evidence of determinism in Ecclesiastes, he nevertheless dated Qoheleth's work firmly in the Persian period, being followed in this position by Scott.[17] Thus, while commentators may differ as to the dating of Qoheleth's work, most accept that it betrays a belief in some form of determinism, even if many are wary of ascribing such an idea to the well-known catalogue of times in ch. 3.[18]

The single greatest problem associated with understanding 3.1-8 as a deterministic text, is that Qoheleth appears elsewhere to presuppose a certain amount of free will in human existence.[19] If all, including human thought is predetermined, there would appear to be little point in producing a work of wisdom that offers advice on how to approach life. Qoheleth regularly uses the imperative form in his work (4.17 [ET 5.1]; 5.2 [ET 1], 4 [ET 3], 6-8 [ET 5-7]; 7.9, 10, 13, 14, 16-18, 21; 8.3; 9.7-10; 10.4, 20; 11.1, 2, 6, 9, 10; 12.1, 13): again, a rather futile exercise if we have no control over our actions.

The problem of free will and how such an idea might be reconciled with those texts in Ecclesiastes that appear to have deterministic tendencies is fundamental to our understanding of Qoheleth's worldview. Nevertheless, no work of which I am aware has attempted to consider the one in the light of the other. The tendency of commentators has been either to ignore the problem completely, or to argue that

---

14. Delitzsch, *Ecclesiastes*, pp. 255-59; Scott, *Proverbs Ecclesiastes*, pp. 220-21; Fox, *Contradictions*, p. 192.

15. Among those who have posited direct Stoic influence on Qoheleth's work are Tyler (*Ecclesiastes*, pp. 10-18); Gammie ('Stoicism and Anti-Stoicism in Qoheleth', pp. 169-87).

16. Murphy, *Ecclesiastes*, p. xlv.

17. Delitzsch, *Ecclesiastes*, p. 214.

18. Whybray, *Ecclesiastes* [NCBC], p. 67.

19. Podechard, *L'Ecclésiaste*, p. 192; Blenkinsopp, 'Ecclesiastes 3.1-15', p. 62.

contradictions in Qoheleth's work are a deliberate reflection of the contradictory nature of life.[20]

1. *Humanity and God (Ecclesiastes 5.18; 6.2; 2.19)*

Seow is the latest of a long line of commentators who have pointed to the strongly Aramaizing tendency of the Hebrew in the book of Ecclesiastes.[21] If Qoheleth's use of √שׁלט can be linked to its legal/economic sense of 'delegated authority', 'right of disposal' or 'proprietorship' in Aramaic texts, then one of the ways in which the idea of free will can be combined with a concept of determinism becomes evident. The context in which Qoheleth uses √שׁלט usually makes it clear that he is speaking of some kind of delegated authority: indeed, it is a sine qua non in the argument of many commentators.

In 5.18 and 6.2 God is depicted as a divine ruler who grants to certain of his human subjects 'wealth and riches and authorization to eat of them', refusing this same authorization to others. Ultimately the picture drawn of God and his relationship with humanity is very similar to that of these Aramaic texts in which the שׁליט ('proprietor') has authorization from above to dispose of (other people's) goods. In this instance, the goods, described as 'wealth and riches' (עשׁר ונכסים—5.18; 6.2) are part of the gift of God. That is to say, they are not earned but apportioned by God and the individual has no right to retain the goods or to treat them as his without the deity's authorization to do so. Indeed, the parallel becomes still closer when one considers passages such as 2.26:

> God gives wisdom, knowledge and joy to the one who pleases him, while to the sinner is given toil: to gather and to heap up and to give to one who pleases God.

The riches and wealth 'given' by God then may come indirectly through another's labour.[22]

---

20. So Delitzsch (*Ecclesiastes*, p. 183) and Fox (*Contradictions*, pp. 19-28).

21. Seow, 'Linguistic Evidence', p. 650. On this basis, others have argued that the Hebrew of Ecclesiastes represents a translation of an originally Aramaic text (F.C. Burkitt, 'Is Ecclesiastes a Translation?', *JTS* 23 [1921–22], pp. 22-27; F. Zimmerman, 'The Aramaic Provenance of Qohelet', *JQR* 36 [1945–46], pp. 17-45; C.C. Torrey, 'The Question of the Original Language of Qohelet', *JQR* 39 [1948–49], pp. 151-60; Ginsberg, *Studies in Koheleth*, pp. 16-39).

22. Most commentators understand 2.26 in the sense that the 'sinner' has these activities inflicted on him as a punishment. Gordis is alone in claiming that 'the

By way of contrast, the situation of the sinner in 2.26 is remarkably similar to that of the one in 6.2 'to whom God grants wealth, riches and substance...but not given him authority to eat of these things: instead, a stranger eats of them'. The picture of God that begins to emerge is of a capricious king whose actions cannot be determined by his subjects.[23] The terms טוב לפני האלהים ('good before God') and חוטא ('sinner'), which are devoid of moral content but which provide the reasons for some of his actions vis-à-vis his subjects only reinforce this view.[24]

The use of √שלט in 2.19 remains close to the parallel usage in Aramaic documentation. There the term is specifically used of the inheritance of Qoheleth's wealth by another. A question mark remains over the source of the authorization that √שלט denotes here. It may simply refer to the right of disposal given by (earthly) legal authorities to Qoheleth's heir. Yet Qoheleth himself seems unaware of who is to inherit (ומי יודע החכם יהיה או סכל ['and who knows whether he will be wise or foolish']): in this case the hand of the inscrutable deity would seem once more to be at work.[25]

In a world in which all, or nearly all, is predetermined, the meaning that √שלט has here of authority (delegated by God) to act in some way makes it equivalent to a limited form of free will.[26] It is significant that here the term √שלט is used in the context of 'eating' or utilizing the material benefits that life has to offer, for this one area in which Qoheleth uses imperative forms of the verb (9.7, 8, 9; 11.9, 10).[27]

man who misses God's purpose, the enjoyment of life, is a sinner (*Koheleth*, p. 227). In other words, Gordis limits God's determinism by claiming that 'to gather and to heap up' is the sin itself rather than the consequence.

23. Crenshaw comments on the 'element of arbitrariness' in God's rule and the inability of human beings to perceive God's actions in the present or future. Both ideas, in his opinion, are suggestive of determinism (*Old Testament Wisdom*, p. 136).

24. Hertzberg, *Prediger*, pp. 82-83; Ginsberg, 'The Structure and Contents of the Book of Koheleth', p. 139; Zimmerli, *Prediger*, pp. 161-62. The idea that both terms are devoid of moral content is now generally accepted.

25. Fox, *Contradictions*, p. 186.

26. Cf. Murphy on 5.18; 6.2 who emphasizes the role of the deity. The situation in which שליט is not given to the rich person is seen as an active intervention by God ('[the] rich person...is prevented by God from enjoying his riches' [*Ecclesiastes*, p. 53]).

27. Whybray sees a sevenfold 'joy' leitmotiv in which emphasis increases with each new affirmation of the worth of joy ('Preacher of Joy', pp. 87-88). Although

These, as I have pointed out, are indicative of the idea that human beings have a degree of control over their actions. One may indeed be granted שִׁלְטוֹן ('authority') to enjoy life by God, but the individual may not exercise that authority: the aim of Qoheleth's investigation is to exploit those areas in which human beings are granted the power to act independently, 'to see what is that good which humanity should do under the heavens' (2.3).[28]

2. *Misuse of Free Will (Ecclesiastes 8.9-13)*

The use of √שלט is not restricted to the idea of having 'right of disposal' over material goods however. Just as in the Aramaic texts that form the background to Qoheleth's thought (cf. esp. the Samaria Papyri), one may have 'right of disposal' over other people.

Qoheleth also speaks of 'a time in which one person has authority over another to his hurt'. The meaning of the ambiguous לְרַע לוֹ ('to his hurt') has sometimes been understood to be that those who have power may injure themselves (so Symmachus, εἰς κακὸν ἑαυτοῦ and AV, 'to his own hurt', perhaps influenced by the similar idiom לְרָעָתוֹ ['to their own hurt'] in 5.12 [ET 13]). However, 8.9 may also be construed in the sense that one person has power over another to the detriment of the inferior party. This rendering is supported by the LXX, Peshitta, Vulgate and Targum as well as the vast majority of modern translations (cf. esp. RSV, 'man lords it over man to his hurt').[29]

Two things should be noted about this verse. The word עֵת '(appointed) time' is generally used in Ecclesiastes to denote those events that are determined by God (cf. esp. 9.11, 12 in which the net cast over humanity is a divine weapon), so that God is ultimately the source of the authority that is enjoyed by the subject of this verse over his fellow. The second is that this is most likely a *šallīṭ* clause as defined by Gropp, with √שלט followed by an infinitive stating what legal powers the subject enjoys. The elision of הֵ on a hiphil infinitive construct after a preposition is not uncommon in the Hebrew Bible

the ability to enjoy life lies in God's gift (p. 89), the responsibility lies with human beings to make use of this ability.

28. In fact, the objective of Qoheleth's search is described in several different ways, connected in particular with finding 'the work which is done under the sun' or 'the work of God', a necessary step before discovering the relevance of his findings for human beings.

29. The same meaning is upheld by almost all commentators.

(GKC §53q). In this case, one person apparently has the legal right to harm another (לרע לו).

In this instance, the subject which Qoheleth is probing is one of theodicy.[30] In a predetermined world, how can wickedness and evil be explained? To follow the implications of determinism to its logical conclusion would be to say that God is not merely directly responsible for human wickedness, but actually acts wickedly himself through his creatures. Unconventional as his thought sometimes is, Qoheleth's Jewish background militates against such an idea.

Qoheleth's solution to this problem, and it is, he realizes, a partial one, is that a person may be granted licence (שׁלט√) by God to dominate his fellows. This licence empowers the individual to act to the detriment of his fellow. It does not follow that God wishes or intends wickedness: a choice is presented to humanity and evil chosen rather than good. This is the negative side to free will. The deterministic God is not therefore directly the author of wickedness but he does bear a certain degree of responsibility in that שׁלטון ('authority', 'licence') is granted to those who misuse it.

This is the idea explored in the succeeding verses,

ובשׁן ראיתי רשׁעים קרבים ובאים מקומסקדושׁ יהלכו וישׁתבחו בעיר אשׁר
כן עשׂו

and so I saw the wicked draw near and approach the place of the holy, walk about and boast in the city that they had done right (Driver's emended text: 8.10.[31]

The wicked may indeed boast that their actions are *morally right*, or at least 'legal', because the deterministic God has shown his approval by allowing them to be carried out in the first place.[32] This problem of

---

30. Fox, *Contradictions*, p. 121.

31. The emendations of G.R. Driver ('Problems and Solutions', *VT* 4 [1954], pp. 230-31) to the MT's ובכן ראיתי רשׁעים קברים ובאו וממקום קדושׁ יהלכו וישׁתכחו בעיר אשׁר כן עשׂו 'so I saw the wicked buried, who had come and gone from the place of the holy, and they were forgotten in the city where they had done so', partially dependent on an earlier suggestion by Burkitt ('Is Ecclesiastes a Translation?', pp. 25-26), are accepted by most commentators, though Gordis (*Koheleth*, p. 295); Lohfink (*Kohelet*, p. 62), followed by Murphy (*Ecclesiastes*, p. 79) retain the MT's קברים, 'buried'.

32. Cf. 9.7, 'Go, eat you bread with pleasure...for God has already approved your works'. In Fox's words on this verse, 'If you are given the opportunity to enjoy life, that is in itself evidence that God has approved of the pleasurable

theodicy is explored further in the next verse: 'because sentence against an evil act is not carried out speedily, the mind of humanity is fully made up to do evil'.[33] The fact that evil may be judged is a logical corollary of Qoheleth's belief that evil stems from a misuse of שׁלטון rather than from actions directly determined by the deity. However, Qoheleth is perplexed by the fact that God appears not to judge the wicked nor to strip them of their authority to act as they do. It is this divine inaction that the wicked are able to construe as divine approval, giving fresh encouragement to further evil.

3. *Limitations of Free Will: Death (Ecclesiastes 8.8)*

Qoheleth's deterministic beliefs naturally mean that free will is limited: while much in life is determined by God, there are some things in life over which human beings are allowed no control under any circumstances. The example par excellence of this is death: 'no one has authorization (שׁליט) over the breath of life to retain the breath of life, no one has authority (שׁלטון) over the day of death'.[34] Again, the final arbiter of life and death is God (11.5; 12.7) and he alone determines the moment at which the life breath passes from the body and returns to its maker.

Death is associated with עת ('appointed time') in the catalogue of divinely ordained times which limit and control human life (3.2), but Qoheleth also speaks of the possibility of dying 'before your time' (בלא עתך—7.17). The implication of this verse is that God may alter a previously appointed time as a response to the 'overly foolish' or 'overly wicked' behaviour of the individual.[35] Commentators have generally been puzzled by the advice not to be 'overly wicked'. Is Qoheleth advising people to be somewhat wicked? The general consensus is that Qoheleth is a realist who recognizes that everyone does wrong at some point: he advises his reader not to abandon himself utterly to such practices.

---

activities you undertake' (*Contradictions*, p. 259). The same view, however, equally applies to wickedness: the fact that God allows the opportunity for it to be committed, means that God has approved it. The wicked have 'done right'.

33. Fox in particular, emphasizes God's apparent injustice in this verse, 'Since the punishment which Qoheleth has in mind is a divinely imposed death sentence, delaying punishment is tantamount to not carrying it out' (*Contradictions*, p. 249).

34. Murphy suggests the divinely determined nature of death in this verse, alluding to 3.2 'a time to give birth, a time to die' (*Ecclesiastes*, p. 84).

35. Strange, 'The Question of Moderation in Eccl 7:15-18', p. 87.

The meaning of √שלט which has been established in 8.9 and its implications for the interpretation of the succeeding verses again offers some explanation of this difficult passage. Wickedness is only possible as a result of the use/misuse of divinely granted שלטון, and may apparently go unpunished in the short term. The thrust of 7.17 would suggest that in the case of a major act of wickedness, God will intervene with the ultimate sanction: the punishment of death in this verse is aimed at those who are *extreme* in their behaviour.[36] Although God may be rebuked for being tardy in his punishment of the wicked, Qoheleth clearly does believe in some form of judgment.[37]

4. *The King as Supreme Expression of Free Will (Ecclesiastes 8.2-7; 10.5)*

Kings, according to Qoheleth, also have שלטון. This is a significant remark because the king normally grants authority: he does not receive it. Should such a use of the term שלטון therefore be understood in a non-legal sense? This may be possible, but the fact that elsewhere Qoheleth uses the term כח for 'power' or 'force' (4.1), would appear to suggest that the idea behind the term שלטון in this particular context would again be one of authority delegated to the king by God.

The phraseology of 8.2

אני פי מלך שמור ועל דברת שבועת אלהים

> I counsel you to obey the king's command and that in respect of the oath of God

has again been something of a puzzle for commentators.[38] The use of √שלט by Qoheleth as signifying authority delegated by God, 'free will'

36. Fox sees the expression 'do not be very wicked' not as recommending moderate wickedness but as a concession to human weakness (*Contradictions*, pp. 235-36).

37. Fredericks defends the idea that Qoheleth has a traditional conception of divine retribution ('Life's Storms', p. 101).

38. Interpreters are divided as to whether the phrase שבועה אלהים 'oath of God' is a subjective or objective genitive. Hertzberg understands the genitive as subjective, referring to God's oath concerning kingship (*Prediger*, p. 143), along with Tyler (*Ecclesiastes*, p. 101). Plumptre (*Ecclesiastes*, p. 175), Barton (*Ecclesiastes*, p. 149), Podechard (*L'Ecclésiaste*, p. 391) and most subsequent commentators understand the genitive as objective referring to a human oath of loyalty to the king with God invoked as a witness (Gordis, *Koheleth*, p. 288; Scott, *Proverbs Ecclesiastes*, p. 240; Galling, *Prediger*, p. 110; Lauha, *Kohelet*, p. 148).

as it were, lends substance to the arguments of those commentators who have in the past suggested that the oath mentioned here is God's oath concerning kingship and not a human oath of loyalty to the king. The way in which Qoheleth goes on to describe the king in 8.3 elucidates the idea of שלטון as free will:

כל אשר יחפץ יעשה באשר דבר מלך שלטון

> he does what he chooses, for where the word of the king is, there is authority

The statement that the king 'does what he chooses' is a remarkable one in the light of Qoheleth's deterministic philosophy, for it suggests that the king enjoys a special relationship with God, acting as the deity's viceregent (cf. Ps. 2.7; Dan. 4.14 [ET 17], 22 [ET 25], 29 [ET 32]; 5.21).[39]

The suggestion that שלטון may retain its legal sense of (delegated) authority is lent support by the work of A. Hurvitz who has shown that the expression כל אשר חפץ עשה ('he has done what he chose'/'he may do what he chooses') is used in a distinct legal sense.[40] It would appear then, that Qoheleth is being consistent in his usage of the technical legal sense of שלט√ as referring to 'authorization'. In this case, however, the extent of the legal authority denoted by שלט√ is not defined by the use of one or more infinitives. This is replaced by the legal phrase כל אשר יחפץ יעשה ('he does what he chooses') to denote total freedom of action. Where most of humankind is constricted by the actions which God has determined for them (לכל זמן ועת לכל חפץ תחת השמים [to everything there is a season, a time for every business under heaven]— 3.1), the king is given legal authority to act as he pleases (כל אשר יחפץ יעשה—8.3). He is, as it were, the supreme embodiment of free will. The fact that the king has such authority from God also makes the command of the king almost a *commandment*.[41]

In 10.5-7 Qoheleth goes on to consider some of the practical consequences of שלטון allotted to rulers by God. He observes 'an error

---

39. Hertzberg points to parallels in 2 Sam. 7.14; Pss. 2.7; 20; 21; 45 *et al.* (*Prediger*, p. 143) which suggest the special status of the king vis-à-vis God.

40. A. Hurvitz, 'The History of a Legal Formula: *kōl 'ăšer ḥāpēṣ 'āśāh* (Psalms CXV 3, CXXXV 6)', *VT* 32 (1982), pp. 257-67.

41. Hertzberg understands God's oath having given the king almost a semi-divine status: 'Gott hat dem König geschworen…, er ist persona sacra, "von Gottes Gnaden"' (*Prediger*, p. 143).

which goes forth from the ruler (שׁליט)'. Again, the term שׁגגה ('error') implies free will, for it suggests that the ruler has the power not to act in the negative way which he does.[42] Just as wickedness and evil may be blamed on a misuse of שׁלטון granted by God, inequity in life may to some extent be assigned to the wrong application of שׁלטון by the ruler to whom God gives it. This is not to undermine the often ambivalent nature of God towards the individual: many passages in Ecclesiastes assert such a concept (2.26; 5.19 [ET 18]; 6.2; 7.14, 26; 9.1). However, the misuse of שׁלטון or free will accounts for many of the problems observed by Qoheleth in life.

Qoheleth apparently dwells on this problem in 10.16-17, although √שׁלט itself does not appear. The licence enjoyed by the king in v. 16 is wrongly extended to the court because the king is too weak to enforce proper rule as God's subordinate: his princes 'eat in the morning'. By contrast the king who is brought up to rule in v. 17, rules wisely: the course of events determined by God is maintained.[43] The princes eat בעת, which on one level means 'at the appropriate time', but also has deterministic nuances. Kings as divine agents have an obligation to rule as God envisions, despite the שׁלטון granted to them.

5. *Qoheleth as King (Ecclesiastes 1.12–2.12)*

Qoheleth too proclaims himself as a king (1.12). Hitherto, his reason for so doing has been considered in the light of the material goods which he enjoys in the course of his investigation into existence.[44] A king has access to all possible pleasures and comforts in life. The so-called 'Solomonic identity' may or may not be incidental, but what is certain

---

42. Whitley is probably correct in understanding ב in כשׁגגה שׁיצא מלפני השׁליט as asseverative: 'Indeed it is an error which goes forth from the ruler', rather than comparative (*Koheleth*, p. 85).

43. Glasser draws a parallel between the situation in 10.16 and the repercussions for a land in which the powerful are not answerable to the king in Eccl. 3.16 and 5.7-11 (*Qohelet*, p. 158). If correct, this is one more illustration of wickedness which may be attributed to a human misuse of שׁלטון rather than divine injustice.

44. Kidner, *A Time to Mourn*, p. 28; Crenshaw also cites the tradition of kings dispensing wisdom as a factor in Qoheleth's adoption of a royal persona (*Ecclesiastes*, p. 70). E. Jones suggests that the literary device of the Solomonic persona 'was really a means of expressing Qohelet's conviction that neither wealth nor wisdom provided the clue to the final meaning of life' (*Proverbs and Ecclesiastes* [London: SCM Press, 1961], p. 282).

is that Qoheleth claims to have acquired more wisdom and more material possessions 'than all who were before me in Jerusalem (1.16; 2.7, 9)'.[45]

As I have argued elsewhere, the expression לִפְנֵי הָיָה ('to be before') is attested in the Hebrew Bible in connection with kingship as an idiom meaning 'to be subject to' (1 Sam. 19.7; 29.8). Qoheleth therefore appears to be claiming not that he has become wiser and wealthier than all his royal predecessors (assuming that Qoheleth = Solomon, almost all interpreters have commented on the strangeness of this remark, since only David ruled in Jerusalem before Solomon), but that he has become wiser and wealthier than any of his subjects.[46] Qoheleth is ideally placed in the here and now to carry out his task of investigating existence, but his role as king rather than subject gives him an extra advantage: the one that is all important for a determinist—he is free to carry out his search without divine interference.[47]

The reason for Qoheleth's adoption of a kingly persona therefore is not simply that a king enjoys access to material wealth. Any wealthy person can replicate Qoheleth's experiment by surrendering themselves to a life of pleasure. Indeed, Ginsberg argues that מֶלֶךְ in 1.12 and 2.12 might just as well be, and indeed should be, repointed as מֹלֵךְ 'land-owner'.[48] It is that the king has שָׁלְטוֹן—authority to act on his own initiative rather than being subject to the deterministic force that appears to control the life of the individual. As a free agent, only a king is fully qualified to investigate existence: Qoheleth's qualifications for the search are not merely wisdom and wealth, but wisdom, wealth and *kingship*. That is to say, the finances to allow access to material things, the wisdom to distinguish profitable from profitless activities and the freedom from divine interference to conceive and carry out the search for what is good.

5. *Conclusion*

Although questions remain about Qoheleth's worldview, his coherent use of שׁלט√ and the implied parallel between God and a human king

---

45. Emending עַל יְרוּשָׁלַם in 1.16 to בִּירוּשָׁלַם as in 2.7, 9, a reading attested by all the Versions and many MSS.

46. Rudman, 'Qohelet's Use of לִפְנֵי', pp. 143-50.

47. Murphy comments on the strangeness of the fact that Qoheleth does not mention his own 'kingly' status in 8.2-5 (*Ecclesiastes*, p. 83).

48. Ginsberg, *Studies in Koheleth*, pp. 12-15.

whose commands have the force of law, but who grants certain sub-
ordinates authority to act on their own initiative is a sophisticated and
relatively successful attempt to explain the problems of human wickedness and social inequality in terms of determinism. It also explains the
reasons why Qoheleth portrays himself as a king, why the attainment of
wisdom is necessary, and why Qoheleth can advise his audience to
pursue certain courses of action when he apparently believes that God
determines all or most of the events making up existence. The pre-
supposition to all of these problems is that God has apportioned some
individual שׁלטון, which gives him the ability to act on his own authority. On another level, the apportionment or not of שׁלטון (cf. 5.18
[ET 19] and 6.2) is another instance of the inscrutable nature of God's
gifts to humanity, underlining their dependence on the deity for
everything.

Seow's conclusion as to the chronological distribution of √שׁלט in
this legal/economic sense requires some qualification, however. Linguistic usage is highly subjective, both from the point of view of the
speaker and that of the interpreter, but it would seem that even in the
third century BCE, √שׁלט could still retain the sense of 'right of disposal', 'delegated authority' or 'proprietorship' which it had in the
Persian period, and that in Hebrew this sense could not be applied to
√רשׁה at that time, even though it may be true that this root occurs in
some texts of the very late Hellenistic period (i.e. the Christian era)
where we should expect to see √שׁלט. On linguistic grounds at least, the
dating of the book of Ecclesiastes remains as problematic as ever, and
Qoheleth's use of √שׁלט can be reconciled with a dating of that work to
the third century BCE.

Chapter 8

DETERMINISM IN EARLY JEWISH LITERATURE

1. *Introduction*

How does Qoheleth's conception of determinism relate to his biblical background? The determinism in the catalogue of times and seasons does, as has been pointed out, have parallels in the Hebrew Bible. The Psalmist states concerning his relationship with God in 31.15, 'My times are in your power' (עתתי בידך) in the sense that God is able to determine what happens to the Psalmist and to rescue him from his enemies if he so desires.[1] This position, however, is not far removed from the traditional view of God in the Hebrew Bible who intervenes in history to rescue or punish Israel, the community, or the individual. Such activity, though it may be called 'Providential' is certainly far from deterministic.[2]

Before continuing further, it would be as well to redefine the criteria by which one may properly call a particular view of the world deterministic. Determinism is the belief that some outside force (usually God) controls the thoughts and actions of the individual and thereby intervenes in one's life not merely on a regular basis, but constantly. This intervention must be true of all individuals, so that God can be said to control the workings of the world down to its smallest details. A limited amount of free will may be presupposed (particularly in the moral/ethical sphere) but generally the room for humanity having control over their own impulses may be said to be severely restricted.

However, it is clear that 'deterministic' is a term that is applied to Ecclesiastes by some commentators in a very loose sense. For example,

1. Fox, *Contradictions*, p. 195; Murphy, *Ecclesiastes*, p. 33.
2. Whybray (*Ecclesiastes* [NCBC], p. 66) points out Qoheleth's negative view of human freedom as contrary to conventional wisdom. This, in fact, is true of the Hebrew Bible generally.

Blenkinsopp argues that Qoheleth is a determinist, yet is reluctant to see the catalogue of seasons as asserting this idea because of the extent to which this would subordinate human free will to that of the deity. For him, as indeed for Whybray, Qoheleth's determinism means that events are 'predisposed' to happen rather than preordained.[3] Most recently, this position has also been echoed by de Jong, who, when he states that 'God acts deterministically' in Ecclesiastes, means by this statement that the deity acts 'according to non-moral standards'.[4]

The rationale for de Jong's article is to demonstrate that the God of Qoheleth is '...the same as the God of Abraham, Isaac and Jacob', and by defining the concept of determinism so loosely (that is, by saying that it refers to God's action outside the narrow bounds of reward–retribution imposed by the sages), he naturally finds many parallels within the Hebrew Bible (Prov. 16.1, 4, 9, 33; 18.22; 20.24; 21.1, 31; Job 1.21; 2.10; 3.23; 9.17-20, 22-24, 28-31; 10.3, 15; 12.4, 6, 16-25; 16.7-17; 19.6; 21.7-9; 23.13-17; 24.1, 12; 27.2; 30.20-23; 33.9-11).[5] Relatively few of these passages can be said to be deterministic in the truest sense of the word (Prov. 16.1, 4; 20.24), with God controlling the thoughts and actions of the individual: most simply contain the idea of God's inscrutability, or of God controlling the outcome of one's actions, or the events that happen in one's life. This is not determinism, but God acting in a way that is similar to an impersonal Fate. While this idea is evident in Ecclesiastes, it is important to distinguish between God as 'Fate', and God as a deterministic force in existence.

An example of something approaching determinism in the Hebrew Bible may be found in Exod. 7.2-3, where God states to Moses:

> You shall speak everything which I command you and Aaron your brother shall speak to Pharaoh, that he shall send the Israelites out of his land. Then I will harden Pharaoh's heart and multiply my signs and wonders in the land of Egypt.

Thus God is shown to control Pharaoh's thoughts and actions in this particular instance in order to fulfill a wider plan. However, this idea seems more designed to provide an explanation for Pharaoh's continuing (and successful) resistance to the God of Israel in the narrative rather than genuinely to express a deterministic worldview (cf. Gen.

---

3. Whybray, *Ecclesiastes*, p. 66; Blenkinsopp, 'Ecclesiastes 3.1-15', pp. 61-63.
4. De Jong, 'God in the Book of Qohelet', p. 156.
5. De Jong, 'God in the Book of Qohelet', pp. 154, 166.

20.6). In 2 Sam. 24.1-10, we find a story in which God incites David to sin by making a census and then punishes Israel for this act.[6] An example of near-determinism may be seen in the story behind Ahab's decision to fight at Ramoth-Gilead in 1 Kgs 22.20-23 in which Yahweh allows a 'lying spirit' to speak through Ahab's prophets in order that the king should go to his death. This however, is a rather indirect form of determinism (indeed Ahab's free will is presupposed in the necessity for Yahweh to go to such lengths to ensure his death). Other texts in the Hebrew Bible can be said to have a quasi-deterministic element to them. For example, in Ps. 139.16, the Psalmist states: 'Your eyes saw my limbs unformed in the womb, and in thy book they are all recorded; day by day they were fashioned, not one of them was late in growing' (NEB translation). A rather more overt example may be found in the call narrative of Jeremiah (Jer. 1.4-10).

In general, however, these texts seem to be the exceptions that prove the indeterministic rule. Generally speaking, the Hebrew Bible cannot be said to advance a concerted idea of determinism. The indeterminacy of events is captured in particular by von Rad when he cites Jer. 18.7-10:[7]

> Sometimes I threaten a nation or a kingdom, to uproot it and demolish it and destroy it; but if the nation which I threaten turns from its wicked-ness, then I shall repent of the evil which I have decreed for it. Some-times I promise a nation or a kingdom, to build it and plant it; but if it does something that displeases me and does not heed my words, then I repent of the good which I had promised to it.

This is the very opposite of determinism, for here it is God's activity which is determined by the deeds of humanity and not vice versa. Noth-ing is preordained. No decision of God is irrevocable. Everything depends on the decisions that free human beings make in the present. This position is echoed in numerous texts in the Hebrew Bible (e.g. Judg. 2.11-19; 2 Chron. 34.11-13; Jon. 2.10–4.2).

Despite the general indeterminacy of the Hebrew Bible, it is possible to say that there may be links between Ecclesiastes and its biblical background as regards the concept of a deterministic God. More likely, however, is a connection with the literature of the Hellenistic period,

---

6.   Cited along with Exod. 11.10 by A.A. Di Lella, 'Wisdom of Ben Sira', *ABD*, VI, p. 942.

7.   Von Rad, *Wisdom in Israel*, p. 270.

which shows a more overt interest in the idea of determinism than the older biblical texts.[8] Some of these later writings contain close parallels of language and thought to the work of Qoheleth.

2. *Text and Context*

1. *The Book of Daniel*

A few similarities between the thought of Qoheleth and that of the author of the book of Daniel have already been mentioned in Chapter 7. On the one hand, the author of Daniel and Qoheleth both use שׁלט√ ('have authority over') in its technical legal sense, which is characteristic of earlier periods. However, the usage of both is differentiated from that of say, the authors of Ezra–Nehemiah, by the metaphorical sense in which the root is employed: God in these later texts, is seen as the supreme holder of שׁליט ('authority') and dispenses it at will to his favoured human subjects. Moreover, Eccl. 4.13-16 appears to make use of the court story genre in much the same way as the author of Daniel.[9] This need not mean that Qoheleth was actually familiar with the book of Daniel. It would, however, appear to suggest that there is a common background to both.

The idea of 'time' also appears in Daniel in its deterministic sense. Thus in 2.21, Daniel praises God, saying 'He changes times and seasons (והוא מהשנא עדניא וזמניא), deposes kings and sets up kings'.[10] This is an idea that is quite similar to the thought of Qoheleth: indeed, the terms used in this verse, זמן ('season') and עדן ('time'), are direct Aramaic parallels to the terms זמן ('season') and עת ('time') which Qoheleth uses together in 3.1.

The same idea of determinism underlies Apocalyptic literature, and so it should come as no surprise to find similar uses of the term עדן in the sense of a time appointed by God in the later portions of the book of Daniel. Thus, in 7.12 Daniel states that subsequent to the stripping of power from three of the four beasts which appear in 7.4-7 'their lives

---

8. Von Rad (*Wisdom in Israel*, p. 264) also picks up on the sudden increase of the usage of the term עת in both Ecclesiastes and Ben Sira. Deterministic texts cited by von Rad include Ben Sira (c. 180 BCE), Daniel (c. 250–160 BCE), Judith (late second century BCE).

9. Rudman, 'A Contextual Reading of Ecclesiastes 4:13-16', pp. 61-63, 65-69, 72.

10. Von Rad, *Wisdom in Israel*, p. 268.

were prolonged until a season and a time (עַד זְמַן וְעִדָּן)'. At the appropriate preordained moment in history, God will crush the enemies of the saints. Likewise, the fourth beast is permitted by God in 7.22 to have dominion over the earth 'until the ancient of days came...and the appointed season came that the saints possessed the kingdom (וְזִמְנָא מְטָה מַלְכוּתָא הֶחֱסִנוּ קַדִּישִׁין)'.

Thus, there are similarities between the author of Daniel's conception of time and that of Qoheleth. The most striking is in the use of the terms עִדָּן or זְמַן for a divinely appointed time, which is indicative of a deterministic worldview. In this respect, Qoheleth would appear to be indebted for the idea of determinism to his Hebraic background. However, it should be noted that the determinism of Daniel (and indeed of the Apocalyptic literature as a whole) is largely a global phenomenon. God determines the rise and fall of kings and empires, but relatively little interest is shown in smaller events applicable to the life of the individual such as we find in Ecclesiastes.

2. *Apocalyptic Literature*

As has been suggested already, the concept of determinism is most often associated with Apocalyptic literature, and it is for this reason that von Rad suggests that the roots of such literature lie ultimately in Wisdom (of the Mantic variety), rather than in prophetic eschatology.[11] This position has found partial support among scholars but remains controversial.[12]

God's foreknowledge of earthly events, which provides the very basis for apocalyptic literature, is asserted in a number of texts.[13] Thus,

---

11. Von Rad, *Wisdom in Israel*, p. 277.

12. H.-P. Müller, 'Mantische Weisheit und Apocalyptik', in *Congress Volume, Uppsala, 1971* (VTSup, 22; Leiden: E.J. Brill, 1972), pp. 271-80; M.E. Stone, 'Lists of Revealed Things in the Apocalyptic Literature', in F.M. Cross *et al.* (eds.), *Magnalia Dei: The Mighty Acts of God* (Garden City, NY: Doubleday, 1976), pp. 414-52; J.J. Collins, 'Cosmos and Salvation: Jewish Wisdom and Apocalyptic in the Hellenistic Age', *HR* 17 (1977), pp. 121-42; K.J.A. Larkin, *The Eschatology of Second Zechariah: A Study in the Formation of a Mantological Wisdom Anthology* (Kampen: Kok, 1996), pp. 248-53; M.A. Knibb, '"You are indeed wiser than Daniel': Reflections on the Character of the Book of Daniel', in A.S. van der Woude (ed.), *The Book of Daniel in the Light of New Findings* (BETL, 106; Leuven: Leuven University Press/Peeters, 1993), pp. 399-411.

13. A. Yarbro Collins (ed.) (*Early Christian Apocalypticism* [Semeia, 36; Decatur: Scholars Press, 1986], p. 7) defines apocalyptic as 'a revelation...mediated

in *Ass. Mos.* 12.4; *1 En.* 39.11, one reads that God has foreseen everything that will happen in the world. Several Qumran texts also express this idea (1QS 3-4; CD 2.3-10; 1QH 1.7-8, 23-25; 4Q180 1; 1QpHab 7).[14] Implicit in this idea of divine foreknowledge of earthly events is that of determinism, since these events must be fixed in order to be foreseen. From this must arise the question of what is the predetermining factor at work in human history. Von Rad, on the basis of *1 Enoch* 85–90, claims that this is God himself.[15]

In the book of *Jubilees*, God shows to Moses all of past and present history (1.4), which is recorded on tablets stretching from the moment of creation to the day of the new creation (1.29). Even relatively small details in the lives of the patriarchs are preordained: the giving of the name Isaac (16.3) and Isaac's curse on the Philistines (24.33). Likewise, Isaac's son Jacob read from the heavenly tablets of destiny 'what would happen to him and his sons for all eternity' (32.21). Such ideas are, however, not confined to apocalyptic literature. The same theme of Yahweh determining the history of Israel may be found in Judith's prayer:

> You designed the things that are now and are yet to be, and what you intended happened. The things you have ordained present themselves and say, 'Here we are'. For all your ways are prepared and your judgment has already taken place (Jdt. 9.5-6).

In this context, it is interesting to note the idea of God's determination of events as a form of judgment (cf. Eccl. 8.5, 6), and of this judgment having taken place prior to the occurrence of the action that is being judged. One may compare Eccl. 9.7, 'Go, eat your food with pleasure and drink your wine with a cheerful heart, for God has already approved your works' for a similar thought (albeit aimed at the individual rather than the nation).

The determination of events in history is typically demonstrated in apocalyptic thought with reference to the nation or the community

---

by an otherworldly being to a human recipient...intended to interpret present earthly circumstances in the light of the supernatural world and of the future'.

14. G.W.E. Nickelsburg, 'Eschatology (Early Jewish)', *ABD*, II, p. 585.

15. Von Rad, *Wisdom in Israel*, p. 272. The identification of God and 'destiny' (εἱμαρμένη) is also made several times by Josephus (*War* 4.297; 6.250, 268, cf. 6.288-315)—so H.W. Attridge, 'Josephus and his Works', in M.E. Stone (ed.), *Jewish Writings of the Second Temple Period* (CRINT; Assen: Van Gorcum; Philadelphia: Fortress Press, 1984), pp. 185-232 (205).

rather than the individual, although the implications for the latter are clear and are sometimes alluded to. However, no real attention is given to the problem of how human free will fits into this deterministic scheme. D.S. Russell remarks on this situation and states:

> The clash of human freedom and divine control had not as yet become a conscious problem, so that these two apparently contradictory points of view could be expressed side by side without any intellectual difficulty. For the most part, the point of view of the apocalyptic writers is that of 'normative' Judaism as expressed in Rabbi Akiba's celebrated statement: 'all is foreseen, but freedom of choice is given' (Pirke 'Abot 3.16).[16]

Thus, in *1 En.* 30.15, the idea that human beings are free to make moral choices concerning good and evil is stressed, despite the fact that elsewhere in the same book it is stated that one's future actions are written down before one is created (*1 En.* 53.2). Likewise, it is stated in *Apoc. Abr.* 26 that God is free to do as he sees fit, but that humanity also have free will. Nevertheless, this statement is juxtaposed with a scene in which God shows Abraham what will befall his descendants in the future (*Apoc. Abr.* 27). In *2 Bar.* 48.40 and 85.7, human free will in the moral sphere is also given emphasis.[17] The fundamental illogic of this position is outlined by J.J. Collins, who remarks concerning the clash between determinism and free will in the book of *Jubilees* that 'If "the judgment of all is ordained and written in the heavenly tablets in righteousness", this is especially a warning for "all who depart from the path" that "if they walk not therein, judgment is written down for every creature and for every kind" (5.13)'.[18]

Thus, in general, early Jewish writings would appear to mask the problem of determinism and its ethical implications for human beings by emphasizing divine foreknowledge over determinism (although one cannot exist without the other). Such an approach is fundamentally different to that of Qoheleth, who mentions divine foreknowledge only in 9.7. Elsewhere in Ecclesiastes God's activity as the determining force in existence is constantly asserted and human freedom severely restricted.

16. D.S. Russell, *The Method and Message of Jewish Apocalyptic* (OTL; London: SCM Press, 1964), p. 232.

17. Russell, *Method and Message*. Cf. also G.H. Box, *The Apocalypse of Abraham* (London: SPCK; New York: Macmillan, 1918), pp. 74-75.

18. J.J. Collins, *The Apocalyptic Imagination* (New York: Crossroad, 1984), p. 66.

3. *Ben Sira*

In Chapter 1 of the present work, Sirach's deterministic thought was mentioned briefly with reference to its possible relationship either to Stoic philosophy or a biblical background. It is at this point that a full consideration of the nature of Sirach's determinism is appropriate. First of all, it is noticeable that Sirach concerns himself with the ethical dilemmas that the theory of determinism raises. Logically, blame for human wrongdoing in a truly deterministic scheme lies with the deity, but this is an aspect of deterministic thought which is for the most part ignored in the Jewish authors mentioned thus far. However, it is this very problem which is considered in Sir. 15.11-20:

> Do not say, 'The Lord is to blame for my failure'; it is for you to avoid doing what he hates.
> Do not say, 'It was he who led me astray'; he has no use for sinful men.
> The Lord hates every kind of vice; you cannot love it and still fear him.
> When he made man in the beginning, he left him free to take his own decisions;
> if you choose, you can keep the commandments; whether or not you keep faith is yours to decide.
> He has set before you fire and water; reach out and take which you choose;
> before men lie life and death, and whichever he prefers is his.
> For in his great and mighty power the Lord sees everything.
> He keeps watch over those who fear him; no human act escapes his notice.
> But he has commanded no man to be wicked, nor has he given licence to commit sin.
>
> (NEB translation)

In Chapter 7, it was argued that Qoheleth makes a concerted attempt to find an explanation for the presence of human wickedness in the light of his deterministic worldview. The way this is done is by advancing the idea that God in some circumstances gives an individual 'authorization' (שלטון) to act as he will. Indeed in 8.9, Qoheleth states that there is 'a time in which a man has authorization over another to harm him'. This could be interpreted as saying that God not only allows wickedness but actually commands it in some circumstances. This, as I have argued leads logically on to the thought of Driver's suggested emendation of 8.10, 'and so I saw the wicked approaching and entering the holy place, walk about and boast in the city that they had done right'.

It is this point of view that is explicitly attacked by Sirach when he states that 'he has commanded no man to be wicked, nor has he given licence to commit sin (לא צוה אנוש לחטא ולא החלים אנשי כזב)'.

Although Sirach does not utilise √שׁלט in this context, the same view-point provides the basis for both passages. The wicked men whom Qoheleth describes in Eccl. 8.10, who 'walk about in the city and boast that they had done right' are addressed by Sirach when he says: 'Do not say, "the Lord is to blame for my failure"... Do not say, "it was he who led me astray"'. Under the circumstances, it may well be that a moral crisis was provoked by the general acceptance of deterministic thought in the third to second centuries BCE as its ethical implications became apparent, and that both Qoheleth and Sirach bear witness to a growing awareness of this problem in certain circles.

Despite his condemnation of those who would argue against the existence of free will in the moral/ethical sphere, Sirach (like other Jewish authors) does in fact assert divine foreknowledge of earthly events. Thus in 23.20 he states, 'Before it happens, everything is known to him, and similarly he sees it before it is finished' (טרם נברא הכל נודע לו וכן אחרי כלות הכל יראה).[19] Yet divine foreknowledge of an event need not necessarily imply the presence of God as the motivating force behind it. Thus far, Sirach's view can be argued to be consistent with his rejection of theological determinism in the moral/ethical sphere.

Like the apocalyptic writers, Sirach is torn between the wish to present God as the prime mover in earthly events, but also to exonerate God from possible blame for human wickedness. Thus, ethical freedom, as well as being explicitly stated, is also implicit in texts such as Sir. 4.26; 7.1-3, 8, 12-13; 8.5; 21.1-2; 23.18-20; 27.8.[20] At the same time, a limited form of determinism is also asserted in 33.7-15:

> Why is one day better than the others, while all the daylight of the year
>   is from the sun?
> They were separated by the wisdom of the Lord, and he made the times
>   and feasts different.
> Some of them he made exalted and holy, and some he counted as
>   ordinary days.
> Men are all made of clay, and Adam was created from the earth.
> In the fullness of his wisdom the Lord separated them and made their
>   destinies different.

---

19. The Hebrew of this passage is ambiguous. Here I have followed the translation offered in von Rad (*Wisdom in Israel*, p. 265). The NEB translates, 'Before the Universe was created, it was known to him, and so it is since its completion'. However, this still expresses the idea of divine foreknowledge of the actions of the sinner in 23.18.

20. Di Lella, 'Wisdom of Ben Sira', p. 942.

Some he blessed and exalted, and some he made holy and brought near
to himself.
Some he cursed and humbled, and hurled from their place.
Like the potter's clay in his hands, to form it as he pleases,
So are men in the hands of their Creator to give to them as he decides.
As good is the opposite of wicked and life is the opposite of death, so the
sinner is the opposite of the godly.
So look upon all the works of the Most High; they are in pairs, the one
the opposite of the other.[21]

Several themes found in Ecclesiastes appear in this passage. God's
determination of individual days finds some echo in Eccl. 7.14. Sirach
considers the inscrutability of God's gifts to humanity (cf. Eccl. 2.26;
5.18 [ET 19]; 6.2). No causal connection is suggested between human
righteousness or sin and God's blessings and curses. God's reasons for
acting as he does are shown to be inexplicable.

In Chapters 2 and 4, it was argued that the catalogue of seasons was
effectively a list of divinely determined human activities. In this context, one may point to Sirach's comment 'Look upon all the works of
the Most High; they are in pairs, the one the opposite of the other' (cf.
Eccl. 3.1-8). Even Sirach's exhortation to 'look upon all the works of
the Most High' finds its parallel in Qohelet's exhortation 'Look upon
the work of God' (7.14) and his claim that 'I saw all the work of God'
(8.17).

However, it is doubtful whether Sirach is in actual fact asserting full
determinism in this passsage: what is envisioned here is a world in
which God may 'give to (the individual) as he decides', rather than
controlling his thoughts and actions. In other words, God controls what
happens to the individual rather than what that individual says and does.
God is shown to be an inscrutable distributor of favours but he is not a
puppet master.

In the light of this conflict between determinism and free will, of
which both Qoheleth and Sirach are aware, it is notable that the ways in
which these two authors approach the problem differ markedly.
Qoheleth is forced to recognize, at least partially, the truth of the
wicked man's claim that the responsibility for human misdeeds lies
with God. Sirach protects God from such a charge by arguing that
human beings are entirely free to make their own ethical decisions. The

---

21. Translation from von Rad (*Wisdom in Israel*, pp. 266-67).

determinism of Sirach is therefore broadly similar to that of the apocalyptists and unlike that of Qoheleth.

4. *Psalms of Solomon*

Certain of the themes that we find in Ben Sira concerning divine determination of events and human free will are also apparent in the *Psalms of Solomon*, which probably date from the first century BCE.[22] In 9.4, for example, the Psalmist states 'Our works are in the choosing and power of our souls, to do right and wrong in the works of our hands'.[23] This clearly demonstrates an awareness of the ethical dilemmas presented by deterministic beliefs, since the Psalmist's avowal of free will implicitly argues against the suggestion that God may be responsible for human iniquity: such a statement would not be necessary if there were no doubt that human beings retained control over their own thoughts and actions.

Yet the Psalmist does not reject the idea of determinism outright, for he states in 14.5 that God 'knew the secrets of the heart before they happen', meaning at the very least that God is able to foresee whether a given individual will turn out good or bad, but possibly implying that God has more specific foreknowledge of the thoughts and actions of the individual. In 5.6, the Psalmist states that the portion of the individual in life is predetermined by God and is unchangeable.[24]

Again, it is important to remember that an assertion of God's foreknowledge of an event is not the same as saying that God himself has determined it. Hence the Psalmist, as we have seen, can state that God knows the motivations of the individual and how they will be acted upon (14.5), without himself being the cause of that motivation (9.4). Because of this foreknowledge, God can prejudge the individual's portion in life (5.6). The theology of the *Pss. Sol.* is therefore, in its essentials, in line with the statement of Akiba that 'all is foreseen, but freedom of choice is given'.

---

22. J.L. Trafton, 'Solomon, Psalms of', *ABD*, VI, p. 115.

23. Verse numbers and translations from the Psalms of Solomon are from *OTP*, II, pp. 639-70.

24. The tension between divine determination and human free will in these passages is noted by Russell (*Method and Message*, pp. 232-33).

3. *Conclusion*

Qoheleth's conception of determinism clearly owes a great deal to his Hebraic background. Yet, while there exist deterministic echoes in the Hebrew Bible, these are relatively few. In general, the Hebrew Bible may be said to be indeterministic in the sense that although God regularly intervenes in history, human beings remain in control of their own moral choices and, generally speaking, over their own actions. It is only in the Hellenistic period that we find anything like an idea of determinism consistently being advanced in the apocalyptic literature of that time.[25]

One way in which his debt to his Hebraic background is evident is in his choice of the terms עת ('time') and זמן ('season') to express the idea of divinely appointed times for events which impinge upon human existence. Both terms appear in this context in the book of Daniel, a product of the Hellenistic period. Even more striking are the parallels that can be made with extrabiblical texts. Determinism is at the heart of Jewish apocalypticism, and though this concept is typically expressed through global events, reference is sometimes made to its implications for the individual.

There are, however, differences between Qoheleth's approach to the consequences of determinism and that of the apocalyptic writers. Broadly speaking, the apocalyptic writers attempted to claim complete sovereignty for God over earthly events, so that everything was said to be predetermined.[26] However, the same writers also wished to retain the idea that human beings were free to make moral/ethical choices since the alternative, that God was responsible for the actions of the wicked, would have denied the goodness and justice of God and indeed would have rendered the law invalid.[27]

Thus a tension is clearly apparent in apocalyptic thought: one may find juxtaposed visions of a future that is preordained with an assertion of human free will. Clearly such writers were aware of the conflict between determinism and free will and a partial solution is offered by

25. D.S. Russell (*Divine Disclosure* [London: SCM Press, 1992], p. 14) sees apocalyptic as essentially a product of the Hellenistic period, from 250 BCE on.

26. L. Morris, *Apocalyptic* (London: Inter-Varsity Press, 1973), pp. 47-48.

27. Russell (*Divine Disclosure*, pp. 113-14) makes the connection between the apocalyptists' assertion of free will and of the consequent necessity of obedience to the law.

emphasizing divine foreknowledge rather than divine determinism per se (although foreknowledge implies determinism). Yet even where determinism is emphasized, it is typically the determination of events rather than human action that is depicted. The same approach to this problem is also evident in the *Psalms of Solomon* and Ben Sira. Faced by the conflict between determinism and free will, both assert the orthodox idea that human beings are entirely free moral beings, but also make claims of divine foreknowledge elsewhere.

The form of determinism advanced by Qoheleth therefore differs significantly from that of his fellows. Faced with moral evil in humanity, Qoheleth does not entirely absolve the deity of blame. Although God is removed from the implication of direct responsibility for wickedness, he is still accused of giving the wicked freedom to commit evil. Moreover, a question mark hangs over even the morally upright as to whether they can take credit for their own actions, for in 9.1, Qoheleth states that 'the righteous and the wise, and their works, are in God's power...' The wicked are conspicuously absent from this observation, so that a situation appears to exist in which a deterministic God can take the credit for the actions of the good, while he is distanced at least to some extent from the evil. This position, in fact, has a direct parallel in Stoic thought.

Chapter 9

QOHELETH AND STOIC DETERMINISM

1. Introduction: A Note on Methodology

As was suggested in Chapter 1 of this work, the idea that the book of Ecclesiastes was subject to Stoic influence is not a new one. Indeed, this position was widely held in some scholarly circles at the end of the last century.[1] Since then, the emphasis in more recent years has been on understanding Qoheleth solely in the context of his Hebraic background,[2] and although some commentators have detected a certain Hellenistic colouring to his work, this has been attributed to the influence of a general *Zeitgeist* rather than to direct contact with Greek philosophy.[3]

Nevertheless, the idea that the author of Ecclesiastes was influenced by specific ideas from Greek philosophy is still advanced by a small but significant minority of scholars.[4] Recent years have also seen several new attempts to claim links between Ecclesiastes and Stoic thought.[5] To

---

1. Tyler, *Ecclesiastes*, pp. 10-29; Plumptre, *Ecclesiastes*, pp. 30-32; Siegfried, *Prediger*, pp. 8-10.

2. Earlier commentators who held that Qoheleth was not subject to Greek influence include Renan (*L'Ecclésiaste*, pp. 62-63); McNeile (*Ecclesiastes*, pp. 43-44), Barton (*Ecclesiastes*, p. 34). More recently their ranks have been joined by Loretz (*Qohelet und der Alte Orient*, p. 134), Seow (*Ecclesiastes*, p. 16).

3. Hengel, *Judaism and Hellenism*, I, pp. 115-30, 126-27; Fox, *Contradictions*, p. 16; Murphy, *Ecclesiastes*, pp. xliv-xlv.

4. Recent exceptions include Braun (*Popularphilosophie*, pp. 167-71); Lohfink (*Kohelet*, pp. 7-15 esp. 9).

5. Gammie, 'Stoicism and Anti-Stoicism in Qoheleth', pp. 169-87; Blenkinsopp, 'Ecclesiastes 3.1-15', pp. 55-64; Levine, 'The Humor of Qohelet', *ZAW* 109 (1997), pp. 71-83 (78). O. Kaiser ('Determination und Freiheit beim Kohelet/Prediger Salomo und in der Frühen Stoa', *NZSTh* 31 [1989], pp. 251-70) makes no attempt to prove dependence, restricting himself largely to a comparison between the thought-systems of the author of Ecclesiastes and the first three Stoic leaders.

this extent, a comparison between Qoheleth's deterministic worldview as I have attempted to reconstruct it in this work and that of the early Stoics, who similarly held that all earthly events were preordained by God, is a worthwhile exercise; the more so since Qoheleth's approach to the subject of determinism has been shown in the previous chapter to differ in some essentials from those of his Jewish contemporaries.

In considering the possibility of Stoic influence on Qoheleth, it is important to restrict material for comparison to known Stoic beliefs of the third century BCE. It is therefore necessary, as far as possible, to distinguish between the ideas of different Stoic philosophers and common Stoic belief.[6] While it is true that our knowledge of early Stoicism is entirely dependent on reports and quotations found in other ancient writers such as Cicero (c. 106–43 BCE) and Diogenes Laertius (fl. 200–20 CE), there remains evidence enough to reconstruct the worldviews of the first three leaders of the Stoic school, Zeno (fl. 300–261 BCE), Cleanthes (fl. 261–232 BCE) and Chrysippus (fl. 232–208/4 BCE) whose dates straddle the period in which the current scholarly consensus would place the composition of Ecclesiastes.

2. *Determinism and Stoic Thought*

The philosophy known as Stoicism may be divided into three main branches: physics, logic and ethics. Much of Stoic thought was profoundly influenced by the work of Heraclitus (fl. 500 BCE), who taught among other things that there was a universal *logos*, or rationality, which controlled the workings of the universe.[7] Although only fragments of Heraclitus's work survive, making it impossible to say for certain whether he was a determinist, this concept is a logical corollary of his philosophy and was advanced enthusiastically by the Stoics.

There are, however, other precursors to the deterministic philosophy of the Stoics. The mechanistic atomist Democritus (b. 460–457 BCE) argued that all events occur in a predictable way through a series of atomic collisions: this comes close to the idea of determinism advanced by the Stoics, but Democritus appears not to have considered the

6.   Gammie, 'Stoicism and Anti-Stoicism in Qoheleth', p. 173. This necessity is also emphasized by J.B. Gould (*The Philosophy of Chrysippus* (Leiden: E.J. Brill, 1970), pp. 1-6.

7.   Guthrie, *History of Greek Philosophy*, I, p. 428; M.C. Nahm, *Selections from Early Greek Philosophy* (New York: Appleton-Century-Crofts, 1968), p. 62.

implications of his philosophy for human free will.[8] Another proponent
of an idea close to determinism was the Pre-Aristotelian philosopher
Diodorus Cronus, one of the school referred to by Aristotle as the
Megarians. The philosophy of determinism is not fully developed in
Diodorus's thought, but he does attempt to advance a logical (albeit
flawed) argument for its existence.[9]

1. *Chrysippus (fl. 232–208/4 BCE)*

It was the Stoics who first propounded a far-reaching and elaborate
form of determinism.[10] In particular, this idea is generally attributed to
Chrysippus, the third leader of the Stoic school and indeed those
commentators who have argued for Stoic influence on the thought of
the author of Ecclesiastes have typically suggested a link with
Chrysippus.[11]

This position is not without its problems, however. The most significant of these is that Chrysippus's leadership of the Stoic school
began in 232 BCE. Commentators have generally been reluctant to date
Qoheleth's work much after 225 BCE, since the social conditions that
are presupposed therein suggest that Qoheleth lived in a time of peace
and prosperity (at least as far as the upper classes were concerned).[12]
The invasion of Palestine by Antiochus III in 219–17 BCE saw the
country change briefly from Ptolemaic to Seleucid hands, bringing to an
end over 100 years of peaceful economic development under the
Ptolemies. Although Antiochus was forced to withdraw after the Battle
of Raphia in 217 BCE, Ptolemaic rule during the closing years of the
third century BCE was marked by poor administration and internal dis-
sension. Palestine fell into Seleucid hands, this time permanently, after
the Battle of Paneion in 200 BCE.[13]

Assuming, therefore, the dating of Ecclesiastes to 250–25 BCE to be
correct, this would leave a period of only seven years for Chrysippus's
distinctive teachings as leader of the Stoa to be formulated and to reach

8. J.B. Gould, 'The Stoic Conception of Fate', *JHI* 35 (1974), pp. 17-32 (19).

9. Taylor, 'Determinism', p. 360.

10. J. den Boeft, *Calcidius on Fate: His Doctrine and Sources* (Leiden: E.J. Brill, 1970), p. 2.

11. Gammie, 'Stoicism and Anti-Stoicism in Qohelet', p. 184; Blenkinsopp, 'Ecclesiastes 3.1-15', pp. 58, 62.

12. Crenshaw, *Ecclesiastes*, p. 50.

13. Hengel, *Judaism and Hellenism*, I, pp. 7-9.

Palestine. Having said this, Chrysippus had taken on the role of Stoic-ism's chief apologist much earlier. Gould states:

> Cleanthes did not possess a combative nature, and even while he was nominally heading the Stoa, Chrysippus, his student, was the prime defender of the Porch against the assaults of the Epicureans...and those of the academics.[14]

So effective were these attacks on Stoicism that by the mid third century BCE, Stoicism as a philosophy was in serious danger of being discredited. That it not only survived but even flourished thereafter may be attributed to the work of Chrysippus in countering objections from rival schools (*SVF* 2.6).[15] Under the circumstances then, Chrysippean ideas may well have influenced the direction of Stoic thought at a rela-tively early stage. This idea is certainly reflected in a saying attributed to Chrysippus who remarked to his teacher Cleanthes that all he wanted was to be told what the main Stoic theories were, and he himself would find the proofs for them (*SVF* 2.1).

The question of to what extent Chrysippus's thought differed from that of his predecessors is a moot one. In general, it would be fair to say that his deterministic philosophy can be distinguished from that of his predecessors by its comprehensiveness, but also by its complexity; a result of attempting to find room for human free will in the moral sphere. This is in fact alluded to by Plutarch:[16]

> Anyone who says that Chrysippus did not make fate the complete cause of these things (right and wrong actions)...will reveal him as once again in conflict with himself, where he extravagantly praises Homer for saying of Zeus 'Therefore accept whatever evil or good that he may send to each of you'...and himself writes many things in agreement with this, and ends up saying that no state or process is to the slightest degree other than in accordance with the rationale of Zeus, which he says is identical to fate.
>
> (Plutarch, *De stoic. repugn.* 1056b-c [*SVF* 2.997])

In a similar vein, Chrysippus is quoted by Gellius as saying that 'Fate is a certain everlasting ordering of the whole: one set of things follows on and succeeds another, and the interconnexion is inviolable' (Gellius

---

14. J.B. Gould, *The Philosophy of Chrysippus* (Leiden: E.J. Brill, 1970), p. 35.

15. Gould, *The Philosophy of Chrysippus*, p. 9.

16. Translations of Stoic texts in this chapter are derived from Long and Sedley (*The Hellenistic Philosophers*, I). The texts in their original languages may be found in the second volume of the same work.

7.2.3 [*SVF* 2.1000]). Two things are emphasized by these quotations. First, Chrysippus's view of fate is that it controls all events on earth, all human action and even human thought (*SVF* 2.913, 925, 997). To this extent, it may justly be said that Chrysippus's worldview is deterministic in the truest sense of the word. Second, human beings are powerless to resist the dictates of Chrysippus's deterministic fate: it is an utterly implacable force.

Naturally, there are some general similarities between the thought of Chrysippus concerning fate and that of Qoheleth. I have argued in Chapters 2 and 3 of this work that Qoheleth's statement in 3.1 that 'there is a time for everything, and an appointed time for every business under heaven' and the catalogue of times in 3.2-8 outline a deterministic worldview in which all human actions and emotions are controlled by the deity. This also appears to be the purport of other key passages within the book of Ecclesiastes, such as 7.14, 26-29; 8.5-6; 9.7, 11-12. Like Qoheleth, who expresses the concept of determinism by equating 'the work of God' with 'the work which is done under the sun', Chrysippus sees fate as ultimately one and the same as the will of the deity (cf. Calcidius 204 [*SVF* 2.933]).[17] Bearing in mind the evidence adduced in the last chapter about the nature of Jewish determinism, Qoheleth's constant emphasis on the determination of human action and thought by God, rather than on God's foreknowledge, might in some ways appear closer to Stoicism than Jewish thought.

As has been suggested in Chapters 7 and 8 of this book, the espousal of a belief in determinism, particularly when the deterministic force is depicted as a benevolent God, results in a moral problem. How can life's injustices and the presence of human evil be explained? More importantly, does the presence of injustice and evil in life mean that God is the author of these things? With whom does responsibility lie for such actions: with the human doer, or with the deity who in theory controls all human actions? This problem is again discussed in the light of Chrysippean determinism by Gellius, who outlines a philosophical position against Chrysippus similar to that of Plutarch (i.e. in terms of the criminal who may appeal to deterministic philosophy to escape justice, cf. *De stoic. repugn.* 1056b-c [above]):

> If Chrysippus they (holders of rival views) say, thinks that all things are
> moved and governed by fate and that the causes of fate and their turns

17. Long and Sedley, *The Hellenistic Philosophers*, I, p. 331.

cannot be changed or surmounted, then the faults and misdeeds of men ought not to cause anger or to be referred to themselves and their wills, but to a certain imperious necessity, which stems from fate; and this is the mistress and arbiter of all things, by which everything which will happen must happen; and for this reason punishments of criminals have been established by the law unjustly, as men do not come to their evil deeds willingly, but are led to them through fate.

(Gellius 7.2.13 [*SVF* 2.1000])

Such objections to Chrysippus's scheme of determinism must have surfaced early, for he is forced to make elaborate attempts to explain the presence of evil in a divinely determined world. For example, he suggests that the 'good' things in life such as justice, truth or beauty derive their significance from the presence of their opposites in the world (Gellius 7.1.1-13 [*SVF* 2.1169-70]). Evil may also be the necessary consequence of God's wider plan for good. Adversity may be a good thing in that it teaches the individual fortitude or other good qualities. Good may come from evil: an earthquake may rid the world of evil people as well as good. War may relieve overpopulation (Plutarch, *De stoic. repugn.* 1049a-d [*SVF* 2.1125]).

Yet Chrysippus (like Qoheleth and Sirach) explicitly considers the problem of the criminal denying responsibility for his crimes, and despite his deterministic beliefs argued that such people should be punished.[18]

Thus, Gellius states on this subject:

(Chrysippus) denies that those who, whether through laziness or through wickedness, are harmful and reckless, should be tolerated and given a hearing, if when caught red-handed they take refuge in the necessity of fate, as if it were a temple-asylum, and say that their worst misdeeds are attributable to fate, and not to their own recklessness.

(Gellius 7.2.13 [*SVF* 2.1000])

An apocryphal story told about Zeno suggests a similar approach to the problem of moral responsibility for wrongdoing: 'The story goes that Zeno was flogging a slave for stealing, "I was fated to steal", said the slave. 'And to be flogged', was Zeno's reply' (*DL* 7.23). Another attempt to resolve the problem was to state that while determinism was a real force which controlled the cosmos, there were certain things over

---

18. Gould (*The Philosophy of Chrysippus*, p. 149) suggests that Chrysippus 'must have been somewhat bitter towards the wicked who thought that the Stoic doctrine of fate bestowed upon them the right to do evil deeds with impunity'.

which human beings have control (*SVF* 2.974), described as το ὑφ' ἡμιν, 'what depends on us'.[19]

Examples of 'what depends on us' focus on presentations in the mind, which we may enact and make real or refrain from enacting. We do not have any control over how presentations enter out mind, so that for example, a man who has a picture in his mind of himself overeating, or of sleeping with a neighbour's wife, is not responsible for what he is thinking. It is, however, within his power to choose whether or not he enacts these things, and therefore human beings must bear responsibility for their own wickednesses (*SVF* 3.177).[20] Thus Chrysippus ends up asserting total determinism and moral free will side by side in much the same way as we have seen in some Jewish writings of this period. That is not to say that the position of these Jewish writers is influenced by Chrysippus: one can clearly see how they arrived at the same conclusions independently, but the parallel remains nevertheless.

At a superficial level, there are similarities between the thought of Qoheleth and Chrysippus in their approach to the question of fate. Both authors lay an emphasis on determinism in their consideration of existence, and on God as the deterministic force behind earthly events. Both are conscious of the theological problem that this philosophy poses in considering human injustice and wickedness. Many other cultures, however, have expressed like concerns about the moral problems consequent from a belief in fate or determinism.[21] Despite the similarities, it is also evident that Qoheleth makes no such convoluted attempts as Chrysippus to explain human evil, nor does he demonstrate any knowledge of Chrysippus's position by attempting to argue against it. The position that Qoheleth takes with the question of human evil in fact brings him somewhat closer in thought to Chrysippus's predecessor, Cleanthes, the second leader of the Stoic school.

19. Blenkinsopp ('Ecclesiastes 3.1-15', p. 62) in fact argues that it is this concept of free will that lies behind the series of actions enumerated in 3.2-8, as does Levine ('The Humor of Qohelet', p. 78) who sees the actions in this passage as denoting 'human freedom in foolish opposition to determinism'.

20. M.E. Reesor, *The Nature of Man in Early Stoic Philosophy* (London: Gerald Duckworth, 1989), pp. 49-58.

21. B.C. Dietrich (*Death, Fate and the Gods* [London: Athlone Press, 1965], pp. 3-5) cites the examples of a serpent in the *Mahabharata* (13.1) who devours a child and disclaims responsibility for the deed on the grounds that it was fated. Similar, in the Koran (35.8) is the assertion that 'God leads astray whom he pleases and guides whom he pleases'.

2. Cleanthes (fl. 261–232 BCE)

Although Stoicism even from its inception laid great emphasis on the role of God in the workings of the world, it is Cleanthes who is generally credited with being the most religious of the Stoic leaders.[22] Cleanthes' pupil Chrysippus, as we have seen, is often asserted to be the first Stoic leader to advance the idea of an all-embracing deterministic force that controls existence. Generally speaking, the viewpoint ascribed to his predecessors by some modern commentators is not dissimilar to traditional Greek conceptions of fate as a force that determines the major milestones in one's life, but in which the details remain under human control.[23]

Such a view is misleading, however. If it is clear that Zeno and Cleanthes were not fully determinist in their outlook, they nevertheless advanced viewpoints very close to it.[24] Cleanthes in particular argued for the activity of Providence lying behind every walk of human life. This 'Providence' was not a series of isolated acts of divine generosity but a continual and thoroughgoing intervention in the affairs of the individual and the world. Indeed, so extensive was God's interaction with existence that one may basically characterize Cleanthes' position by calling it a kind of 'positive determinism'. Such a view of life gives rise to the very same problem that Chrysippus faced later. How can this divine Providence be reconciled with wickedness? Cleanthes writes:

> No deed is done on earth, God, without your offices, nor in the divine ethereal vault of heaven, nor at sea, save what bad men do in their folly. But you know how to make things crooked straight and to order things disorderly.
>
> (Cleanthes, *Hymn to Zeus* 1.537)

22. Gould, *The Philosophy of Chrysippus*, pp. 34-35; Long and Sedley, *The Hellenistic Philosophers*, I, p. 332.

23. Long and Sedley, *The Hellenistic Philosophers*, I, pp. 342, 392.

24. Some classical scholars have indeed asserted that Chrysippus is totally beholden to his predecessors for his philosophy and made no original contribution to Stoic thought: in essence he recapitulated the ideas of Zeno and Cleanthes and systematized them (so A.C. Pearson, *The Fragments of Zeno and Cleanthes* [London: Clay, 1891], p. 48; E.V. Arnold, *Roman Stoicism* [New York: Humanities, 1958], p. 91). Not dissimilar (at least as far as the concept of determinism is concerned) is the view of Gould (*The Philosophy of Chrysippus*, p. 206), who argues that Chrysippus did not so much build his own deterministic world view as systematize that of his two predecessors.

As may be observed from this passage, the solution to the problem of human wickedness and how this can be reconciled with a belief in a benevolent deterministic God was a very simple one. Cleanthes assigned blame for humanity's wickedness with humanity itself and apportioned credit for human good deeds with the providential deity. Cleanthes speaks not just of major events being subject to external control but every human action not tainted by folly or wickedness.

If one considers the view of Providence offered by Cleanthes, it appears to be quite similar to that of Qoheleth. I have argued in this book that the latter reconciles the concepts of free will and determinism by means of a parallel from the legal sphere. God gives שׁלטון, 'author-ization' to certain people to act as they wish (5.18; 6.2; 8.4, 9; 10.5). Qoheleth recommends that this freedom be used to derive enjoyment from life (5.18) but others are also free to gain dominion over their fellows or to act wickedly (8.9). Others, perhaps well-meaning, make errors of judgment and upset the social order by giving preferential treatment to people of low rank at the expense of those who really ought to be honoured (10.5-6).

The implication of this is that while God in theory controls every-thing, he is not directly responsible for human injustice, folly or wickedness. Both Cleanthes and Qoheleth stress the universality of God's intervention in existence, yet are careful not to assign blame for human wickedness directly to the deity. It is as if the wicked stand outside the control of the deterministic force, retaining freedom over their actions, while the good are enslaved by Fate, God, or whatever this power is called.

The same implication is made by Qoheleth, who states 'the righteous and the wise, and their works, are in God's power' (9.1). What Qoheleth claims here is that God controls the thoughts and actions of 'good' people.[25] One might object that this verse could simply mean that the righteous and wise are dependent on the will of an inscrutable God for their 'just' reward and that God alone can ensure that their

---

25. So Crenshaw, who states 'The destiny of just people and wise is entirely at God's disposal, contrary to the sage's belief that they controlled their own destiny [*sic*]. The term "and their actions" refers either to what the wise and just think they accomplish in their own strength, or to their inability to do anything apart from the deity's prior approval' (*Ecclesiastes*, p. 159). Cf. Delitzsch, *Ecclesiastes*, pp. 354-55; Hertzberg, *Prediger*, pp. 153-55; Galling, *Prediger*, pp. 112-13; Loader, *Polar Structures*, pp. 101-102.

actions have a successful outcome.[26] However, the position of 9.1 following 8.16-17 would appear to be significant. Qoheleth has just linked 'the work of God' with 'the work which is done under the sun' and stated the impossibility of achieving his intention of 'finding out' these things. No 'wise man' can do so because, as 9.1 explains, 'the righteous and the wise are in God's power'.[27]

Nothing is said of the foolish or wicked—they are apparently *not* in God's power. The parallel between this thought and that of Cleanthes: 'No deed is done on earth, God, without your offices...save what bad men do in their folly' is striking, but it is, as I have suggested, borne out by the way that Qoheleth uses √שׁלט ('authorize') to denote a degree of freedom from divine control in contexts having to do with human wickedness and injustice.

Yet while Qoheleth is apparently sympathetic to the basic position adopted by Cleanthes, he also notes its weaknesses. The fact that human evil is a consequence of free will does not absolve the deity of all responsibility for the inequities of existence: it is God, after all, who gives freedom to people who will use it wickedly in the first place, enabling them to 'boast that they had done right' (8.9). Moreover, God is often tardy in his judgment of such people: sometimes they may even go unpunished.

Qoheleth's God therefore has a darker side than that of Cleanthes. While Cleanthes can say that the function of the Stoic god is 'to make crooked things straight', Qoheleth charges God with doing the exact opposite: 'Consider the work of God—who can make straight what he has made crooked?' (7.13) and in a similar vein he says of existence in general, 'The crooked cannot be made straight, nor the missing counted' (1.15).

Thus, there are similarities between the deterministic thought of Qoheleth and ideas expressed by the early Stoic philosophers, notably Cleanthes: if this could be said to indicate some form of influence, it would support the generally accepted dating of Ecclesiastes to 250–25 BCE, typically advanced on the basis of the social situation described by the book and its close correspondence with the situation in Palestine as

---

26. McNeile, *Ecclesiastes*, p. 19; Barton, *Ecclesiastes*, pp. 157-58; Glasser, *Qohelet*, pp. 140-41.

27. Fox (*Contradictions*, p. 257) also understands 9.1 in the light of 8.16-17, although his interpretation of the former is somewhat ambiguous.

depicted in the P. Zen. (c. 265–55 BCE).[28] On the basis of the evidence adduced so far however, one may well object that these similarities can only be considered as parallels (albeit striking ones), rather than the product of direct contact. This is a not unreasonable position. Although Murphy, commenting on criteria for demonstrating Hellenistic influences on the book of Ecclesiastes, is correct in warning against expecting evidence to be too specific and thus discounting more general connections as mere parallels,[29] more evidence (indeed, more *specific* evidence) is required before Stoic influence on Ecclesiastes should be given serious consideration.

Significantly, as the next section will demonstrate, Qoheleth appears to show a more specific awareness of the concept of a controlling mechanism of the cosmos, which the Stoic philosophers called the *logos*.

3. *Qoheleth and the* Logos

1. *The Meaning of* חשבון *in Ecclesiastes*

Traditionally, commentators have interpreted the noun חשבון ('account') in one of two ways. On the one hand, there are those who have argued that Qoheleth uses the term in a concrete way to refer to an account of existence that Qoheleth hopes to piece together from his observations. On the other, it has also been suggested that the term חשבון has an abstract meaning, and that it has an existence outside Qoheleth's imagination.

Among those who hold to the first of these options is Fox, who suggests that חשבון 'refers to both the process of reckoning and the solution reached'. In other words, the term denotes the sum total of knowledge that Qoheleth is able to establish as a result of his observations.[30] Glasser follows the same line of thinking. For him, חשבון refers to 'les estimations de la sagesse' ('the estimations of wisdom').[31] The logical conclusion that follows from the arguments of both commentators is that the book of Ecclesiastes is itself the חשבון that

---

28. Crenshaw, *Ecclesiastes*, p. 50; Whybray, *Ecclesiastes* [NCBC], pp. 11-12.

29. Murphy, *Ecclesiastes*, p. xliv.

30. Fox, *Contradictions*, p. 241.

31. Glasser, *Qohelet*, p. 124. Michel (*Untersuchungen zur Eigenart des Buches Qohelet*, pp. 235-36) also argues for this understanding of the term חשבון, which defines further the nature of the wisdom that Qoheleth utilizes.

Qoheleth sought and which he has succeeded in finding.

This position is supported by the LXX which translates חשבון in 7.27, 29 and 9.10 with the Greek noun λογισμός, derived from the verb λογίζεσθαι, which has the sense of reckoning, evaluating, charging up a debt and typically denotes the act of (human) thought according to strict logical rules.[32] In 7.25, חשבון is translated by ψῆφος, which refers to a small stone (Hdt 3.12.1). Such stones were often used in counting (Hdt 2.36.4), and hence the term comes to have the alternative meanings 'number' or 'account' (P. Lips. 1.64.7; 1.105.17-19).[33] The use of both terms emphasizes the translator's belief that the term חשבון was used in the concrete sense of an 'account' given by Qoheleth of his investigations.

The second option, that the term חשבון refers to an abstract 'account' or 'sum' which is already in existence is upheld by Tyler, who argues for the meaning of:

> ...plan, i.e. of the moral administration of the world. The idea represented by חשבון is, probably, the thought underlying and manifest in the condition of man viewed as the subject of a moral government.[34]

McNeile follows much the same path when he states that 'Here, and in v. 27 it means "the rationale of things", a law by which the perplexing phenomena of life can be explained'.[35] Likewise, Whybray follows RSV, 'the sum of things' and remarks that Qoheleth is seeking 'something which makes sense of the whole of "That which is"'.[36]

Both arguments have their adherents, and yet neither understanding of the term חשבון appears to be appropriate to every occurrence of the term in Ecclesiastes. In 7.25, for example, חשבון is parallel to that of חכמה ('wisdom') and indeed both Glasser and Whybray have suggested that the expression חכמה וחשבון is a hendiadys. The wisdom that Qoheleth seeks, as Whybray well observes, is 'not the superficial, conventional, "practical" wisdom'.[37] It is termed 'very deep' in 7.23 and Qoheleth alludes to it in 7.24 as 'far from me'. In the sense that it is

32. H. Heidland, 'λογίζομαι, λογισμός', *TDNT*, IV, p. 284.

33. G. Braumann, 'ψῆφος', *TDNT*, IX, p. 904.

34. Tyler, *Ecclesiastes*, p. 137.

35. McNeile, *Ecclesiastes*, p. 75. Similar is Podechard (*L'Ecclésiaste*, p. 385) who understands the חשבון to be 'l'explication du monde et des événements'.

36. Whybray, *Ecclesiastes* [NCBC], p. 124. Barton (*Ecclesiastes*, p. 146) describes the חשבון similarly, calling it 'the ultimate reality'.

37. Whybray, *Ecclesiastes*, p. 124

a wisdom designed to enable him to see the whole of that which is, it is something analogous to divine wisdom. Crenshaw describes it as 'wisdom par excellence, as opposed to practical knowledge', which is one and the same as 'the substance of human thought, the sum total of all knowledge'.[38] Thus, there would appear to be good reason for thinking that the term חשבון in 7.25 refers to an abstract preexistent 'account' or 'sum of things' as Whybray terms it, which is coextensive with Wisdom. Whether it be seen as 'wisdom par excellence' or 'the reason of things', it is something more than the purely human-made account described by the LXX's ψῆφος in this location. The finding of this חשבון (and 7.28 suggests that Qoheleth failed in this regard) would give Qoheleth a degree of mastery over existence. In the sense that it appears (as Crenshaw suggests) to denote the substance of human thought and (as Whybray suggests) to define 'the whole of "That which is"', it would appear to be coextensive with 'the work of God'/'the work which is done under the sun'.

It is noteworthy that the verbs בקש ('seek', 7.25, 28, 29) and מצא ('find out', 7.24, 26, 27 [×2], 28 [×3], 29; 9.10) are constantly used in those passages which speak of חשבנות/חשבון. This suggests that Qoheleth's חשבון which he seeks is already in existence, there (in theory) to be found by those with the wisdom to find it: in other words it is an abstract concept (like 'Wisdom'). The verbs בקש and מצא are also concentrated in 8.17 which, like 7.23-29, sums up Qoheleth's investigation and in which Qoheleth admits defeat:

> Then I beheld all the work of God, that a man cannot find out [מצא] the work which is done under the sun, because though a man labour to seek it out [בקש], yet he shall not find it [מצא]; indeed, though a wise man think to know it, yet he shall not be able to find it [מצא].

This verse, in which בקש occurs once, and מצא three times with 'the work of God', or 'the work which is done under the sun' as their object, suggests that the term חשבון may be synonymous with 'the work which is done under the sun', and/or 'the work of God'.[39] The verbs בקש and מצא occur almost exclusively in those passages in which Qoheleth speaks of the work of God, or the חשבון (3.11; 7.23-29; 8.17; 9.10).

---

38. Crenshaw, *Ecclesiastes*, p. 145.

39. Like Gordis (*Koheleth*, pp. 298-99), Fox (*Contradictions*, p. 175) and Murphy (*Ecclesiastes*, p. 13), I argue that 'the work of God' is one and the same as 'the work which is done under the sun'.

חֶשְׁבּוֹן therefore appears to connote the divine order, the מַעֲשֵׂה הָאֱלֹהִים ('the work of God') which should be apparent in 'the work which is done under the sun' (מַעֲשֶׂה שֶׁנַּעֲשָׂה תַּחַת הַשֶּׁמֶשׁ) but, as the expression חָכְמָה וְחֶשְׁבּוֹן in 7.25 shows, it also denotes the wisdom by which that work is done or by which that work may be understood. Whybray's assertion that חֶשְׁבּוֹן constitutes the whole of 'That which is', as well as the suggestions that חֶשְׁבּוֹן is the 'rationale of things', or the 'plan' for the 'moral administration of the world' by McNeile and Tyler respectively seem to be borne out by the context in which מָצָא and בָּקֵשׁ appear.

In 7.27, Qoheleth clearly considers that he may come to know the 'account' by which God works by adding 'one to one' from his observations. In doing so, he plays on the idea of a numerical account. This is a theme which runs throughout Ecclesiastes: Qoheleth considers the 'profit' (יוֹתֵר מוֹתַר יִתְרוֹן—1.3; 2.11, 15; 3.9, 19; 5.15; 6.8, 11) and 'loss' (חֶסְרוֹן—1.15) inherent in the 'account' which governs the world. Interestingly, in 3.14, Qoheleth uses similar language of the work of God, affirming that 'what God does is eternal: there is no adding to it, and no taking away from it' (3.14).[40] Again, if the חֶשְׁבּוֹן is to be identified with 'the work of God' (as I have suggested in Chapter 5), the 'adding to' (יָסַף) and 'taking away' (גָּרַע) would refer to human attempts to interfere with the balance of the divine account which ensures that 'That which is , is that which will be' (3.15). Thus, in the context of 7.27, חֶשְׁבּוֹן could, and probably does, have a double meaning indicating the supreme account governing the world and the account which Qoheleth himself intends to form in the course of his calculations: one which will hopefully balance with the account par excellence. Rather than choosing between the opposing views of modern commentators, it may be as well to accept the idea that Qoheleth uses the term חֶשְׁבּוֹן in both its abstract and concrete senses.

It would appear that Qoheleth plays on words again in 7.29, in which he remarks that 'they (humankind) have sought out many חִשְׁבֹנוֹת'. The MT points as חִשְּׁבֹנוֹת, a word used elsewhere only in 2 Chron. 24.6 of 'devices'. Certainly, Lohfink argues that the fact that Qoheleth uses this word so soon after his uses of חֶשְׁבּוֹן in 7.25, 27, suggests a double

---

40. W. Staples ('Profit in Ecclesiastes', *JNES* 4 [1945], pp. 87-96 [88]) also links the idea of the absence of 'profit' to humanity's inability to act outside 'the work of God'.

meaning.[41] Fox goes further, however, and sees the use of בקשׁ as indicative that חשׁבנות is merely the plural of that חשׁבון which is described in 7.25, 27.[42] For him, the context of this verse demands that a meaning such as 'explanation, solution' be attached to חשׁבנות.

I would argue for the correctness of Fox's assertion, although I would not go as far as to claim that the whole of Ecclesiastes details 'Qohelet's search for *hiśśᵉbonot*'. Qoheleth in fact seeks a single 'account' which will allow him to understand existence. The thrust of 7.29 may suggest a changeable abstract חשׁבון or possibly refer to the individual 'accounts' which human beings have attempted to form of it. Qoheleth's thought at this point is extremely obscure and no interpretation enjoys unqualified acceptance. On balance however, Fox's suggestion as to the meaning of חשׁבנות in this context would appear to make most sense.

Thus, in contrast to 7.25, 7, in which חשׁבון appears to have a double meaning as a divine account governing the cosmos and an accurate human 'account of the account' which Qoheleth sets out to form, 7.29 appears to refer solely to human accounts of existence which have been sought. The context seems to militate against a divine 'account' controlling existence, and this is reflected in the MT's pointing חִשְׁבֹנוֹת ('devices') and in the Vulgate's rendering, 'infinitis...quaestionibus' ('many questionable things'). Nevertheless, the fact that Qoheleth uses the singular חֶשְׁבּוֹן, in 7.25, 7, and 9.10 suggests strongly that the occurrence in 7.29 is merely the plural of חשׁבון as Fox indeed argues.

Eccl. 9.10 is interesting in its usage of the term חשׁבון outside the immediate context of the passage 7.23-29 which has been under consideration:

> Whatever your hand finds to do (מצא ידך לעשׂות), do mightily (עשׂה בכח);
> for there is no work (מעשׂה), nor חשׁבון nor knowledge (דעת), nor
> wisdom (חכמה) in Sheol, where you are going.

Here the term חשׁבון appears not to mean a divine account which governs existence (although Qoheleth once again plays on words, for it is placed parallel to the noun מעשׂה ['work'] and elsewhere contextual evidence would appear to suggest that the חשׁבון is coextensive with 'the work which is done under the sun'). Nor, however, does the term

41. Lohfink, *Kohelet*, pp. 58-59.
42. Fox, *Contradictions*, p. 243.

חשׁבון here seemingly refer to a human 'account of the account'. In its position parallel to attributes such as action (מעשׂה), knowledge (דעת) and wisdom (חכמה), the generality of which seem to be emphasized, it would appear to have a much more pedestrian sense than is found in 7.25, 27 (although here as in 7.25, it is parallel to 'wisdom' and 'knowledge'), and is therefore often translated 'thought'.[43] This is a particularly strange usage of the term חשׁבון, and one which finds no echo elsewhere in Hebrew.

In summary, it appears that Qoheleth does not use the term חשׁבון with any one meaning in all locations. In some locations (7.25, 27) it refers to 'the rationale of things' but also appears to be connected to 'the work of God' or 'the work which is done under the sun'. Qoheleth indulges in a certain amount of wordplay in 7.27, however, so that it has a double meaning of the 'account' which governs existence and the account which Qoheleth hopes to make of it. In 7.29, the plural occurs of the individual accounts made by others of existence, or perhaps suggests a changeable account. Finally, in 9.10, the term חשׁבון is used parallel to 'wisdom', 'knowledge' and 'work/action' and may be rendered by commentators in yet another way, as 'thought'. Thus, the term as Qoheleth uses it has an extremely extended semantic range which apparently encompasses thought, wisdom, deed and calculation in both the human and divine spheres.

2. *Stoicism and Qoheleth: Two Accounts*

In his consideration of the possible links between Stoic philosophy and the thought of Qoheleth, Gammie remarks that 'Stoic philosophy is perhaps closest to Qoheleth in its affirmation of the operation of a universal logos, cosmic nature or God'.[44] In Stoic thought, this *logos* was the rationality and structuring principle that governed the cosmos. It was therefore identified both with God and Fate.

Since the *logos* played such a central part in Stoicism, we should perhaps expect to find some trace of this idea in the book of Ecclesiastes if Qoheleth's deterministic worldview owes anything to Stoic thought. A study of this term is therefore appropriate at this point.

---

43. Crenshaw, *Ecclesiastes*, p. 158.
44. Gammie, 'Stoicism and Anti-Stoicism in Qoheleth', p. 180.

a. *The meaning of the term* Logos

The Greek verb λέγω, from which the noun λόγος is derived, has two main senses: (1) to count, recount; (2) to say, speak. Although the derived verbal noun λόγος has a broad semantic range, its diverse meanings are connected to those of its parent verb: from (1) are derived the senses 'computation, reckoning, (financial) account, measure, esteem'; (2) provides the senses 'explanation, argument, theory, law, saying'.[45]

The term *logos* became very much a key word in the thought of the pre-Socratic philosopher Heraclitus of Ephesus (c. 500 BCE), who used it in the sense of a system or rationality which governed existence. This Heraclitean doctrine was taken up by the Stoics in the third century BCE. This in turn provides a remarkable parallel with the thought of Qoheleth. One aspect of the Heraclitean/Stoic concept of the universe being based on a *logos* ('proportion, explanation, account'), is that it suggests an underlying mathematical basis for life and the events that occur in it.

As we have seen, Qoheleth also shows a familiarity with and an interest in the concept of a universe definable by numbers. Significantly, the semantic parallel between the Heraclitean/Stoic *logos* and Qoheleth's חשׁבון is almost exact. Both have a mathematical sense of an account that may be added up, but both are basically used in the sense of 'explanation' to describe 'the whole of that which is' by their different authors. Qoheleth's חשׁבון as I have already suggested, is described in terms which suggest that it is equivalent to 'the work of God' or 'the work which is done under the sun'. This, as we shall see, is also true of the Heraclitean/Stoic *logos*. In the words of Kleinknecht concerning this sense of the term:

> It is presupposed as self-evident by the Greek that there is in things, in the world and its course, a primary λόγος, an intelligible and recognisable law, which then makes possible knowledge and understanding in the human λόγος. But this λόγος is not taken to be something which is merely grasped theoretically. It claims a man. It determines his true life and conduct.[46]

---

45. A. Debrunner ('λέγω A', *TDNT*, IV, p. 73) notes this sense of 'calculation' in Herodotus 3.142, 143 and in the sense of 'total' in IG 4.1485, 145, 151, 154, 155, 161, 173, 178 and 1487.12, 18. Documents from Hellenistic Roman Egypt also, as he points out, use the term in the sense of a financial account or balance.

46. H. Kleinknecht, 'λέγω B', *TDNT*, IV, p. 81.

b. Logos *in Greek philosophy*

As noted in the previous section, Heraclitus' use of the concept of *logos* was distinctive and had far-reaching repercussions for the course of later philosophical inquiry into the nature of existence. Indirectly, it also exerted a powerful influence on later Jewish ideas about God's government of the cosmos. Since it is Heraclitus and not Zeno, Cleanthes or Chyrisippus who is ultimately responsible for the development of the Stoic logos, it makes sense to begin with an examination of his ideas as mediated by the extant fragments of his work.

Most of the time, Heraclitus uses the term *logos* in its more common meanings of 'proportion', 'explanation' or 'account'. Two examples of this usage will suffice for the present. The first is a simple proverb: 'a fool delights in getting excited on any account (λογω)' (Plutarch, *De Aud. Poet.* 28D [D. 87]). Here, 'account' is used in the sense of 'reason', although Heraclitus may well be indulging in a wordplay here and be suggesting that fools will swallow any old philosophy, even if its propositions are nonsense. The second is broadly similar: 'Of all those whose accounts (λογους) I have listened to, none has gone as far as this: to recognize that which is wise, set apart from all' (Stobaeus 3.1.174 [D.108]). Here 'account' refers to an individual explanation of existence (though once again there may be a deeper wordplay, with 'account' also referring to the individual's perception of the true 'account').

However, Heraclitus also used the term *logos* in the sense of an underlying cosmic principle of order...

> Although this account (λόγος) holds forever, men ever fail to comprehend, both before hearing it, and once they have heard. Although all things come to pass in accordance with this account (λόγος), men are like the untried when they try such words and works as I set forth.
> (Sextus Empiricus, *Adv. Math.* 7.132 [D.1])

Heraclitus is unique among the early Greek philosophers in seeing the *logos* as a rationality governing the universe, a cosmic principle controlling events on earth, and one, moreover which is established by God. In this, he is followed by the Stoics, who refer to *logos* as 'the craftsman god...by which it is established both at which time each thing will come to birth and when it will perish' (Calcidius 293). The *logos* is evident as the wisdom governing the universe, but it is also the wisdom of humanity.[47] Hence, Heraclitus can say: 'Although the account (*logos*) is shared, most men live as though their thinking was a private possession' (Sextus Empiricus, *Adv. Math.* 8.133 [D.2]). All human thought and action forms a part of the all-pervasive *logos* which controls existence—as a result, Heraclitus can claim that human thought is 'shared' rather than 'private' to the individual.[48]

As I have already suggested, Qoheleth's חשבון, like the Heraclitean/ Stoic *logos*, has the idea of an 'account' or 'rationale' which defines the nature of existence, but which also serves as its controlling mechanism (7.25, 27). But Heraclitus also uses the term *logos* in the latter quotation in a dual sense. Primarily, it refers to the 'account' which governs existence, but Heraclitus also plays on the idea of thinking that is inherent in the term. Thus, because the account is common, human thought is common. Qoheleth also uses the term חשבון with this play on meaning, for in 7.25, 27, it refers to the account which orders the world. However, Qoheleth also plays on the background meaning of חשב√ ('think', 'consider') in 9.10 so that the noun there refers apparently to human thought.

This parallel usage is striking enough, but like Qoheleth, who links the terms חשבון and חכמה in Eccl. 7.25, Heraclitus also directly links the *logos* with wisdom: 'It is wise, listening not to me but to the account to agree that all things are one' (Hippolytus, *Refutatio* 9.9.1 [D. 50]). Again, this fragment emphasizes that the *logos* has an independent existence of its own. Underlying the idea of the *logos* is the statement that 'all things are one': they are all a reflection of the action of a common *logos*, the system by which the events of life play themselves out. Wisdom lies in finding and listening to this *logos*, and agreeing with it.

The Stoic concept of *logos*, which goes on to play such an important part in Jewish wisdom speculation, is the direct descendant of this

---

47. Guthrie (*History of Greek Philosophy*, 2.428), Nahm (*Selections from Early Greek Philosophy*, pp. 67-69) and G.S. Kirk (*Heraclitus: The Cosmic Fragments* [Cambridge: Cambridge University Press, 1954], p. 39) translate λόγος as 'law' and 'formula of things' respectively. These are both aspects of the *logos* but Guthrie argues convincingly for a dual rendering as human thought and the governing principle of the universe.

48. Long and Sedley (*The Hellenistic Philosophers*, I, p. 491) typically translate λόγος by the term 'reason', rather than 'account', although it can have both these and many other senses according to context.

Heraclitean *logos*. As such, it serves as the controlling mechanism of the cosmos, and was thus identified with Fate or God (Diogenes Laertius 7.134 [*SVF* 2.300]).[49] Once again, it is the thought of Cleanthes as evidenced by the *Hymn to Zeus* which offers the best parallel with Qohelet:

> You (God) direct the universal *logos* which runs through all things... No deed is done on earth, God, without your offices... For you have so welded into one all things good and bad that they all share in a single everlasting *logos* (*Hymn to Zeus*, ll. 12-21 [*SVF* 1.537]).

Significantly, the concept of *logos* as coextensive with wisdom and the divine work plays a part in Jewish wisdom speculation of the Hellenistic period. The work of Aristobulus (fl. 150 BCE) indicates that acceptance of the concept of a *logos* had taken place at an early stage. Aristobulus (who is mentioned in 2 Macc. 1.10) sought to interpret the LXX in the light of Greek (especially Stoic) philosophy and thus connected divine wisdom (σοφία) with *logos* in its guise as the cosmic ordering principle (Eusebius, *Praep. Evang.* 13.12.10-13).[50] This connection between Wisdom and the *logos* is also notable in the Wisdom of Solomon. Here, God's *logos* and God's wisdom occur side by side, describing the means by which the world and human beings were created (Wis. 9.1-2). Philo used the term *logos* in its Stoic sense of a rationality that pervaded the cosmos (*Rer. Div. Her.* 188; *Fug.* 111), and also connected it with wisdom (*Leg. All.* 165; *Rer. Div. Her.* 191; *Somn.* 2.242-45). According to Philo, the *logos* served as the medium through which the work of God found expression but was also the source of the universe's intelligibility.[51] The use of the concept of *logos* in early Jewish writings is analogous to the way in which Qoheleth uses the term הַשֶּׁבוֹן, for this too is a 'rationale', apparently coextensive with 'the work which is done under the sun' or 'the work of God', but also

---

49. Long and Sedley, *The Hellenistic Philosophers*, I, pp. 268, 270. Debrunner, 'λέγω', p. 84; F.H. Sandbach (*The Stoics* [London: Chatto & Windus, 1975], p. 72) captures the manifold meanings of the term *logos* as used by the Stoics when he explains that it means 'the explanation of a thing, which may be the account or formula of its constitution, and the statement of its purpose. But to give the grounds for anything is a rational activity... Perhaps "plan" has something of the same ambiguity... (A Plan) implies the intentions of a rational being...'

50. Charlesworth, *OTP*, II, pp. 834-35.

51. Tobin, 'Logos', pp. 350-51.

the means by which Qoheleth seeks to make sense of the universe around him.

The term *logos* is therefore used in the philosophical tradition represented by Heraclitus and the Stoics to denote a divine 'account', a rationale that governs existence and through which existence can be understood by the wise individual. This 'account' is in effect the sum total of human thought and action but is also an abstract concept, a controlling mechanism for the cosmos.

One might object that here we have a parallel thought between Qoheleth and Greek philosophy rather than direct influence, but what is striking about Qoheleth's usage is that he does not restrict the term חשבון to the idea of a numerical account: in 9.10, for example it appears to mean 'thought' (a meaning which it has nowhere else in Hebrew).[52] This is an example of wordplay analogous to that which we have seen in Heraclitus. Often, there is an ambiguity about whether Qoheleth is using the term in an abstract or concrete sense (again, paralleled by Heraclitus's use of the term *logos* in his philosophy). It is, however, in its dual sense of rationality and rationale, placed parallel to wisdom, that Qoheleth's חשבון appears most like the *logos* as it appears in Stoic and early Jewish thought.

The concept of the *logos* is used by Heraclitus and the early Stoics in all the ways in which Qoheleth used the term חשבון. One is forced to conclude that there is more than a simple parallel of thought here. Qoheleth has borrowed the concept of the *logos* as the governing mechanism for existence and is aware of the many ways in which it is used. This in itself, if one accepts the Hellenistic dating of Ecclesiastes, need not be surprising. The *logos* as a concept was subsumed into Judaism very early on (appearing in Jewish Greek writings from 150 BCE onwards), and played a major part in Jewish wisdom thereafter.

---

52. In Sir. 42.3, חשבון is used in the sense of a business account, a usage which is extremely common in the later period (cf. *Exod. R.* 51; *Deut. R.* 4; *t. b. Qam.* 10.21). In *b. B. Bat.* 9b too, it has the meaning of a financial total. In only two locations of which I am aware is there any figurative usage: *b. B. Bat.* 78b and *Ab.* 4.22 both speak of a חשבון in the sense of an account in contexts having to do with divine judgment. Thus, in *b. B. Bat.* 78b one may speak of God balancing a loss incurred in obeying the law by rewarding an individual (and a gain occasioned from breaking the law by punishing the individual) after death, and in *m. Abot.* 4.22 of the individual rendering an account of one's deeds before God on the day of judgment. Nowhere is it used either with the range of meanings that Qohelet applies to it, nor in the same context.

We do not know how early this idea entered Judaism, and it is entirely possible that Qoheleth came into contact with this idea and adapted it for his own ends. This need not detract from Qoheleth's originality, nor need it suggest that Qoheleth's determinism does not ultimately stem from his Jewish background: his language elsewhere is fundamentally in line with other Hebrew deterministic writings of this time. It is, however, precisely at such interfaces between different cultures that the borrowing of general ideas is most likely. In this case, it is the specific contexts in which the concept is expressed by Qoheleth that suggests that the connection between חשבון and *logos* is more than a parallel.

4. *History*

An important part of the Stoic message focuses on the idea that history is repeated in periodic cycles, and some commentators have argued that Qoheleth echoes this idea in Eccl. 1.4-11.[53] Specifically, Qoheleth states in Eccl. 1.9-10:

> That which has been is that which will be,
> That which has been done is that which will be done:
> There is nothing new under the sun.
> Is there a thing of which it may be said 'See, this is new?'
> It has already been in ages which were before us.

Gammie rightly goes on to draw a parallel to the Stoic statement of Cicero, although some caution should be exercised since Cicero was writing in the first century BCE:[54]

> If there were some human being who could see with his mind the connection of all causes, he would certainly never be deceived. For whoever grasps the causes of future things must necessarily grasp all that will be... The passage of time is like the unwinding of a rope, bringing about nothing new.
>
> (Cicero, *De Divinatione* 1.127 [*SVF* 2.944])

It may be objected that the idea that 'there is nothing new' in existence is the sort of general thought that might easily be arrived at independently by different people in their consideration of life. As we shall

---

53. Gammie, 'Stoicism and Anti-Stoicism in Qoheleth', pp. 174-76; Most recently this position has been adopted by Levine ('The Humor in Qohelet', pp. 78-79).

54. Gammie, 'Stoicism and Anti-Stoicism in Qoheleth', p. 176.

see however, the content of the rest of this passage supports the idea that Qoheleth is borrowing from Greek, and specifically Stoic, thought.

The majority of commentators already accept, albeit tacitly, some form of Greek influence when they point out the fact that Qoheleth's depiction of the cycles followed by the wind, rivers, sun and earth itself makes use of the doctrine of the four elements.[55] This idea of the cosmos and everything therein being composed of these elements was canonical in Greek thought, and in Greek thought alone: it was also a major feature of Stoic philosophy (DL 7.136 [*SVF* 1.102]; 7.137 [*SVF* 2.580]; Nemesius 164.15-18 [*SVF* 2.418]; Plutarch, *Comm. not.* 1085c-d [*SVF* 2.444]). The doctrine of the four elements is also found at the very earliest stages of Stoic thought. Stobaeus, a Greek anthologist writing in the fifth century CE, states:

> Chrysippus has the following views on the elements formed out of substance, following Zeno the leader of the school. He says that there are four elements <fire, air, water, earth, out of which everything is composed–animals,> plants, the whole world and its contents–and that they are dissolved into these.
>
> (Stobaeus 1.129.2-3 [*SVF* 2.413])

Qoheleth's use of this concept is therefore of some significance for the argument that Ecclesiastes is a product of the Hellenistic era. Again, one might argue that Qoheleth's mention of earth, fire (sun), air (wind) and water is coincidental. Against this, however, not only are each of the four elements mentioned in turn, they serve as an initial illustration of Qoheleth's thesis that '*everything* is הבל ("vanity")' (1.2) as they do of the statement that '*all things* are full of labour' (1.8). Both statements presuppose that 1.4-7 represents something more than four isolated examples of natural forces at work. Only by understanding the four elements in their Greek/Stoic role as being the basic building blocks for all things can one understand the logic of Qoheleth's jump from the use

---

55. Gammie, 'Stoicism and Anti-Stoicism in Qoheleth', p. 174; Crenshaw, *Ecclesiastes*, p. 62; Whybray, *Ecclesiastes* [NCBC], p. 39; Lohfink, *Kohelet*, p. 22. This common interpretation was seemingly first advanced by Ibn Ezra who was heavily influenced by Aristotelian philosophy (Gordis, *Koheleth*, pp. 56-57; Zimmerli, *Prediger*, p. 143; Hertzberg, *Prediger*, p. 61; S. Japhet, 'Goes to the South and turns to the North' [Ecclesiastes 1:6] The Sources and History of the Exegetical Traditions', *JSQ* 1 [1994], p. 319). Fox is in a minority in understanding the term הארץ as referring not to the earth as such but to humanity as a whole, of which each generation forms a part (*Contradictions*, p. 171).

of these four examples of the elements in their natural (i.e. unmixed) state, showing how each one engages in ceaseless activity, to the claim that 'all things' are full of labour. Indeed, just as Qoheleth does in 1.8, Cleanthes drew a parallel between the ceaseless movement of the four elements in the cosmos and the human frame.[56]

Qoheleth, however, also demonstrates influence from his own Semitic background in the way that these elements are depicted. The earth cannot be said to 'move' as such, and so ceaseless activity in this realm is shown by the generations of human beings dying and coming to life.[57] Chrysippus argued that animals were made up of all four elements. Qoheleth sees earth as their primary element, in line with general Hebrew thought (3.20; 12.7; cf. Gen. 2.7; 3.19) and thus the cycle of birth and death (or death and birth) serves as an example of unending activity in the realm of the element earth.

Many commentators have also pointed out the parallel between Qoheleth's statement that 'all rivers flow to the sea yet the sea is never full' (1.7) with that of Aristophanes, who remarks 'The sea, though all rivers flow to it, increases not in volume' (*The Clouds* 1294; cf. Lucretius 6.608).[58] The same commentators have, generally speaking, been rather more cautious in drawing parallels between Qoheleth's apparent application of these cycles to history with the Stoic doctrine of the periodic repetition of events. Thus, the Stoics held that fate was so constructed that the whole of history, down to the smallest detail, would be repeated periodically. One of the strangest consequences of this idea was that in order for history to repeat itself, the same people had to appear in it and thus every person who has ever lived would be reborn:

> Chrysippus…when speaking of the world's renewal, drew the following conclusion: 'Since this is so, it is evidently not impossible that we too after our death will return to the shape we now are, after certain periods of time have elapsed'.
>
> (Lactantius, *Div. inst.* 7.23 [*SVF* 2.623])

56. Gould, *The Philosophy of Chrysippus*, p. 35.

57. Ogden argues against this interpretation, although it is upheld by almost all commentators. For him, the term דור refers to the 'generations' (i.e. individual cycles) of the remaining three elements; fire, wind and water ('The Interpretation of דור in Ecclesiastes 1.4', pp. 91-92).

58. Gordis, *Koheleth*, p. 206; Plumptre, *Ecclesiastes*, p. 106; Zimmerli, *Prediger*, p. 143.

The same idea is also attributed to the Stoics in Nemesius 309.5–311.2 [*SVF* 2.625]; Eusebius, *Praep. evang.* 15.19.1-2 [*SVF* 2.599]; Origen, *Contra Cels.* 4.68, 5.20 [*SVF* 2.626] and many other sources, although the sources agree in its attribution to Chrysippus. Qoheleth certainly does not suggest that the cycles of the four elements are indicative of such a periodic repetition of history. However, his use of these cycles of the elements before the statement that 'there is nothing new under the sun' (1.9) is evidently of some significance.

Certainly, Hertzberg is right in pointing out that Qoheleth's thought here is unique in the Hebrew Bible (Ps. 96.1; Jer. 31.22, 31; Isa. 43.19; 65.18).[59] This becomes more significant if it is remembered that in most of the previous examples, it is God who does a 'new thing'. In Ecclesiastes, the actions that occur in the human realm are also divinely controlled, yet there is 'nothing new'.

Having said this, however, the majority consensus views Qoheleth's statement that 'there is nothing new under the sun' as referring in the most general way to human actions.[60] One might sing a new song, but it still falls into the category 'song'. One might make a new covenant but this too conforms to an archetypal 'covenant'. In this sense the events that go to make up existence do repeat themselves. One problem with this view is that in 1.10 Qoheleth forestalls possible arguments against his statement by remarking that 'there is no remembrance of former things'. The repetition cannot therefore be one of general 'archetypes' or of general actions as Fox supposes: these archetypes are well known to humanity. Based on the contextual evidence, one can come to no other conclusion than that Qoheleth is referring to specific actions or events which are being repeated. This brings the passage much closer to the literal repetition evident in the depiction of the four elements in 1.4-7, and also to the Stoic view of history.

The essential difference between Qoheleth and the philosophy of the Stoics in this area lies in the Stoic claim that the world was subject to periodic conflagration (ἐκπύρωσις) which recreated the world anew, after which history would repeat itself down to the smallest detail (Eusebius, *Praep. evang.* 15.14.2 [*SVF* 1.98]; DL 7.141 [*SVF* 2.589]). Qoheleth, on the other hand, clearly states that 'the earth remains forever' (1.4).

59. Hertzberg, *Prediger*, p. 62.
60. Fox, *Contradictions*, pp. 172-72; Murphy, *Ecclesiastes*, p. 8.

There is no denying that this doctrine appears to have been advanced by the first three leaders of the Stoic school. However, it remained extremely controversial and subsequent leaders were forced to revise their arguments, either withholding judgment on the question or altogether denying the doctrine of ἐκπύρωσις. Thus Philo writes:

> Boethius of Sidon and Panaetius...gave up the conflagrations and regenerations, and deserted to the holier doctrine of the entire world's indestructibility. Diogenes too is reported to have subscribed to the doctrine of the conflagration when he was a young man, but to have had doubts in his maturity and suspended judgment.
>
> (Philo, *Aet. Mund.* 76-77)

The philosophers mentioned in this passage Boethius (second century), Panaetius (c. 185–110) and Diogenes of Babylon (c. 220–152) are too late to provide a reasonable parallel with a third-century dating for Ecclesiastes but are nevertheless indicative of a debate going on within Stoicism at an early date concerning the doctrine of ἐκπύρωσις. More significantly, even among the earliest leaders there was no agreement about the precise nature of the conflagration: Cleanthes argued that the world would change into flame, while his pupil Chrysippus suggested that it changed into light (Philo, *Aet. Mund.* 90 [= *SVF* 1.511]). Under the circumstances, it is not impossible that Qoheleth had contact with the Stoic theory of cycles without accepting the idea of ἐκπύρωσις as indeed both Gammie and Levine have previously claimed.

5. *Conclusion*

In conclusion, we can perhaps say that although the differences between the thought of Qoheleth and the earliest Stoics are many, there are also significant parallels that are sufficiently frequent and close to suggest some kind of connection. First, Qoheleth appears to diverge to some extent from his Jewish background in emphasizing God's determination of human thought and action rather than his foreknowledge of the same. Free will in Ecclesiastes appears extremely limited, in a way that is rare elsewhere in early Jewish literature.

Qoheleth's position on moral/ethical free will is also similar in many respects to that of the second leader of the Stoic school, Cleanthes: the righteous are stated to be under God's deterministic control, while the wicked are said to act outside it. Indeed, Qoheleth may even cite Cleanthes' dictum about the nature of the Stoic god against him.

Whereas the Stoic god is said to 'make crooked things straight', Qoheleth's god does the exact opposite and makes that which is straight crooked. Qoheleth appears to demonstrate some knowledge of the deterministic mechanism which the Stoics called the *logos*, and which he calls by an equivalent term, the חשׁבון ('account').

Finally, Qoheleth shows an awareness of the four elements that were canonical in Greek thought, and has a cyclical view of history, similar in many respects to that of the Stoics. Qoheleth's partial acceptance of Stoic thought, evident perhaps in his veiled criticism of Cleanthes, may also be reflected in his apparent rejection of the idea of ἐκπύρωσις.

Qoheleth is not a Stoic. This much is clear. This need not mean, however, that he was ignorant of its doctrines, nor that some of these ideas are not reflected in his work. Since the evidence for the date of Ecclesiastes in general points to the Hellenistic period, this means that some attempt must be made to understand Qoheleth's thought against the cultural backdrop of Hellenistic thought, both Jewish and Greek.[61] The work of Qoheleth, I would argue, owes something to both milieus, although as this book has also demonstrated, he can and frequently does view things from a standpoint unique to himself.

---

61. Gammie's justification for his attempt to link Stoicism with Qoheleth's thought is worth citing in this regard: 'even though the exegete may fall into erroneous expositions (should his or her assessment of date or background subsequently be proven to be wrong), the worse error would be to attempt to interpret with little or no reference to the relation of the biblical author to hs or her own cultural environment' ('Stoicism and Anti-Stoicism in Qoheleth', p. 173). This view is also echoed to some extent by Fox (*Contradictions*, p. 16).

Chapter 10

CONCLUSION

The object of this work has been to demonstrate that Qoheleth is a determinist and that his work is a product of the Hellenistic period. In Chapter 1, the evidence for a Hellenistic dating was reviewed, and the current scholarly consensus upheld, although with some reservations. Subsequently, several of the key terms (מקרה, 'occurrence, happening'; פגע, 'meeting'; עת, 'time', 'appointed time'; משפט, 'judgment'; חלק, 'portion'; מעשה שנעשה תחת השמש/מעשה האלהים, 'the work which is done under the sun'/'the work of God') occurring in passages which have been traditionally interpreted in a deterministic sense were examined (Chapter 2). Perhaps the most important conclusion of this chapter for the future direction of studies on Ecclesiastes is that Qoheleth does not consider chance to be a force operative in existence, contrary to the assertion of many commentators.

The term מקרה, contrary to its usage elsewhere in the Hebrew Bible, has the sense of '(unpredictable/uncontrollable) happening' rather than 'chance happening', for it is used primarily of death, which is clearly stated by Qoheleth to be predetermined. Likewise, √פגע, which is translated 'chance' by many commentators, is in fact used elsewhere only of some form of encounter or meeting which is planned by at least one of the parties thereto. When used of an event that befalls human beings, as Qoheleth does, one may conclude that it is of an event that is predetermined.

Many commentators already understand the term עת in the sense of a time for human action which is predetermined by God, and in accordance with which human beings must act. A consideration of the contexts in which Qoheleth uses this term concludes that this is indeed the case, and that Qoheleth therefore advances the concept of a far-reaching form of determinism over all, or nearly all, human activities. Related to this topic is the question of what Qoheleth means when he speaks of 'judgment' (מֹשָׁפְט), particularly in the difficult passage 8.5-6. Follow-ing an examination of the two different interpretations currently advanced by modern commentators, that Qoheleth either refers to the judgment of the wise man and his ability to act at the appropriate time, or to the idea that at a certain predetermined moment, God will enact a traditional judgment on human beings, it was concluded that neither interpretation answered the problems evident both in this passage and in the wider context. A new interpretation was therefore advanced, in which Qoheleth understood the divinely determined times which befall human beings as a form of judgment. This was demonstrated to fit Qoheleth's worldview and to all contexts in which √שָׁפַט is used of God's activity except 11.9b, thus supporting the view of many com-mentators that 11.9b is the work of a glossator.

Qoheleth's usage of the term חלק ('portion') was also considered: this usage was shown to be fundamentally different to that of other texts in the Hebrew Bible. Primarily, this dfference was apparent in the fact that God gives 'portion' to the individual. More remarkably, however, this 'portion' was shown to be not so much connected with material goods as with human emotions. The 'portion' which God gives to hum-anity is joy, love, hate, envy. Qoheleth's deterministic worldview finds clear expression in the idea that God is responsible for the emotions that human beings feel as well as the actions that they perform. Finally, an examination into the phrases מעשׂה שׁנעשׂה תחת הׁשמׁש/מעשׂה האלהים ('the work which is done under the sun'/'the work of God') was carried out. Many of those who support the idea that Qoheleth is a determinist argue for the equivalence of 'the work of God' and 'the work which is done under the sun'. Yet current translations of 8.17a translate the particle כִּי as if it were introducing an object clause, so that Qoheleth in this text apparently states that the work of God is to prevent human beings from finding out the work which is done under the sun. An examination of the form in which such object clauses are expressed in Hebrew in GKC, however, led to the conclusion that it had been wrongly classified and that the particle כִּי should therefore be translated affirmatively (i.e. 'surely'). This finding reinforces the argument that 'the work of God' and 'the work which is done under the sun' are more or less equivalent phrases, and thus bolsters the argument that Qoheleth is a determinist in the true sense of the word.

The depiction of the cycles of nature in 1.3-8 is often termed the prologue of the book of Ecclesiastes, and understood to give expression to the main themes of that book. Chapter 3 focused specifically on this text. As well as the idea of futile but toilsome activity, it was noted that the text described the four elements as engaged in activity that was set within well-defined boundaries, leading to the conclusion that this too was a passage that expressed a deterministic view of existence. Just as the courses of the sun, wind, rivers etc. are mapped out by God, so those of humanity are also set before them. Human beings have as little chance of breaking free of the divine decrees that determine the progress of their lives as have the elemental forces which bind the cosmos together.

The question of the meaning of the term עֵת ('time', 'appointed time') is perhaps the most important one for establishing the nature and extent of Qoheleth's deterministic worldview. If one can say that Qoheleth uses the term עֵת in the sense of predetermined time in 3.1, 'for everything there is a season, a time for every matter under heaven' and in the list of human activities in 3.2-8, then one can say that Qoheleth is in the truest sense of the word a determinist. This position has been challenged by Joseph Blenkinsopp, and to this extent a response to Blenkinsopp's paper formed the body of Chapter 4. Blenkinsopp's thesis, that Qoheleth is a determinist (in a looser sense of the word) but that this was not the idea which 3.2-8 was intended to express, was refuted on the basis of evidence brought out in the previous chapter, joined with fresh evidence to support the idea that 3.2-8 was Qoheleth's own work and that it was intended to express a deterministic worldview.

In Chapter 5, consideration was given to what is perhaps the most difficult passage in the book of Ecclesiastes (7.23-29). Typically, the woman who appears in this passage has been regarded in one of two ways. The first is that she is a stereotypical 'wicked' woman in line with other misogynistic depictions of such women in Proverbs or Ben Sira. The other has been that Qoheleth quotes such an idea of woman in order to argue against it. A careful consideration of the entrapment imagery associated with the woman, however, revealed that Qoheleth depicts her as a divine agent, for the nets which she uses to entrap men are almost always associated with Yahweh's judgment elsewhere in the Hebrew Bible. Nor could the reference in 7.26 be considered appropriate only to 'a certain type of woman', for her activity was shown not to affect the stray individual, but the many. Whether her potential victim was caught or escaped was wholly in the hands of God. Thus,

Qoheleth's depiction of woman demonstrated that there was indeed 'a time to love', in line with Qoheleth's statement in 3.8.

Having given consideration to the *nature* of the woman, who is apparently a morally neutral figure, and whose actions (like the rest of humanity) are determined by God, attention was turned to the *purpose* for which the woman was introduced into this text, which essentially admits Qoheleth's failure to achieve the kind of knowledge of existence which he seeks. Tentatively, it was concluded that the woman acts as a defence against human beings gaining mastery over existence and thus finding the work of God. She is symbolic of the pleasure that God allots to humanity in order to keep them occupied. As far as Qoheleth's own search goes (for Qoheleth is apparently one of the lucky few who have escaped), it would appear that the danger that the woman represents prevents him from carrying out his purpose.

These ideas lead on naturally to the subject of Chapter 6, in which Qoheleth's attitude towards human joy is considered, as evidenced in those texts in which Qoheleth makes the recommendation to seek out pleasure (as defined by Whybray and de Jong). Although this subject is considered to some extent in Chapters 2 and 5, the evidence provided in this chapter shows that while a certain amount of human free will is presupposed in the seeking of pleasure, human beings remain entirely dependent on God for its attainment. This is particularly underlined by Qoheleth's reference to pleasure as 'the gift of God'. The conclusion reached in this chaper is fundamentally in line with the current thinking of the major commentators of Ecclesiastes (e.g. Crenshaw, Whybray), who themselves are only the latest in a long line of commentators who have understood Qoheleth's thinking thus.

Chapter 7 produced two new contributions to the debate on the nature and date of Ecclesiastes. Seow has recently argued powerfully against the current consensus that would make the book of Ecclesiastes a product of the early Hellenistic period. His argument that Qoheleth's work can only be dated to the Persian period hinges, however, on Qoheleth's use of √שלט in its legal/technical sense of '(delegated) authority' or 'proprietorship', a sense that he claims falls out of use after the Persian period. A closer examination of this claim found that, on the contrary, examples of √שלט used in this sense could clearly be seen in the books of Daniel and Ben Sira, both products of the early Hellenistic period. Moreover, this technical sense of the root occurs several times in Hebrew in the Talmud, in Syriac slave sale documents of the early

Christian era, in Mediaeval Aramaic marriage contracts and finally in a Yiddish proverb which has been used up to modern times. These findings allow us to conclude that Qoheleth may well have written his work in the Hellenistic period, and indeed the figurative use in which Qoheleth uses √שׁלט has clear affinities with the usage in the Hellenistic book of Daniel, in contrast to the purely pedestrian sense in which it is found in Persian period texts.

Consideration was then given to Qoheleth's use of the root in the light of Seow's claims as to its meaning. It was found that by and large, God is seen by Qoheleth as the distributor of שׁלטון ('authority') to human beings (in contrast to Seow, who considers it to be, in the main, allocated by earthly authorities). This finding has particular relevance for understanding Qoheleth's worldview, since Qoheleth uses this idea of divinely allocated שׁלטון in the context of finding happiness, but also to explain human evil and inequities in an existence that he believes to be divinely controlled. This idea of שׁלטון may therefore be understood as a limited form of free will. This in turn explains why Qoheleth can advise his disciple on the manner of finding happiness (when 'there is an appointed time for every matter'), and also shows that Qoheleth gave some thought to the problem of human evil in the context of determinism. By explaining evil and inequity as a product of human volition, the deity is to some extent distanced (although not wholly absolved of responsibility for) the existence of these things. It was also noted that Qoheleth uses a special legal formula ('he does whatever he chooses') of the king and apparently considers the king to have a special relationship with God. Kings are effectively free of the deterministic mechanism that otherwise controls existence. This in turn may explain, at least to some extent, the royal fiction in Ecclesiastes 1 and 2 and the paradox of how Qoheleth is free to conduct his investigations when all is predetermined, although such an idea is not made explicit therein.

Having to some extent reconstructed Qoheleth's worldview in the preceding chapters, the final two chapters of this work turned to consider the question of how this view of existence meshes with the background in which Qoheleth is supposed to have lived and written. In Chapter 8, Qoheleth's deterministic depiction of life was considered in the light of Jewish thought. It was concluded that in general there is no consistent belief in determinism in the Hebrew Bible, although a few scattered ideas consistent with this concept may be found therein. There is, however, a strongly deterministic element to be found in early

Jewish extra-biblical literature from the Hellenistic period on. This is particularly true of the apocalyptic literature, a fact which has led many to argue that this genre stems ultimately from the wisdom tradition in which Qoheleth wrote. Again, this apparent flowering of the idea of determinism in the Hellenistic period would appear to support the consensus dating of Ecclesiastes to this time. Similarities were, moreover, noted between the way that both Qoheleth and the author of the book of Daniel expressed this concept of determinism. The thought of Qoheleth was also demonstrated to show some affinity with Sirach in that both consider the problem of human wickedness in the light of determinism and allude to the idea that God may thereby be construed by the wicked as supporting their wrongdoing.

Nevertheless, several important differences were noted between Qoheleth's consideration of the problem of evil and that of the normative tradition that is expressed by other Jewish writers. In other texts of this time, where consideration is given to the problem of evil at all, total free will for human beings is asserted in the moral/ethical sphere. Yet this clearly contradicts the idea that God may determine the course of history or the life of the individual, for it is through the choices made by human beings that history is made.

In line with the similarities noted beween Ecclesiastes and Hellenistic literature in previous chapters, suggesting that Qoheleth's work is a product of this time, Chapter 9 then considers the question of a possible interface between the form of determinism advanced by the Stoics in the third century BCE. Discussion in the first part of this chapter was limited to those areas in which Qoheleth appears to diverge from contemporary Jewish thought, specifically the question of how human evil can be reconciled with a benevolent deterministic God.

Again, general similarities were noted between the form of determinism advanced by the Stoics and that of Qoheleth. These are less striking by and large than the similarities with Jewish thought. Unlike Jewish writers of the Hellenistic period, however, the Stoics paid a great deal of attention to the question of how human evil and wickedness may be reconciled with a belief in determinism. Qoheleth makes no such convoluted or complicated attempts to reconcile the two and neither does the third leader of the Stoic school, Chrysippus, with whom his work is most often linked. An analogous explanation for the presence of evil was, however, found in the work of Cleanthes, the predecessor of Chrysippus, and a contemporary of Qoheleth according to the current consensus for the date of Ecclesiastes. According to Cleanthes, God was held to control all things that happened on earth, with the exception of those actions that were performed by the wicked. This thought is a good parallel to that of Eccl. 9.1 in which Qoheleth sees God's activity as being expressed through 'the wise and the righteous and their works'. It is an open question however, as to whether this is an example of influence or of two original thinkers reaching the same conclusion independently.

That the former may be the case, however, and that Qoheleth may have been aware of the basic ideas of Stoic determinism is suggested by his use of the term חשבון. Elsewhere in Hebrew and cognate languages, this term typically means 'account' in a numerical sense. Qoheleth, however, uses it to describe the system by which the events of life play themselves out. As such, the חשבון appears to be coextensive with 'the work of God' or 'the work which is done under the sun', but it is also the means by which these things may be understood. Qoheleth also uses the term in a concrete (numerical) sense to refer to the account which he himself hopes to form, and of the accounts which others form of existence. Finally, he also uses it in the sense of 'thought', a meaning that it has nowhere else in Hebrew, although this meaning is implicit in √חשב from which the noun is derived. Qoheleth's use of this noun is unique in Hebrew, but the meanings with which he invests it are almost exactly those in which the corresponding Greek term *logos* occurs in the philosophies of Heraclitus and the Stoics. As such, Qoheleth's usage appears to be more than a parallel of thought, but to be indicative of contact with this, the most fundamental aspect of Stoic determinism. This need not detract from Qoheleth's originality, nor need it imply that Qoheleth takes on board the ideas of Stoicism wholesale. In many respects, his thought differs quite fundamentally from that of the Stoic philosophers, although other similarities with Stoic thinking (his reference to the four elements, his apparently cyclical view of history) have in the past been noted. The evidence adduced in this thesis supports the idea that Qoheleth's thought is primarily to be related to his Jewish background. At the same time, however, those aspects of Greek thought (limited though they may be) which find expression in his work should not be ignored.

BIBLIOGRAPHY

Ackroyd, P.R., 'דִּין', *TDOT*, V, pp. 409-10.

Attridge, H.W., 'Josephus and his Works' in M.E. Stone (ed.), *Jewish Writings of the Second Temple Period* (CRINT; Assen: Van Gorcum; Philadelphia: Fortress Press, 1984), pp. 185-232.

Arnold, E.V., *Roman Stoicism* (New York: Humanities, 1958).

Ausejo, S. de, 'El género literario del Ecclesiastés', *EstBib* 7 (1948), pp. 394-406.

Baltzer, K., 'Women and War in Qohelet 7:23–8:1a', *HTR* 80 (1987), pp. 127-32.

Barton, G.A., *Ecclesiastes* (ICC; Edinburgh: T. & T. Clark, 1908).

Barucq, A., *Ecclésiaste* (Paris: Beauchesne, 1968).

Bickerman, E., *Four Strange Books of the Bible* (New York: Schocken Books, 1967).

Blenkinsopp, J., 'Ecclesiastes 3.1-15: Another Interpretation', *JSOT* 66 (1995), pp. 55-64.

Boeft, J. den, *Calcidius on Fate: His Doctrine and Sources* (Leiden: E.J. Brill, 1970).

Box, G.H., *The Apocalypse of Abraham* (London: SPCK; New York: Macmillan, 1918).

Braumann, G., 'ψῆφος', *TDNT*, IX, pp. 604-607

Braun, R., *Kohelet und die frühhellenistische Popularphilosophie* (BZAW, 130; Berlin: W. de Gruyter, 1973).

Brenner, A., 'Some Observations on Figurations of Woman in Wisdom Literature', in A. Brenner (ed.), *A Feminist Companion to Wisdom Literature* (The Feminist Companion to the Bible, 9; Sheffield: Sheffield Academic Press, 1995), pp. 50-66.

Brockelman, K., *Lexicon Syriacum* (Hildesheim: Georg Olms, 1966).

Burkitt, F.C., 'Is Ecclesiastes a Translation?', *JTS* 23 (1921–22), pp. 22-28.

Castellino, G.R., 'Qohelet and his Wisdom', *CBQ* 30 (1968), pp. 15-28.

Collins, J.J., 'Cosmos and Salvation: Jewish Wisdom and Apocalyptic in the Hellenistic Age', *HR* 17 (1977), pp. 121-42.

—*The Apocalyptic Imagination* (New York: Crossroad, 1984).

Condamin, A., 'Etudes sur l'Ecclésiaste', *RB* 9 (1900), pp. 30-44.

Corré, A.D., 'A Reference to Epispasm in Koheleth', *VT* 4 (1954), pp. 416-18.

Cowley, A., *Aramaic Papyri of the 5th Century B.C.* (Oxford: Clarendon Press, 1923).

Crenshaw, J.L., 'The Eternal Gospel (Eccl 3:11)', in J.L. Crenshaw and J.T. Willis (eds.), *Essays in Old Testament Ethics* (New York: Ktav, 1974), pp. 23-55.

—*Old Testament Wisdom: An Introduction* (Atlanta: John Knox Press, 1981).

—'The Expression *mî yôdēa* in the Hebrew Bible', *VT* 36 (1986), pp. 274-88.

—*Ecclesiastes* (OTL; Philadelphia: Westminster Press, 1987).

Cross, F.M., 'The Oldest Manuscripts from Qumran', *JBL* 74 (1955), pp. 147-72.

—'The Discovery of the Samaria Papyri', *BA* 26 (1963), pp. 110-20.

—'Samaria Papyrus 1: An Aramaic Slave Conveyance of 335 B.C.E. Found in the Wadi ed-Daliyeh', in *Nahman Avigad Volume* (ErIsr 18; Jerusalem, 1985), pp. 7-17.

—'A Report on the Samaria Papyri', in J.A. Emerton (ed.), *Congress Volume, Jerusalem, 1986* (VTSup, 40; Leiden: E.J. Brill, 1988), pp. 17-26.

Dahood, M., 'Canaanite-Phoenician Influence in Qoheleth', *Bib* 33 (1952), pp. 30-52, 191-221.

—'Qoheleth and Recent Discoveries', *Bib* 39 (1958), pp. 302-18.

—'Qoheleth and Northwest Semitic Philology', *Bib* 43 (1962), pp. 349-65.

—'Canaanite Words in Qoheleth 10,20', *Bib* 46 (1965), pp. 210-12.

—'The Phoenician Background of Qoheleth', *Bib* 47 (1966), pp. 264-82.

Davila, J.R., 'Qoheleth and Northern Hebrew', *Maarav* 5-6 (1990), pp. 68-87.

Debrunner, A., 'λόγος [= λέγω A2]', *TDNT*, IV, pp. 73-77.

Delitzsch, F., *Commentary on the Song of Songs and Ecclesiastes* (Leipzig: Dörffling & Franke, 1875; Edinburgh: T. & T. Clark, 1877; repr., Grand Rapids: Eerdmans, 1982).

Devine, M., *Ecclesiastes or the Confessions of an Adventurous Soul* (London: Macmillan, 1916).

Dietrich, B.C., *Death, Fate and the Gods* (London: Athlone Press, 1965).

Dossin, G., 'Une nouvelle lettre d'el Amarna', *RA* 31 (1934), pp. 126-29.

Driver, G.R., 'Problems and Solutions', *VT* 4 (1954), pp. 225-45.

Droge, A.J., 'Suicide', *ABD*, VI, pp. 227-31.

Droge, A.J., and J.D. Tabor, *A Noble Death: Suicide and Martyrdom among Jews and Christians in Antiquity* (San Francisco: Harper-Collins, 1992).

Ellermeier, F., *Qohelet* (Herzberg: Erwin Jungfer, 1967).

Fischel, H.A., 'Stoicism', *EncJud*, XV, p. 410.

Fox, M.V., *Qohelet and his Contradictions* (JSOTSup, 71; Sheffield: Almond Press, 1989).

—*The Song of Songs and Ancient Egyptian Love Songs* (Madison: University of Wisconsin Press).

Fox, M.V., and B. Porten, 'Unsought Discoveries: Qohelet 7:23–8:1a', *HS* 19 (1978), pp. 26-38.

Fredericks, D.C., 'Life's Storms and Structural Unity in Qoheleth 11.1–12.8', *JSOT* 52 (1991), pp. 95-114.

Fuerst, W.J., *The Books of Ruth, Ecclesiastes, the Song of Songs, Lamentations* (Cambridge: Cambridge University Press, 1975).

Galling, K., *Studien zur Geschichte Israels im persischen Zeitalter* (Tübingen: J.C.B. Mohr, 1964).

—*Der Prediger* (HAT, 18; Tübingen: J.C.B. Mohr, 1969).

Gammie, J.G., 'Stoicism and Anti-Stoicism in Qoheleth', *HAR* 9 (1985), pp. 169-87.

Gemser, B., 'The Instructions of; Onchsheshonqy and Biblical Wisdom Literature', in *Congress Volume, Oxford, 1959* (VTSup, 7; Leiden: E.J. Brill, 1960), pp. 102-28.

Giesen, G., 'חרם (II)', *TDOT*, V, pp. 200-203.

Ginsberg, H.L., *Studies in Koheleth* (New York: Jewish Theological Seminary of America, 1950).

—'The Structure and Contents of the Book of Koheleth', in M. Noth and D.W. Thomas (eds.), *Wisdom in Israel and the Ancient Near East* (VTSup, 3; Leiden: E.J. Brill, 1955), pp. 138-49.

—*Qoheleth* (Jerusalem and Tel Aviv: Newman, 1961).

Ginsburger, M., 'Review of *Das Targum zu Koheleth nach sudarabischen Handschriften herausgegeben* von Alfred Levy', *ZDMG* 59 (1905), p. 717.

Glasser, E., *Le procès du bonheur par Qohelet* (Paris: Cerf, 1970).

Goldstein, J.A., 'The Syriac Bill of Sale from Dura-Europos', *JNES* 25 (1966), pp. 11-12.

Gómez Aranda, M., *El Comentario de Abraham Ibn Ezra al Libro del Eclesiastés* (TECC, 56; Madrid: CSIC, 1994).

Gordis, R., 'Was Koheleth a Phoenician? Some Observations on Methods in Research', *JBL* 71 (1955), pp. 105-109.

—*Koheleth: The Man and his World* (3rd edn; New York: Bloch, 1968).

Gould, J.B., *The Philosophy of Chrysippus* (Leiden: Brill, 1970).

—'The Stoic Conception of Fate', *JHI* 35 (1974), pp. 17-32.

Grassi, J.A., 'Child, Children', *ABD*, I, pp. 904-907.

Greene, W.C., *Moira: Fate, Good and Evil in Greek Thought* (Cambridge: Harvard University Press, 1944).

Gropp, D.M., 'The Origin and Development of the Aramaic *Šallîṭ* Clause', *JNES* 52 (1993), pp. 31-36.

Grotius, H., *Annotationes in Vetus Testamentum* (ed. G. Vogel; Halae: Curt, 1875–76).

Guthrie, W.K.C., *History of Greek Philosophy* (6 vols.; Cambridge: Cambridge University Press, 1962–81).

Hengel, M., *Judaism and Hellenism* (2 vols.; London: SCM Press, 1974).

Heidland, H., 'λογίζομαι, λογίσμος', *TDNT*, IV, pp. 284-92.

Hertzberg, H.W., *Der Prediger* (KAT XVI, 4; Leipzig: Scholl, 1932).

Hitzig, F., *Der Prediger Salomo's* (KHAT; Leipzig: Weidmann, 1847).

Hurvitz, A., 'The History of a Legal Formula: *kōl 'ăšer ḥāpēṣ 'āśāh* (Psalms CXV 3, CXXXV 6)', *VT* 32 (1982), pp. 257-67.

Japhet, S., 'Goes to the South and Turns to the North [Ecclesiastes 1:6] The Sources and History of the Exegetical Traditions', *JSQ* 1 (1994), pp. 289-322.

Japhet, S., and R.B. Salters, *Rashbam on Qohelet* (Jerusalem: Magnes, 1985).

Jastrow, M., *A Gentle Cynic* (Phildelphia: Lippincott, 1919).

—*A Dictionary of the Targumim, the Talmud Babli and Yerushalmi, and the Midrashic Literature* (New York: Judaica, 1992).

Johnston, R.K., 'Confessions of a Workaholic: A Reappriasal of Qoheleth', *CBQ* 38 (1976), pp. 14-28.

Jones, E., *Proverbs and Ecclesiastes* (London: SCM Press, 1961).

Jong, S. de, 'A Book on Labour: The Structuring Principles and the Main Theme of the Book of Qohelet', *JSOT* 54 (1992), pp. 107-16.

—'Qohelet and the Ambitious Spirit of the Ptolemaic Period', *JSOT* 61 (1994), pp. 85-96.

—'God in the Book of Qohelet: A Reappraisal of Qohelet's Place in Old Testament Theology', *VT* 47 (1997), pp. 154-67.

Kaiser, O., 'Judentum und Hellenismus', *VF* 27 (1982), pp. 69-73.

—'Determination und Freiheit beim Kohelet/Prediger Salomo in der frühen Stoa', *NZSTh* 31 (1989), pp. 251-70.

Kidner, D., *A Time to Mourn and a Time to Dance* (Leicester: Inter-Varsity Press, 1976).

Kirk, G.S., *Heraclitus: The Cosmic Fragments* (Cambridge: Cambridge University Press, 1954).

Kleinknecht, H., 'λέγω B', *TDNT*, IV, pp. 77-91.

Knibb, M.A., '"You are indeed wiser than Daniel": Reflections on the Character of the Book of Daniel', in A.S. Van der Woude (ed.), *The Book of Daniel in the Light of New Findings* (BETL, 106; Leuven: Leuven University/Peeters, 1993), pp. 399-411.

Knobel, P.S., *The Targums of Job, Proverbs, Qohelet* (Edinburgh: T. & T. Clark, 1991).

Koester, H., *History, Culture and Religion of the Hellenistic Age* (Philadelphia: Fortress Press, 1984).

Kraeling, E.G., *The Brooklyn Museum Aramaic Papyri: New Documents of the Fifth Century B.C. from the Jewish Colony at Elephantine* (New Haven: Yale University Press, 1953).

Kroeber, R., *Der Prediger* (Berlin: Akademie-Verlag, 1963).

Kugel, J.L., 'Qohelet and Money', *CBQ* 51 (1989), pp. 32-49.

Kutscher, E.Y., 'New Aramaic Texts', *JAOS* 74 (1954), pp. 233-48.

Larkin, K.J.A., *The Eschatology of Second Zechariah: A Study in the Formation of a Mantological Wisdom Anthology* (Kampen: Kok, 1996).

Lauha, A., Kohelet (BKAT, 19; Neukirchen–Vluyn: Neukirchener Verlag, 1978).

Lella, A.A. Di, 'Wisdom of Ben Sira', *ABD*, VI, pp. 931-45.

Levine, E., *The Aramaic Version of Qohelet* (New York: Hermon, 1978).

—'The Humor in Qohelet', *ZAW* 109 (1997), pp. 71-83.

Loader, J.A., 'Qohelet 3:2-8—A "Sonnet" in the Old Testament', *ZAW* 81 (1969), pp. 240-42.

—*Polar Structures in the Book of Qohelet* (BZAW, 152; Berlin: W. de Gruyter, 1979).

Lohfink, N., *Kohelet* (Würzburg: Echter Verlag, 1980).

—'War Kohelet ein Frauenfeind? Ein Versuch, die Logik und den Gegenstand von Koh. 7:23–8:1a herauszufinden', in M. Gilbert (ed.), *La sagesse de l'Ancien Testament* (BETL, 51; Gembloux: Duculot; Leuven: Leuven University Press, 1979), pp. 259-87.

—'*Melek, šallīṭ* und *môšēl* bei Kohelet und die Aufassungzeit des Buchs', *Bib* 62 (1981), pp. 525-43.

Long, A.A., and D.N. Sedley, *The Hellenistic Philosophers* (2 vols; Cambridge: Cambridge University Press, 1987).

Loretz, O., *Qohelet und der Alte Orient: Untersuchungen zu Stil und theologischer Thematik des Buches Qohelet* (Freiburg: Herder, 1964).

McKane, W., *Proverbs* (OTL; London: SCM Press, 1970).

McNeile, A.H., *An Introduction to the Book of Ecclesiastes* (Cambridge: Cambridge University Press, 1904).

Mannebach, E., *Aristippi et Cyrenaicorum Fragmenta* (Leiden: E.J. Brill, 1961).

Margoliouth, D.S., 'Ecclesiastes', *Jewish Encyclopaedia* (New York: Funk & Wagnalls, 1907), V, pp. 32-34.

Michel, D., *Qohelet* (Darmstadt: Wissenschaftliche Buchgesellschaft, 1988).

—*Untersuchungen zur Eigenart des Buches Qohelet* (BZAW, 183; Berlin: W. de Gruyter, 1989).

Montgomery, J.A., *Daniel* (ICC; Edinburgh: T. & T. Clark, 1927).

—'Notes on Ecclesiastes', *JBL* 43 (1924), pp. 241-44.

Morris, L., *Apocalyptic* (London: Inter-Varsity Press, 1973).

Muffs, Y., *Studies in the Aramaic Legal Papyri from Elephantine* (Studia et Documenta ad Iura Orientis Antiqui Pertinenta, 8; Leiden: E.J. Brill, 1969).

Muilenberg, J., 'A Qoheleth Scroll from Qumran', *BASOR* 135 (1954), pp. 20-28.

Müller, H.-P., 'Mantische Weisheit und Apokalyptik', in *Congress Volume, Uppsala, 1971* (VTSup, 22; Leiden: E.J. Brill, 1972), pp. 271-80.

—'Neige der althebräische "Weisheit": Zum Denken Qohäläts', *ZAW* 90 (1978), pp. 238-64.

Murphy, R.E., *Ecclesiastes* (WBC23a; Dallas, TX: Word Books, 1992).

Nahm, M.C., *Selections from Early Greek Philosophy* (New York: Meredith, 1962).

Nickelsburg, G.W.E., 'Eschatology (Early Jewish)', *ABD*, II, pp. 579-94.

Nöldeke, T., 'Bemerkungen zum hebräischen Ben Sira', *ZAW* 20 (1900), pp. 81-94.

Ogden, G.S., 'Qoheleth's Use of the "Nothing is Better" Form', *JBL* 98 (1979), pp. 341-50.

—'Qoheleth IX 1-16', *VT* 32 (1982), pp. 158-69.

—'Qoheleth XI 7-XII 8: Qoheleth's Summons to Enjoyment and Reflection', *VT* 34 (1984), pp. 27-38

—'The Interpretation of דור in Ecclesiastes 1.4', *JSOT* 34 (1986), pp. 91-92.

—*Qoheleth* (Readings: A New Biblical Commentary; Sheffield: JSOT Press, 1987).

Pearson, A.C., *The Fragments of Zeno and Cleanthes* (London: Clay, 1891).

Porteous, N., *Daniel* (OTL; London: SCM Press, 1979).

Préaux, C., *Le monde héllenistique: La Grèce et l'Orient de la mort d'Alexandre à la conquête romaine de la Grèce (232-146 av. J.-C.)* (Paris: Nouvelle Clio, 1978).

Pfleiderer, E., *Die Philosophie des Heraklit von Ephesus, nebst Koheleth und besonders im Buch der Weisheit* (Berlin: Reimer, 1886).

Plumptre, E.H., *Ecclesiastes* (Cambridge: Cambridge University Press, 1881).

Podechard, E., *L'Ecclésiaste* (Paris: Lecoffre, 1912).

Rabinowitz, J.J., *Jewish Law: Its Influence on the Development of Legal Institutions* (New York: Bloch, 1956).

Rad, G. von, 'The Promised Land and Yahweh's Land in the Hexateuch', *ZDPV* 66 (1943), pp. 191-204 (= *The Problem of the Hexateuch and Other Essays* [Edinburgh & London: Oliver & Boyd, 1966], pp. 79-93).

—*Wisdom in Israel* (London: SCM Press, 1972).

Rankin, H.D., *Sophists, Socratics and Cynics* (Beckenham: Croom Helms, 1983).

Ranston, H., *Ecclesiastes and the Early Greek Wisdom Literature* (London: Epworth, 1925).

Reesor, M.E., *The Nature of Man in Early Stoic Philosophy* (London: Gerald Duckworth, 1989)

Renan, E., *L'Ecclésiaste traduit de l'Hébreu avec une étude sur l'age et le caractère du livre* (Paris: Levy, 1882).

Rosenthal, F., *A Grammar of Biblical Aramaic* (Wiesbaden: Otto Harrassowitz, 1983).

Rudman, D.C., 'A Contextual Reading of Ecclesiastes 4:13-16', *JBL* 116 (1997), pp. 57-73.

—'The Translation and Interpretation of Ecclesiastes 8:17a', *JNSL* 23 (1997), pp. 1-9.

—'Woman as Divine Agent in Ecclesiastes', *JBL* 116 (1997), pp. 411-27.

—'Qohelet's Use of לפני', *JNSL* 23 (1997), pp. 143-50.

—'The Anatomy of the Wise Man: Wisdom, Sorrow and Joy in the Book of Ecclesiastes', in A. Schoors (ed.), *Qohelet in the Context of Wisdom* (BETL; Leuven: Leuven University Press/Peeters, 1998), pp. 465-72.

—'A Note on the Dating of Ecclesiastes', *CBQ* 61 (1999), pp. 47-52.

Russell, D.S., *The Method and Message of Jewish Apocalyptic* (OTL; London: SCM Press, 1964).

—*Divine Disclosure* (London: SCM Press, 1992).

Salters, R.B., 'The Book of Ecclesiastes: Studies in the Versions and the History of Exegesis' (PhD dissertation; St Andrews, 1973).

—'A Note on the Exegesis of Ecclesiastes 3 15b', *ZAW* 88 (1976), pp. 419-20.

Sandbach, F.H., *The Stoics* (London: Chatto & Windus, 1975).

Savignac, J. de, 'La sagesse du Qôhéléth et l'épopée de Gilgamesh', *VT* 28 (1978), pp. 318-23.

Schoors, A., 'The Use of Vowel Letters in Qoheleth', *UF* 20 (1988), pp. 277-86.

Scott, R.B.Y., *Proverbs Ecclesiastes* (AB, 18; Garden City, NY: Doubleday, 1965).

Seow, C.L., 'The Socioeconomic Context of "The Preacher's" Hermeneutic', *PSB* NS 17 (1996), pp. 168-95.

—'Linguistic Evidence and the Dating of Qohelet', *JBL* 115 (1996), pp. 643-66.

—*Ecclesiastes* (AB, 18C; Garden City: Doubleday, 1997).

Siegfried, C.G., 'Review of T. Tyler, Ecclesiastes', *ZWT* (1875), pp. 284-91.

—'Der jüdische Hellenismus', *ZWT* (1875), pp. 469-89.

—*Prediger und Hoheslied* (HAT II, 3/2; Göttingen: Vandenhoeck & Ruprecht, 1898).

Staples, W., 'The Meaning of *ḥepeṣ* in Ecclesiastes', *JNES* 24 (1965), pp. 110-12.

—'Profit in Ecclesiastes', *JNES* 4 (1945), pp. 87-96.

Stern, E., *Material Culture of the Land of the Bible in the Persian Period 538–332 B.C.* (Warminster: Aris & Phillips, 1982).

—'The Archaeology of Persian Palestine', in W.D. Davies and L. Finkelstein (eds.), *The Cambridge History of Judaism*. I. *The Persian Period* (Cambridge: Cambridge University Press, 1984).

Stone, M.E., 'Lists of Revealed Things in the Apocalyptic Literature', in F.M. Cross, *et al.* (eds.), *Magnalia Dei: The Mighty Acts of God* (Garden City, NY: Doubleday, 1976), pp. 414-52.

Strange, M., 'The Question of Moderation in Eccl 7:15-18' (S.T.D. dissertation; Catholic University of America, 1969).

Strobel, A., *Das Buch Prediger (Kohelet)* (Düsseldorf: Patmos, 1967).

Tarn, W.W., and G.T. Griffith, *Hellenistic Civilization* (3rd rev. edn; London: Methuen, 1959).

Taylor, R., 'Determinism', in P. Edwards (ed.), *Encyclopedia of Philosophy* (London: Macmillan, 1967–72).

Tcherikover, V., *Hellenistic Civilization and the Jews* (Philadelphia: Jewish Publication Society of America; Jerusalem: Magnes Press, 1959).

Tobin, T.H., 'Logos', *ABD*, IV, pp. 348-56.

Torrey, C.C., 'The Question of the Original Language of Qohelet', *JQR* 39 (1948–49), pp. 151-60.

Toy, C.H., *Proverbs* (ICC; Edinburgh: T. & T. Clark, 1899).

Trafton, J.L., 'Solomon, Psalms of', *ABD*, VI, pp. 115-17.

Tsevat, M., 'חלק (II)', *TDOT*, IV, pp. 447-51.

Tyler, T., *Ecclesiastes* (London: Williams & Norgate, 1874).

Verheij, A., 'Paradise Retried: On Qohelet 2:4-6', *JSOT* 50 (1991), pp. 113-15.

Whitley, C.F., *Koheleth: His Language and Thought* (BZAW, 148; Berlin: W. de Gruyter, 1979).

Whybray, R.N., 'Qoheleth the Immoralist? (Qoh 7:16-17)', in J.G. Gammie *et al.* (eds.), *Israelite Wisdom: Essays in Honor of Samuel Terrien* (Missoula, MT: Scholars Press, 1978), pp. 191-204.

—'Qoheleth, Preacher of Joy', *JSOT* 23 (1982), pp. 87-98.

—'Ecclesiastes 1.5-7 and the Wonders of Nature', *JSOT* 41 (1988), pp. 105-12.

—*Ecclesiastes* (NCBC; Grand Rapids: Eerdmans; London: Marshall, Morgan & Scott, 1989).

—*Ecclesiastes* (OTG; Sheffield: JSOT Press, 1989).

—*The Composition of the Book of Proverbs* (JSOTSup, 168; Sheffield: Sheffield Academic Press, 1994).

—'Qoheleth as Theologian', in A. Schoors (ed.), *Qohelet in the Context of Wisdom* (BETL; Leuven: Leuven University/Peeters, 1998).

Wildeboer, G., 'Der Prediger', in K. Budde (ed.), *Die fünf Megillot* (KHAT, 17; Freiburg: J.C.B. Mohr, 1898).

Williams, R.J., 'The Sages of Ancient Egypt in the Light of Recent Scholarship', *JAOS* 101 (1981), pp. 1-19.

Witzenrath, H., *Süss ist das Licht...: Eine literaturwissenschaftliche Untersuchung zu Kohelet 11:7–12:7* (MUSKTF. ATSAT, 11; S. Ottilien: EOS, 1979).

Woude, A.S. Van der, *Micah* (Nijkerk: Callenback, 1976).

Wright, A.G., '"For Everything There is a Season": The Structure and Meaning of the Fourteen Opposites (Ecclesiastes 3, 2-8)', in J. Doré *et al.* (eds.), *De la Tôrah au Messie: Mélanges Henri Cazelles* (Paris: J.G. Gabalda, 1981), pp. 321-28.

Wright, C.H.H., *The Book of Koheleth* (London: Hodder & Stoughton, 1883).

Yarbro Collins, A. (ed.), *Early Christian Apocalypticism* (Semeia, 36; Decatur: Scholars Press, 1986).

Yaron, R., 'Aramaic Marriage Contracts from Elephantine', *JSS* 3 (1958), pp. 9-10.

—'Aramaic Deeds of Conveyance', *Bib* 41 (1960), pp. 248-74.

Zimmerli, W., *Der Prediger* (ATD, 16.1; Göttingen: Vandenhoeck & Ruprecht, 1962).

Zimmerman, F., 'The Aramaic Provenance of Qohelet', *JQR* 36 (1945–46), pp. 17-45.

INDEXES

INDEX OF REFERENCES

BIBLE

Index of References 217

INDEX OF MODERN AUTHORS

JOURNAL FOR THE STUDY OF THE OLD TESTAMENT
SUPPLEMENT SERIES